"Would you rather take battlefield advice from a television analyst or a field general in the trenches getting dirty? Me too. Buy this book. Read it. Learn it. You'll be a better social media strategist for it."

—Jason Falls, CEO of Social Media Explorer and author of *No Bullshit Social Media: The All-Business, No-Hype Guide to Social Media Marketing*

"Over the last several years there have been hundreds of books written on how businesses can tap into the power of social media. Some of these books are useful but many miss the mark because the authors have never worked for or with these same businesses they presume to understand. Finally, a business book on social media by someone that understands business and social media!"

—Aaron Strout, head of marketing, WCG, and coauthor of *Location-Based Marketing for Dummies*

"This book is a MUST READ for anyone implementing social media for a large organization—you'll learn the true, valuable lessons from someone who's been there and learned the craft the hard way."

—Maddie Grant, coauthor of *Humanize: How People-Centric Organizations Succeed in a Social World* and chief social media strategist, SocialFish

"Finally, a book on social media geared for the corporate communications side. Christopher Barger is a pioneer in corporate social media, and in this book he shares insights that you can't get from an outsider. A must-read for everyone in corporate communications, whether you're launching a new social media presence or if you're an established player in the space."

> —Dan Bedore, director of product communications for Nissan North America, formerly senior group manager of public relations and creative director of social media at Hyundai Motor America

"There is no better person than Christopher Barger to teach you how to build a successful social media program from the inside out. Not only was he one of the early adopters; he did exactly what *The Social Media Strategist* recommends for one of the largest companies in the world. He provides theory and philosophy *and* real-world experience—a combination that is rate in today's digital world."

> —Gini Dietrich, chief executive officer, Arment Dietrich and author of *Spin Sucks*

THE
SOCIAL
MEDIA
STRATEGIST

Build a Successful Program from the Inside Out

CHRISTOPHER BARGER

New York Chicago San Francisco Lisbon London Madrid Mexico City
Milan New Delhi San Juan Seoul Singapore Sydney Toronto

The McGraw·Hill Companies

1 2 3 4 5 6 7 8 9 10 11 12 13 14 15 16 17   QFR/QFR   1 9 8 7 6 5 4 3 2 1

ISBN   978-0-07-176825-2
MHID   0-07-176825-4

e-ISBN   978-0-07-176855-9
e-MHID   0-07-176855-6

This publication is designed to provide accurate and authoritative information in regard to the subject matter covered. It is sold with the understanding that neither the author nor the publisher is engaged in rendering legal, accounting, securities trading, or other professional services. If legal advice or other expert assistance is required, the services of a competent professional person should be sought.
>   —*From a Declaration of Principles Jointly Adopted by a Committee of the American Bar Association and a Committee of Publishers and Associations*

Library of Congress Cataloging-in-Publication Data

Barger, Christopher.
    The social media strategist : build a successful program from the inside out / by Christopher Barger.
      p.   cm.
    ISBN-13: 978-0-07-176825-2 (hardback : acid-free paper)
    ISBN-10: 0-07-176825-4 (hardback : acid-free paper)
    1. Social media—Economic aspects.   2. Online social networks—Economic aspects.   3. Public relations.   4. Customer service   I. Title.

HM851.B3665   2012
302.23068—dc23   2011037912

McGraw-Hill books are available at special quantity discounts to use as premiums and sales promotions or for use in corporate training programs. To contact a representative, please e-mail us at bulksales@mcgraw-hill.com.

This book is printed on acid-free paper.

*For my parents
and
for Holly*

CONTENTS

CONTENTS

FOREWORD

"I served with Jack Kennedy, I knew Jack Kennedy, Jack Kennedy was a friend of mine. Senator, you're no Jack Kennedy."

—SENATOR LLOYD BENTSEN,
VICE PRESIDENTIAL DEBATE, OCTOBER 5, 1988

That stinging retort may be lost on recent generations, but for those of us who watched it live, it will forever remain as part of our collective memory. Essentially it has come to mean *you're a pretender to the throne.*

When I was approached with the opportunity to lead Ford Motor Company's social media efforts in late 2007, I was struck with the incredible opportunity and responsibility that holding such a position would entail. Having worked with large brands as a consultant and agency representative, I had a good sense of some of the challenges that were in store for me. But fundamentally, I knew that that there would be situations that could only be understood by someone on the other side of the client-agency relationship.

So I called Christopher Barger.

I had known Christopher for a few short years, having been part of an agency that supported IBM and witnessed IBM's early foray into what has come to be known as "social media." My most recent interaction with him was at an annual conference for the Society for New Communications Research, which he was visiting in his capacity as the director of social media for General Motors. My respect for him was (and still is) profound—a colleague who was tackling new forms of communications at two of the largest corporations in the world—and so I asked for his advice as I considered a role at an equally storied institution.

(This is an ongoing theme in social media—even though many of us may be trailblazers, we realize that the lone wolves don't really fare that well. We absolutely rely on each other for coaching, encouragement, and guidance, even in competitive environments.)

I remember waiting for the reply to that e-mail in which I asked Christopher about the environment on the inside of a large company, what it was like to work within a matrixed team, what it took to convince him to move from New York to Michigan, etc. When the reply came, it was a long and thorough one that delved into many details, weighing the pros against the cons. That he responded at the height of the North American International Auto Show made it even more significant.

I still have that e-mail, and the main points are just as relevant and correct as ever:

1. Make sure senior communications leadership supports the direction you're going to go—not just with lip service but with a true commitment to social media.
2. Make sure you're reporting in to communications, not marketing.
3. Make sure that your management will understand that measurement is different in social media.

All very sensible points, but those that could only truly come from someone who had experience within a company rather than consulting for it.

Based on this very solid advice, I moved my family and my career to join the communications team at Ford to improve the company's reputation and build purchase consideration via the ever-growing segment of social media. Some would say it's been a success story.

Having a friend and colleague at a crosstown rival company has made the ride all the more interesting. Christopher and I managed to have fun with it, publicly play-fighting as "frenemies" but always sharing and reassuring each other behind the scenes. When he left General Motors, I was disappointed, relieved, and optimistic. Disappointed in that I didn't have an equivalent there with whom I could have that back-channel relationship, relieved that a major talent was no longer with a competitor, and optimistic for Christopher and Voce Communications.

For you see, Voce now has a strategic asset—much like the one you're holding in your hand. It has the benefit of the knowledge, passion, and leadership of someone who has actually done what it is it's coaching its clients on. We are very fortunate that Christopher has turned his considerable talent to the written page and supplied us some strong elements to make social media work within a large organization.

And to those who would try to tell you they know how to help you do it despite a lack of experience themselves, I say:

I served with Christopher Barger, I knew Christopher Barger, Christopher Barger was a friend of mine. Senator, you're no Christopher Barger.

SCOTT MONTY
GLOBAL DIGITAL COMMUNICATIONS
FORD MOTOR COMPANY

ACKNOWLEDGMENTS

Everyone who has ever written a book owes a debt of gratitude to people who helped him or her move beyond a great idea to actually getting it on paper and then getting a publisher to agree to put it out. These lists are always longer than the author can realistically include in the acknowledgments at the front of the book. I am no exception to this rule, and I am sure I have not included everyone who has helped or impacted my career. I apologize in advance to those I've missed.

That said, there are a number of people who've made incredible contributions to my professional and personal success, and I'd be derelict if I didn't thank them in writing. First and foremost, my parents, Murray and Helen Barger, whose contributions to my life would fill at least another book and who taught me that I can do anything. My wife, Holly, and my stepson, Anthony, who is my son in every aspect but DNA: if my parents taught me how to be a man, Holly and Anthony have taught me why to be one and the joy of being a family.

My editors, Niki Papadopoulos and Donya Dickerson, who shepherded me through the process from the vague idea that someone ought to write a book like this to the point of your having this book in your hands, and Julia Baxter and her team at McGraw-Hill's publicity department. Andy Sernovitz of GasPedal, who listened to my rant one night on a drive from the Salt Lick Bar-B-Que back to Austin and told me I needed to write a book. Kim Moldofsky of the blog Hormone-Colored Days, who did a blog post at about the same time saying that I should write a book. Thank you for inspiring me, guys.

My close friend Mike Maney of Alcatel-Lucent was also once my boss at IBM, and in the spring of 2003, he suggested so often that I would be really good at blogging that I finally started one just to shut him up. Not only did I enjoy it, but that blog opened the door to everything that has happened or that I've done since.

Mike and his wife, Jenn, were part of my inner circle of friends in New York. To them and the others in this circle—Tim and Donna Blair, Clint and Janet Roswell, Ed and Jane Barbini—thank you for making my New York years happier and for your continued friendship. Ed Barbini of IBM gets a double thank-you as my professional mentor; I've learned more from him about being a pro than anyone else—and I still hope that someday I'm half the leader Ed is.

Within the social media world, Aaron Strout, Allen Mireles, Amber Naslund, Audrey Walker, Brandon Chesnutt, Brian Carter, Brian Simpson, C. C. Chapman, Casey Mullins, Chris Brogan, Chris Moody, Chris Theisen, Danielle Brigida, Danny Brown, Dave Murray, David Armano, David Meerman Scott, Doug Haslam, Ekaterina Walter, Emily Thompson, Erin Kane, Geoff Livingston, Gini Dietrich, Henry Balanon, Jason Falls, Jason Keath, Jessica Randazza, Joseph Jaffe, Josh Hallett, Justin Levy, Kami Watson Huyse, Kristin Brandt, Kristin Hammond, Lucretia Pruitt, Matt Dickman, Mike Manuel, Mitch Joel, Nicole D'Alonzo, Olivier Blanchard, Ramon DeLeon, Richard Brewer-Hay, Ryan Boyles, Shauna Causey, Shel Holtz, Shelly Kramer, Summer Boone, Wayne Sutton, and the Punks (who know who they are) have inspired me in their own ways, driving me to push envelopes and break some eggs, and they deserve thanks for teaching me that not even the sky should ever be a limit.

Lindsay Lebresco of Lilly Pulitzer (formerly of Graco), David Puner of Havas Digital (formerly of Dunkin' Donuts), Zena Weist of H&R Block, Mike Wing at IBM, and Richard Binhammer at Dell were incredibly giving of their time and were willing to sit for either e-mail or phone interviews for this book. Thank you for your perspective and for helping me get this closer to right.

No one achieves success single-handedly; never has that been truer than with me. Everyone who has ever worked with me at General Motors has been partly responsible for what we've achieved together. Len Marsico (who recruited me to Detroit and wouldn't take no for an answer), Steve Harris, Chris Preuss, Edd Snyder, Mary Henige, Lori Arpin, Natalie Johnson, Rick Crooks, Adam Denison, Lesley Hettinger, Robyn Henderson, Wendy Clark, Connie Burke, Annalisa Bluhm, Nuria Baldello-Sole, Mike Morrissey, Phil Colley, Chris Vary, Chris Perry, Laurie Mayers, Jud Branam, Chris Poterala, Gayle Weiswasser, Lisa Bader, Andy Schueneman, Lish Dorset, John Cortez, Bobby Hoppey, Patrick Hernandez, Kameya Shows, Nicole Carriere, Rob Peterson, Jason Laird, Joe LaMuraglia, Lisa Gilpin, Deb Ochs, Jennie Ecclestone, Donna McLallen, Dave Barthmuss, Otie McKinley, Jordana Strosberg, Lauren Indiveri, Ryan Zemmin, Danielle Ciotti, Whitney Drake, Nick Twork, George Jones, Patrick Reyes, Janet Keller, Suzanne Johnson, and Arianna Kughn: thank you for making me look good.

Finally: special appreciation, thanks, and love to the crew who sat in the war room with me on June 1, 2009, and the week that fell in its aftermath. Unless you were there, putting in the 21-hour days, bearing the intense stress of being the social network faces of General Motors during the week of the Chapter 11 filing, you can't know what that group of people dealt with, more admirably than anyone could have expected. In some ways, that week was the proudest week of my career, and the people who went through it with me will always have a place in my heart for being in the foxhole with me. Wendy, Connie, Annalisa, Nuria, Mike, Robyn, Adam, Otie, Mary, Andy, Potsie, Lish: you will always be my Dirty Dozen, and I'll always be grateful for what we did together that week.

INTRODUCTION

If there's one thing you can count on in life, it's the bandwagon. You can see it everywhere, in almost every aspect of culture. On television, whenever one network finds a hit series, you can count the weeks until the other networks come out with something similar. (Witness the explosion of reality TV, for example.) In football, when a team wins the Super Bowl with a particular style of play, you can be assured that next season another team or two will be running similar offenses. Have you ever noticed how a team suddenly gets more fans when it starts to win? We all know people who discovered their "lifelong love" of the Boston Red Sox in 2004 or bought Miami Heat jerseys as soon as LeBron James, Dwyane Wade, and Chris Bosh signed their contracts there.

When the bandwagon phenomenon extends into the business world, it usually results in a rush of companies trying to either (a) duplicate another's success with a particular concept or process or (b) show themselves to be "innovative" by their use of the latest tools, technologies, or concepts. From Six Sigma to Total Quality Management to Knowledge Management, business history is full of concepts that spurred cottage industries, with squadrons of consultants lining up to help willing businesses adopt the latest concept, model, or practice.

Social media is no different. In the past five years, new communications platforms and networks have emerged whose adoption numbers dwarf those of the media that came before them—and the speed at which these platforms and networks emerge can scare the hell out of most marketing and communications departments. As Facebook, YouTube, Twitter, and Foursquare have attracted millions of users and boatloads of media attention, companies still struggling to adjust or react to the emergence of blogs now feel even more overwhelmed by the speed, size, and magnitude of the changes wrought by social media. It's downright scary to many of us—especially when we realize that customers now *expect* us to be not only present within the social Web but also aware, responsive, and engaged.

The sense of imminent change, the reality of consumers taking control of branding and reputation, and the fear of being seen as behind the times have made "social media strategy" one of the hottest specialties in marketing and communications. And predictably, social media "experts" have popped up like mushrooms on a forest floor. Hundreds of agencies and consultants knock at the doors of companies and organizations around the world, proposing programs and emphasizing the urgency of developing a solid social media strategy.

Now, it should be said that there are a lot of very smart social media consultants out there. I'm a fan of Geoff Livingston, Valeria Maltoni, Jeremiah Owyang, David Meerman Scott, Mitch Joel, Olivier Blanchard, Shel Holtz, Jason Falls, Amber Naslund, and Chris Brogan, among others, and consider many of them friends. I read their blogs often, and I've learned from them.

But telling a company from the outside what it should do is one thing; actually making it happen from the inside is quite another.

Over the past seven years, I've had the good fortune to lead social media efforts at General Motors and IBM. At IBM, we built a company-wide blogging and podcasting effort that came to include more than 3,000 employees by the time I left—at a time when Facebook was only for college students, when Twitter didn't exist, and when most of the media and big businesses stereotyped the average blogger as "a guy sitting in his living room in his pajamas writing."[1] At General Motors, I not only had the chance to build the company's social media program from the ground up but also led GM's presence in social networks through its tumultuous decline into, and eventually its successful emergence from, Chapter 11 bankruptcy. At both companies, the programs I led won industry awards and earned positive recognition from the PR, marketing, and business media as being among the best in business use of social media.

I know from that experience and from talking to friends and social media counterparts at other big companies that there can be a lot of frustration when social media "experts" talk about transparency and engagement without realizing some of the barriers a corporate client might face. There's some exasperation out there about how frequently we're pitched with social media strategies by people who don't recognize the real costs of executing them or what a client may face when trying to win support for them within the company. If you're in a position of trying to manage or build a social program at a big organization, this may sound familiar.

Unfortunately, the broad changes in both tactics and mindset necessary for social Web success are often crippled by institutional and cultural resistance. Legal compliance, policy changes, HR buy-in, and the traditionally contentious relationship between marketing and PR are all obstacles that must be overcome. And if you haven't been inside a company or organization—if you don't know corporate culture and bureaucracy, or have no experience navigating internal minefields—then you don't know how to make social media work inside a company. It doesn't matter how many Twitter followers you have, how many people read your blog, or how sound your ideas are.

Why This Book

There are two things I want to say to you if you have this book in your hands right now. The first is a simple "Thank you." I'm a big believer in expressing gratitude, and I don't think people hear it enough.

The second thing I want you to know is that I'm assuming that I know something about you, about why this book interested you among all the others that are out there regarding social media. (Or the "social Web." Or the "real-time Web." Or, God forbid, "Web 2.0." There are as many names for this stuff as there are for carbonated sugar beverages.)

- You work in communications or marketing leadership for a large organization—maybe even a Fortune 500 company—and want to ramp up your organization's social media presence and programs.
- You work in communications or marketing at one of these large organizations but in the rank and file; you're one of the doers as well as one of the thinkers, and your leadership has started putting some pressure on you to develop a social media strategy for your company.
- You're considering a job offer from a big organization to lead the development of its social media program or are about to be given that responsibility. You might know social media very well or be only vaguely familiar with anything beyond Facebook—but either way, you're trying to figure out how you're going to build this ark for your organization.
- You're with a PR or marketing agency with big corporate or organizational clients. Maybe your agency has proposed social media campaigns for your client, only to have them rejected or resisted. Maybe your client is asking for big social media ideas. Or maybe you're just reading the tea leaves and realizing that you're going to need to start including social media ideas in your pitches. Whatever the case, you're

wondering what pitches your client may like or accept, why ideas that you think are surefire winners don't seem to go anywhere with the client or die somewhere inside the client's walls, and what you need to build into your pitches that will get you closer to winning client buy-in.

If you're one of the people I just mentioned, the realities of your social media existence are different from the realities faced by an individual practitioner or consultant. For you, winning at social media isn't just about being first to adopt the next big thing, or coming up with a killer idea, or even being transparent and human. Doing your job well means playing the Game of Internal Politics well enough to enable you to take advantage of those great lightbulb-over-your-head moments or the really creative ideas that some expert, consultant, or agency brings to you. For you, winning means playing the corporate game, gaining the right internal converts at the right time, and building the right infrastructure *inside* the organization. Your job requires that you recognize that demands and expectations of big companies—and even laws governing their behavior—are different from those for individuals or small shops.

My hope for this book is to help you navigate those demands and expectations—to help you understand the mechanics of corporate social media and help you develop a strategy that works for all the stakeholders present in a bigger organization. The experience I've had at two Fortune 20 companies can work for you and help you put the pieces in place for success before you start building. I've learned quite a bit in the past seven years, much of it through trial and error, about how to personally represent a big brand in the social Web; those lessons are here, too. What you'll find in these pages isn't theory or outside analysis or utopian proclamations of what should be; it's the counsel of someone who's been there—more than once—and who's succeeded in the job you're probably faced with if you're reading this book.

I'm not going to spell out some magical genius foolproof formula for how to build a legendary social media campaign. Every campaign and every company is different. You could no more copy a social media strategy template from the automotive industry and apply it verbatim to your industry than you could take the formula for successfully launching a new car model and apply it to launching a new flavor of potato chips. There is no exact recipe for social media success any more than there is a one-size-fits-all formula for success with traditional marketing programs. In the immortal words of Westley from *The Princess Bride*, "Anyone who says differently is selling something."

In this new media environment, a new social network, platform, or technology seems to emerge pretty much every month. What seems like the most innovative strategy one day quickly becomes standard practice. Having a brand presence on Twitter in 2008 made you a leader; by 2009 if you didn't have one, you were behind the curve. Using QR codes in 2010 was innovative; in 2011 everyone's done them, and proudly boasting of your cutting-edge new campaign with QR codes will get you yawned at, laughed at, or both for the claim. If you want to lead in social media, you've got to get comfortable with constantly evolving your tactics and never having an "in stone" strategy or playbook.

But there *are* some general principles and steps you can take to increase your odds of success. I've been fortunate to get to know many of the people who've built leading social media programs at other companies—Richard Binhammer and Manish Mehta at Dell, Zena Weist at H&R Block, Ekaterina Walter at Intel, Scott Monty at Ford, Paula Berg (who built Southwest Airlines' program), Michael Donnelly at Coca-Cola, and many others. Many of us talk to each other at conferences, via e-mail, or on Facebook, sharing the experiences, challenges, and rewards of leading a brand's social presence—and a pattern has emerged from these collective experiences.

Lucky Seven: The Seven Elements to a Winning Social Media Program

A few years ago, when the first companies began to experiment in social media, there wasn't a template or blueprint for putting together a winning presence in the social Web. People like Frank Eliason, then at Comcast, were able by virtue of their mere participation in conversations and networks to establish their company's reputation as a social media leader—and their stories gave rise to the legend of the lone visionary, pounding away at his keyboard, posting comments on blogs, engaging with people on Twitter, joining discussion threads on Facebook, and single-handedly pushing his company into the twenty-first century of communications and marketing.

I'm not sure that the mythology of the lone visionary was ever entirely accurate, but if it was, that time has most certainly passed. The social Web has matured too far and grown too big—and companies' presence alone is no longer enough of a surprise to win favor.

Organizational social media programs are no longer an experiment; they are a facet of every company's go-to-market strategy. And for something that's now as basic as media buys or a PR strategy, you can't make it up on the fly. You've got to cover all the bases, get organized, and be strategic about how you build the capability inside your organization.

It's been my experience that there are seven elements to a winning *corporate* or *organizational* social media program—elements vital to the development of a long-term, strategic initiative capable of not just a winning campaign but also sustained success over time:

- An executive champion inside the organization who, while perhaps not directly involved in executing social media programs, fully endorses the organization's involvement in it and provides internal support for the program and its leader

- Understanding and consensus within the company as to which part of the organization (i.e., communications, marketing, Web development, etc.) will "own" social media and set the strategic direction for the company's social media program
- A strong social media evangelist who leads the strategic and day-to-day execution of a company's social media initiatives and who not only is a social media expert but also has the power and resources to develop and execute programs as well as build the overall strategy
- A well-articulated set of metrics that define a company's expectations and objectives for its social media program and what success looks like as well as tangible measurements to track its progress and effectiveness
- A smooth partnership between the organization's social media team and its legal department, a working relationship in which neither side sees the other as "the enemy" but rather one in which both work together on social media programs and meeting their objectives
- A well-articulated social media policy that is widely communicated to the organization's employees and may even be made available to consumers and observers
- A comprehensive education program that trains the organization's employees not just on the social media policy but also on the technologies and platforms of the social Web, on how to handle specific kinds of situations in social networks, and on the expectations that both audiences and the company have of them within those networks

In the next few chapters, I'm going to explore each of these in detail.

Every program is different, and much of your success depends on factors unique to your organization: the product you're trying to sell, the brand you're building awareness for, and the personalities of the people you have executing your program. But while there are many variables to social media success, these seven elements are the constants, the ones that underpin the most successful programs I've observed. Incorporate all of them, and you've got all the right ingredients in place for a successful social media program. Miss or underperform on any of them, and your program is flawed and wounded from the outset, either preventing it from living up to its fullest potential in a best-case scenario or setting you up for significant failure in a worst-case scenario.

In Chapters 10 through 13, I'll identify some things you need to know—guidelines that should underlie every campaign or effort you undertake: how to work effectively with bloggers, how to drive social media success even if you don't have a huge budget, and what to do when things go wrong. These are just as important to success as building the right infrastructure inside your organization.

Take the process of cooking a gourmet meal. You can be really gifted in the kitchen, but if you don't have the right ingredients, you're not going to be able to make beef Wellington. Likewise, if you don't know sugar from salt, then having all the right ingredients won't help you. You also have to understand the basic principles of cooking—which seasonings and spices work well together, which flavors amuse the palate and which will clash, and what to cook in which order to get the meal just right.

Your social media initiative is very much the same. In order to succeed, you'll need both the right elements and enough gut sense to make a lot of things up on the fly. What we're doing in this book is preparing you for your social media gourmet meal. The seven elements are your basic ingredients; without them, you won't be cooking the dish you want. The guidelines are your principles; understanding them will help you improvise, create signature flavors for your program, and cope with disaster should it arise.

To keep with the cooking analogy, you need to be able to experiment confidently—but more important, you also need to be OK with having some of those experiments ending up tasting awful. It's the only way you learn. It's the only way *I've* learned. When I was leading social initiatives at IBM and General Motors, I didn't have that confidence or knowledge going in to building the programs I've worked on. In fact, more than a few of the recommendations I'm including in this book are things we *didn't* do at GM when I had the chance to build a program from the ground up. That's how I learned that they're things you *should* do!

Social media is not even a decade old. We're all still learning and adding to the canon. No one, not even those of us who've been doing this for a few years, can claim to have it "nailed" so well that we can't still learn to be even more effective.

But for now, every journey of a thousand miles begins with just a few steps. So it's into the conference room we go—because your bosses are waiting, your customers are waiting, and you have miles to go before you sleep.

CHAPTER 1

THE LAY OF THE LAND

The world of social media and Internet communities has been called "the Wild West" so often by so many observers (usually those who aren't directly involved in social media, by the way) that it's become an accepted truth. While I don't think the analogy is 100 percent on target, it's used widely enough that I'll stick with it, drawing a few parallels to make a point.

The most important asset for survival in an Old West town was knowing the lay of the land. A sheriff in the Wild West—at least the one of popular imagination—had to know every foot of his county, know the country like the back of his hand, and understand the unwritten rules of a society that allegedly had no rules. If he did, he was able to keep some order. Maybe he didn't *control* everything, but at least there was a sense that the law was upheld and that the good people of the town didn't have to live in fear of outlaw gangs.

The analogy pretty much holds true in the modern "Wild West" of social media: if you have a lay of the land and understand its nooks, crannies, and unwritten rules, you can master some elements of this "Wild West" and maintain some semblance of order.

So before we do anything else, let's go through the lay of the social media land, as it were. In this chapter, we'll get an understanding of this new environment and the basic rules of survival within it. Once you've got that down, we'll move on to what you need to build a successful social media program.

Social Media Is About *People*, Not Technology

It can often seem as if the world of social media exists because of the development of inexpensive (or free) and simple publishing tools, like WordPress, or the emergence of Facebook or Twitter. The social media "gurusphere" and big businesses and brands often develop a fascination with the latest bright and shiny object—be it location-based services like Foursquare or Gowalla, influence measurement tools like Klout, or emerging community networks like Quora or Google+—and rush to identify their "strategy" for utilizing each tool. The problem with overfocusing on the technologies and platforms is that it misses the point. The phenomenon most people think of as "social media" is merely enabled by technology, not created by it.

"Social media" is an environment in which the barriers to publication have crumbled, making anyone with an Internet connection a potential publisher and trusted source of information. Whether about events or products, it's an environment where traditional sources of information, such as the "traditional media," the government, or a company or organization, are less trusted or viewed with skepticism or cynicism. It sometimes baffles some of my longtime PR colleagues that anyone in an audience might consider "Joe Blogger" to be as credible a source of news as a major publication or as credible a source of company information as the company itself. But in many cases, that's where we are. Decrying it or arguing that it shouldn't be does not make the environment any less open.

In the social media environment, real connections with real people are not only possible but also in many cases more greatly valued than the official voice of a company. Organizational voices (e.g., "Acme Company announced today that . . .") are less trusted and less important, and the voices of real people—even those representing a brand—carry much more weight. In this environment, audiences are looking to connect with a person, not a logo. What you say is still important, but *who says it* is at least equally important, that is, a brand's message is only as credible in these environments as the people from the brand who communicate it. The "social" is always more important than the "media" and always will be. Facebook and Twitter and blogs and podcasts and YouTube may empower these dynamics, but they don't cause them. If you build a social media program thinking that you simply need to shift your attention to these new media without shifting your tactics or approaches, you're going to fail. Few people want to be marketed to in these channels, at least in the traditional sense. They're looking to interact—with *real people* who just happen to work for that brand—and they want to be *listened to*. When someone goes onto Twitter or a brand's Facebook page or blog, she doesn't just want whatever information the brand wants to push today; she can get that from traditional sources. She wants her questions answered, she wants her complaints or comments addressed, and she wants to know that her voice has been heard by the brand. That two-way dynamic is the most important aspect of social media, and if you've not grasped that, then it won't matter which platforms you're on or how quickly you got there. Audiences reward brands and organizations that join social networks or platforms to talk *with* people and increasingly ignore those that are there only to talk *at* them.

For Businesses Using Social Media, Social Media Is Still a *Business Tool*

Businesses and organizations can't use the tools in the same way that individual users do—and the social media community must understand this. Organizational social media is done with purpose, for a purpose.

The individual connections and relationships made within social networks on behalf of organizations and brands don't happen because the brands want to appear more approachable or more human. Those are nice side effects. But make no mistake: as unromantic as it sounds, businesses and organizations get into social media because they want customers (or potential customers) to eventually buy their products, feel better about having purchased their products, and have problems with their products resolved more efficiently, and they want to get insight on what might make a customer more likely to buy those products in the future. "The conversation" and "engagement" are just means to that end. Nonprofits should have similar goals: involvement in social media is a means to spread information and raise awareness about their cause, increase membership, drive a certain action from members, or raise money.

Before you start your social media program, you must know what your organization is looking to achieve or accomplish. Like any other business initiative, your social media program should have identifiable goals and objectives. Build those goals and objectives rather than just engaging in undirected "social media activity."

It's easy to get caught up in the "Kumbaya" talk about "the conversation" and the idea of relationships. But in a business context, those conversations and relationships are meant to lead somewhere. Richard Binhammer, who's one of the main architects of Dell's success in social media, puts it this way: "No company can afford not to be very close to its customers; social media is a viable, valuable tool within your arsenal for this whether you're talking B2B or B2C."[1]

While the conversational and sometimes uncontrolled nature of these media may seem unfamiliar or even frivolous, there is often real business value to even the most casual of interactions. Even a seemingly trivial conversation on Twitter or an occasional blog post that seems to have nothing to do with brand positioning or messaging can be a step in the direction that eventually yields the bottom-line results that the organization is looking for.

Social Media Does Not Change Your Business, Nor Is It a Panacea for All That Ails You

Social media is a fantastic tool for building relationships with audiences and customers, improving customer service, raising awareness of a product or service, and sometimes even helping to sell that product or service. But it is not a set of magic beans that turn chicken poop into chicken salad. If your product is not satisfactory to customers, the best social media program in the world is not going to disguise that reality.

In fact, social media can serve to amplify flaws in your product. If your customer service processes limit what your agents are able to do for customers, then putting a handful or even all of your customer service team on Facebook and Twitter isn't going to improve your customer service ratings. In fact, it will just give your customers one more access point to lousy customer service that frustrates them and makes them feel uncared for.

Social media also is not an elixir that magically changes your company's culture overnight. The existence of hammers and nails doesn't mean that the non-mechanically inclined (like me!) go out and start building things; if it's not something that's in you, the existence of a tool doesn't suddenly infuse you with it. If your culture isn't disposed toward open conversation and genuinely hearing your customers or the audiences you're targeting,

Facebook and Twitter don't suddenly turn you into Zappos; social media tools are as useless to you as a hammer is to a horse. As Richard Binhammer from Dell puts it, "If you don't have a culture that wants to listen with big ears, social media won't change that."[2]

My first experience with social media in a big organization was at IBM in the mid-2000s. We got a lot of credit—I think deservedly so—for the enthusiasm with which IBM embraced the emergence of blogs and empowered its employees to get involved in blogging. But it didn't happen in a vacuum. Mike Wing, IBM's vice president of strategic and executive communications, is quick to point out that IBM's enthusiasm for the openness of blogging was consistent with a longer-term evolution of its culture. From the emergence of an employee-driven and employee-written intranet to the "jams" (targeted, focused brainstorming sessions that welcomed all ideas and criticism) IBM conducted in the years before blogging took off, Mike recalls, IBM was on a gradual progression toward a culture of open dialogue and employee empowerment. "The extent to which social media is embraced depends on what the organization is ready for," he says.[3] It wasn't that social media changed IBM's culture and was a revolutionary step; IBM's culture made the adoption of social media—and the initiatives that resulted that won us so much acclaim—that much easier and likely to succeed.

Mike also points out that technologies and platforms are rarely so complicated that they can't be adopted by a big organization. Instead, it is not complexity but management's attitude that is the key, he says; according to Mike, the most important social media platform is the level of management's comfort with and trust in its employees.[4] In other words, if your organization's leadership is uncomfortable with the idea of giving up some control to audiences external and internal, social media is going to have a rough time gaining traction there. If, on the other hand, your management and culture are open to change and the input of employees and customers, social media is merely an extension of that approach and won't be entirely disruptive.

Because of some of the hype that surrounds social media, a set of perhaps unrealistic expectations for what it can do for an organization has developed. It can amplify your marketing and communications programs and deepen customer relationships. But it cannot make you something you're not, and it won't make you what your culture doesn't allow it to be. A great social media program should—and will—feel like a natural extension of a great company. If your company's culture is stiff and controlled and your products aren't all that great, then your social media program will likely feel stiff, controlling, and false, and your program just won't be all that successful. You're best advised to go about fixing your culture before worrying about launching a social media program.

You Don't Have Control Anymore—Get Used to It

The idea of letting an audience dictate the direction or topic of a conversation is scary enough to make some companies wonder whether they really want to get fully involved in social media. Twitter, with its rapid-fire, real-time pace, open nature, and seeming randomness of trending topics, can seem like an uncontrolled free-for-all to a nervous executive unused to public criticism. The idea of allowing user-generated content on a company's Facebook page or website often draws warnings from multiple corners in an organization. As a PR rep for a major national brand has told me, "Our execs know that the critics are out there on the Web; they just don't think we should provide them a platform to bash us." My friend's company is not alone. From legal concerns about an organization's liability for what a customer might leave on the company website to concerns about impact on the brand if disparaging comments appear on a page designed to get customers to want to buy, this desire to assert control over conversations about the brand is pervasive enough to be familiar to most social media evangelists within corporate settings.

In social media, the audience directs the conversation, and everyday customers are often thought of as equally reliable as or even more reliable than a brand when it comes to information about that brand. When a company tries to reassert control over a conversation happening online, its efforts are often met with scorn, anger, or charges that it "just doesn't get it."

So why would any executive in her right mind want her brand to engage in social media? Why get involved if you can't control the content or conversations that are taking place about your product? Because you already lost control a long time ago—of conversations about your brand, the way your messages are received, and the way your brand is perceived. The ability of anyone and everyone to air an opinion—not to mention the larger breakdown of authority and trust in Western society, especially in America—means that audiences long ago stopped taking your word for how good your product is, what your brand stands for, or whether your news is truly relevant.

They also stopped putting as much stock as you do in what the traditional media has to say about you or your products. Have you checked a trust survey recently? About the only entities that finish below "corporate America" are politicians and the media. We in marketing and communications invest so much effort into influencing traditional media that we sometimes forget that the audience doesn't put as much stock in these media as we do.

The fact of the matter is, people have been talking about us like this and mistrusting us and counteracting our messaging for a long time now; the social Web just amplified this and made it easier for them to share their perceptions. But marketers are kidding themselves if they think they can go back to the days when they were the most trusted source of information about their own brands or organizations or the days when having relationships with a few reporters at a handful of key outlets meant that they could control how a brand was represented and perceived by the public. Those days are long gone; get over it.

The good news is that while you can't control online conversations, you *can* influence them. The more you're involved, the more relationships you build, the more questions you've answered candidly, and the more times you've stood there and taken criticism, the more audiences are going to see you as an equal and valued partner in their community, and the more they'll give you the benefit of the doubt or be willing to hear your position or side on things. Plus, your responses end up showing up in searches on the topic; if you're not out there to counter unfair or inaccurate statements about your brand, the only thing Google or Bing will turn up is your critics. There's a saying that you shouldn't let perfect be the enemy of good; in social media, you shouldn't let control be the enemy of influence. Avoiding a social media presence unless or until you can control it is self-delusional and also misses a tremendous opportunity to actually influence people in the directions you want them to go.

Your Organization Is Now a Media Outlet

With all the fuss and fascination about the emergence of bloggers as influencers or the launch of some new tool, channel, or platform that's attracting lots of users, it's sometimes easy to focus so much on who's influential in which platform or whose blog we want to be mentioned in that we can overlook one of the most fundamental benefits of the social Web to big business: the ability to develop and publish content just like everyone else.

The fact is that these tools really do provide big brands the same opportunities as individuals to publish content and opinion inexpensively. It used to be that in order to get a big publicity hit, an organization's media relations team would have to pitch the idea to big publications and hope something would click. After the Net emerged, media relations started aiming to land placements on popular websites for their content. But whether the clip appeared in print, on television, or on the Web, an organization had to rely on the outlet's or reporter's interpretation of its news, announcement, or messages.

Today, a company no longer has to rely on anyone else's interpretation; if you develop creative and interesting content that draws an audience, you're communicating directly to that audience—no reporter's biases or time and space limitations involved. Instead of trying to get clicks on someone else's website, a company is *competing* with those sites for clicks. You want audiences to click on *your* content rather than content generated by "the media," a blogger, or anyone else. Instead of clicking on a video developed by *USA Today* and placed on its site, audiences can watch videos produced by *you*. Instead of reading the *Wall Street Journal*'s take on your latest announcement, your audience can read your blog posts. The trick here, of course, is creating content that is compelling enough to steal clicks from traditional media. Far too often, brands forget that their "messages" in and of themselves aren't always compelling to someone who doesn't work there.

Think of a company that's not in your industry and doesn't compete with you—one in which you have no professional interest, that you only relate to as a consumer. Would you watch a three-minute video about its new environmentally friendly packaging or its "version 3.1.1" slight upgrade of its flagship product? Would you care if you got an e-mail asking you to like its Facebook page so you could get "exclusive" access to its newest commercial? Would you forward it to your friends or post it on your Facebook page? Now think about the kind of content you *do* share. Which videos do you post on friends' Facebook pages? What makes a story, post, or podcast worthy enough for you to send the link to your friends? When you're developing content you hope will spread through social networks and across the Web, put yourself in the audience's shoes. Give them reasons to choose your content over other sources—whether by entertaining them or giving them access to information they really can't get anywhere else—and don't assume that the audience will be interested just because you want them to be.

Even though you're trying to win clicks to your *content*, these clicks don't always have to happen on your *site*. When an organization invests significant resources in creating "microsites," "online content hubs," or something along those lines, it's overlooking one of the most powerful aspects of social media: if you create great content, the social Web will do the work for you. Rather than spend a lot of money trying to draw people to *your* site, why not focus those resources on building content others will want to share and building up a network to syndicate that content to? It's incredibly easy to make your video content shareable—often, with a simple click of a button or by copying a single line of code, other bloggers and online media can copy or share your content and post it on their sites or pages.

But whether audiences are visiting your website, blog, YouTube channel, or Facebook page or seeing your content for the first time on a site unrelated to you, the point is that the tools of the social Web make your organization a content publisher—a media outlet—as much as anyone else. That's an opportunity you cannot afford to miss out on.

Social Media Are *Two-Way* Tools

It's easy to start thinking about competing with the media for how your story gets told and to start salivating while thinking of those 800 million consumers on Facebook or the nearly 200 million on Twitter just waiting to hear your messages and forget a very important point: all those people aren't just there to have your message thrust at them. They're there to interact with each other—and they expect that you know the etiquette, too. If you expect them to pay attention to you, they *expect* you to interact with them as well. This is a point frequently missed by people new to social media or who see social networks as mass collections of "eyeballs" to be marketed at. But if you only use the promotion/production side of social media, you've not fully grasped the point of its appeal. When you were a little kid, did you ever have walkie-talkies? How much fun was it if you were the only one playing? Sure, you could press the button, and in theory, someone might be able to hear what you had to say, but the game only got fun when someone else talked back to you.

Whether on Facebook, Twitter, YouTube, blog communities, or some other aspect of the social Web, people are there for the interactive nature of what they find. They want to converse back and forth on Twitter, make comments on Facebook pages and blogs, be acknowledged and responded to, get into healthy (or pointless) debates with one another, and create video responses to one another on YouTube. Audience interaction and response is at the core of the social Web. If your organization is going to be involved, your audience *expects* that you won't just be pushing messages—you'll be listening, too.

I'm not the only one to offer you this counsel; many of the successful corporate social media leaders interviewed for this book mention "listening" as the most important element in their success. Richard Binhammer, offering counsel to anyone starting from scratch in building a social media program, says, "Start by listening first; figure out what your audience is doing and what they want. You have to understand your opportunity first."[5] David Puner, who built the Dunkin' Donuts social presence, adds that "social media isn't about having Facebook; it's about knowing your audience, your brand, and what fits. Listening is paramount to everything."[6] Zena Weist at H&R Block says that the most important element to a social media program is "to make sure as you build your program the customer/prospect knows you listened, are listening, and are incorporating their input."[7] Richard also points out that "fundamentally, marketers are about understanding the customer—so it's up to us to *understand*, not fight, customer expectations and needs within social networks. It's not just about messaging!"[8] I'm quite sure that if I had talked to another dozen prominent or recognized corporate social media practitioners, at least 11 of them would have mentioned the importance of *listening* to success.

Listening takes many forms. Sometimes it's responding to customer complaints about your product online; sometimes it's answering questions someone poses about your brand—or even just general questions about products that your brand happens to make. (While I was at GM, for example, if a blogger happened to ask about buying a new car, I might try to respond not by pushing Chevrolet but by asking what he was looking for most, how much he wanted to spend, etc.) Sometimes, it's simply letting a blogger know that you read and liked her post, even if it had nothing to do with your product or brand. Whatever form listening takes, it's the most critical aspect of your social activity—because listening and interacting earn you credibility. We just talked about the importance of building up a network of people who are willing to share or spread your content. People are much more willing to do so once they've engaged in a few conversations with your brand representatives online and gotten to know you and feel a greater affinity for your brand. That doesn't happen because of your "message"; rather, it happens because you interact and listen. Just like in real life, listening to someone else makes him far more willing to listen to you; failing to do so makes him far more likely to tune you out.

Listening to and interacting with social media audiences is not a waste of time, a "necessary evil," or a distraction from your true message; it's a vital and indispensable part of your strategy. And that's something that, culturally, your organization must accept and embrace before embarking on a social media program—not just in letter but also in spirit. If the organization is simply going through the motions or pretending to be open to feedback when in reality it is not, the audience is going to sniff that out pretty quickly. You can't hide your true nature for very long online.

If your social media program or the people behind it focus too much on your message and emphasize content development or "editorial calendars" for social networks at the expense of genuine, honest, and unstructured interaction and listening, you're still looking at social channels as one-way tools instead of taking advantage of the inherent and unique characteristics of the medium. There's a difference between *digital* and *social*: digital is only one way—and if you're not interacting with and actually listening to your audience, then you're not doing social media, only digital.

It's About Transparency, Not "Authenticity"

Some "social media rock stars" will tell you that success in social media requires authenticity and transparency. I'd argue no one can prescribe "authenticity"—what might be authentically within my personality might seem forced from you, or vice versa. But transparency isn't nearly as subjective. You can't start a fake blog pretending to be a customer who just loves your product, and your employees can't participate in conversations on others' blogs to talk about your brand or your products without disclosing their connection to the company. "Nondisclosure is slimy," says H&R Block's Zena Weist. "It still is happening a lot. I call it out whenever I can. All brands need to call out nondisclosure when they see it."[9]

Transparency is not only a smart strategy. It's mandatory. If you're not 100 percent committed to transparency in your social media efforts, you'll experience consequences not only with your online audience but also with the FTC. In October 2009, the Federal Trade Commission issued its first guidelines around how brands interact with social media influencers and bloggers—or more accurately, the kinds of disclosures that must take place whenever a blogger writes an endorsement or voices support for your product or brand.[10]

While these guidelines continue to evolve and there are still questions as to how they'll be enforced, the bottom line is clear: the FTC is watching. Brands and bloggers alike need to be aware not only of the guidelines but also of the sentiment supporting them. The appetite is there to ensure full disclosure of relationships between bloggers and brands, as well as of any exchange of perceived value (free product, access to an event, etc.), and to enforce *transparency* by brands in the social Web.

It's a simple thing, really: be who you say you are, make sure that anyone who's received anything from you discloses the relationship, and don't try to "pull one over" on anyone in the social Web.

Big Brands *Can* Innovate and Be Creative in Social Media

There's a stereotype of big companies or organizations as colossi, stodgy in nature and too weighted by their bureaucracies and procedures to move quickly or innovate. This stereotype isn't unique to social media—it's generally shared across multiple industries and is embraced and even promoted by some entrepreneurs who argue that "start-up culture" is superior to that of big organizations and more conducive to innovation—but it certainly has adherents in the social media world. I've heard some social media consultants claim that they would never want to work with a big client, suggesting that organizational hubris and inertia would prevent the client from adopting anything truly groundbreaking or game-changing. Any example of a big organization's failure or struggles in social media is often treated as emblematic.

It's a silly argument. For starters, it ignores the fact that many of the most notable success stories in social media—Dell, Southwest Airlines, ComcastCares, Dunkin' Donuts, H&R Block, IBM, Graco, Best Buy, Disney, Coca-Cola, Pepsi, Starbucks, Chevrolet's SXSW program, and the Ford Fiesta Movement, among others—were generated by large organizations. But it's also neglectful of the fact that big organizations carry a lot of inherent advantages—name recognition, usually some financial resources, a marketing and PR team to help raise awareness, and larger groups of advocates or fans within an online community—that contribute to social media success.

Yes, bigger organizations have bigger bureaucracies. Yes, there can be organizational inertia or fear of risk. But entrepreneurs, start-ups, and small organizations have their own sets of challenges to overcome, from finding the money to carry off a good social media campaign to making sure enough people are paying attention. The truth is, when it comes to social media savvy or success, size doesn't matter. Big brands come up with great campaigns; small brands and individuals come up with great uses for social tools. Success comes from creativity, and creativity isn't inherently present in small organizations and missing from big ones. So don't worry about whether "the audience" thinks you should be out there as a bigger brand or organization. If you develop great content, invest time interacting in the communities you hope to influence, indulge your more creative instincts, and remain transparent (there's that word again!), your audience will come to respect and appreciate what you're doing. They might even forgive you an occasional misstep.

Now that we've established some of the basic ground rules and gotten the lay of the social media landscape, here's hoping that you not only are still convinced that you should be getting involved in social media but also feel that you have a little better sense of the environment you're about to experience. We'll move on now to the elements you'll need in place internally before you actually launch your public program.

CHAPTER 2

THE EXECUTIVE
CHAMPION

Success in social media requires the collective effort of lots of people within an organization. Marketing, communications and PR, customer service, product-line managers, product development people, and business leadership all have roles to play in making a corporation's program take shape and execute smoothly and successfully. But of all the players and roles, two are most critical to an organization's success.

The first is the social media evangelist—the person actually tasked with building the strategy and program and representing the brand in social networks. Most of the public focus and attention falls to this person, the social media expert who is the online public face of the company. We'll discuss that person more in Chapter 4.

To demonstrate the nature and importance of the second person, let's use an example from one of the most beloved films of the past quarter century. *Bull Durham* is considered by many baseball fans (including me) to be the best baseball movie ever made. Viewers are treated to a bus ride through the peculiarities and culture of minor-league baseball while following the developing relationship between worldly-wise, grizzled veteran catcher Crash Davis and his high-potential pitcher, Ebby Calvin "Nuke" LaLoosh, who, despite his golden arm, is arrogant, eccentric, and naive. Over the course of the minor-league season, the Davis-LaLoosh relationship becomes one of sports movies' most recognized and beloved mentor-mentee stories.

But if you know the movie, you know that none of it would have happened without manager Joe Riggins—who brings Davis to the team in the first place to make sure the young pitcher succeeds. While Davis focuses on making the kid as good as he can be, Riggins keeps his attention on the eventual success of the whole team on the field, at the same time being there for Davis when his support is needed. He knows enough to let Davis alone and to do the job he is there to do: make the team successful while empowering Davis to succeed in his role.

When it comes to implementing social media within a large organization, every Crash Davis needs a Joe Riggins—someone in leadership who makes the whole team successful while empowering the social media evangelist to do her specific job of bringing the organization along and maturing its social initiatives. Call this leadership role the *executive champion* of social media. This can be a different person in different organizations. Frequently the head of communications or PR plays this role, sometimes it's one of the senior people in marketing, and sometimes it's even someone forward thinking in business leadership. The executive champion isn't directly involved in developing strategy or executing social media initiatives or campaigns—but he is just as important as the evangelist in building a winning social program. The executive champion clears the path inside the organization to give social media a chance and a foothold in the first place.

This is the most critical element for social media success at any company. A strong executive champion can help make even a lesser evangelist successful. Absent such leadership (or if the executive champion is weak or only halfheartedly supports social media), even the best social media evangelist will find it difficult to truly drive adoption across the company and get full buy-in for the company's social media efforts.

David Puner, who, as the architect of Dunkin' Donuts' social presence, rose to online prominence as "Dunkin' Dave," puts it this way: "Unless you've got somebody *way* up there supporting social—somebody senior taking the leap of faith and saying 'let's go for it, let's do it'—it's hard to have a program backed with enough resources or support."[1] Zena Weist, who has led H&R Block's social media program since January 2010, is equally blunt. "You need a leader to make social media a priority within the organization," she says. "If it's not a priority, it will not get resources, and without resources, you will not have cachet to get your social media foundation built."[2]

Characteristics of the Executive Champion

First and foremost, it's not necessary to fully understand or "get" social media or be immersed in social networks for an executive champion to be effective in his role. I've been fortunate enough to work with two great ones during my corporate career, Jon Iwata at IBM and Steve Harris at General Motors. Neither man is extensively active in social networks, and unless you work in the communications field or at IBM or GM, you may not even know who they are. But neither IBM nor GM would have as extensive or well reputed a social media program without them.

The executive champion isn't the person at the organization who handles the Twitter conversations, updates the Facebook page, appears at tweetups, or decides which social media events to sponsor or attend. But he does have at least a grasp of the importance of social media and a commitment to it. When Jon asked me to be IBM's blogger-in-chief in early 2005, he was forthright about what he expected. "There will be a business application for blogs," he told me, "and we want you to help us find out what that is and make IBM a leader in blogging for business." (This was well before Twitter, before Facebook opened to noncollegiate audiences, before even MySpace exploded; at that time, "social media" largely consisted of blogs and podcasts.) When I was considering going to GM, Steve Harris won me over during our interview by telling me that what he wanted more than anything else from me was for me to "scare the hell" out of him on a regular basis—to push the company out of its comfort zones and do the innovative, "we've never done this before" kinds of things that would announce GM to be a serious player in social media. Neither Iwata nor Harris was a social media expert—that's what they were hiring someone for—but both instinctively understood the communications and media landscape well enough to know the importance of building a solid social media presence and program, and both were committed to the premise that their brand would be a leader in the space. They didn't just want their company to be active in the online social realm; they wanted to be out in front.

Your organization may not have the size or breadth of an IBM or a GM, but you're going to need someone in leadership who shares Iwata's or Harris's vision and commitment to social media. An effective executive champion has to be senior enough in the organization to:

• **Hire someone into the position of social media lead (even possibly building a team if the organization is big enough).** Both Iwata and Harris were senior vice presidents of communications at their respective companies. Depending on the organization, it might be someone in marketing, communications, or customer service, and it may not be an SVP—but wherever he comes from, the organization needs someone with the authority to make this kind of hire or create this kind of position.

- **Establish ownership and authority over the social space**. If an executive champion claims that his department will staff up for social media or lead in executing social programs but is not high enough or credible enough within the organization to be granted that leadership, the stage is set for internal clashes later. If multiple departments or leaders claim that social belongs to them, disaster will soon follow. The executive champion has to have the gravitas and clout such that when he says, "My department will lead here," the rest of the organization recognizes that leadership.
- **Mediate disputes with authority**. With social media having become as big as it has, large organizations often have multiple departments, sub-brands, or teams wanting to execute a social media program or initiative. Ideally these groups are working together and agree on the right course of action. But when differences of opinion or direction cannot be worked out or when disputes aren't getting solved at the working level, the executive champion needs both the wisdom to mediate and make a decision and the seniority to have his word stand. If the executive champion hears two possible courses of action or is asked to choose between direction A or direction B and says "we're going to do A," all parties in the organization need to recognize that executive's authority and not go off saying, "Well, Smith said go with A, but we don't have to listen to that."

Achieving that kind of authority doesn't just come with a title or position, however. An executive champion who claims leadership in social media without any demonstrated knowledge or reason for that leadership is not going to be credible. The executive champion also will need to be organizationally adept and agile enough to support his claim to social media leadership and responsibility. The executive champion will need to do the following:
- **Sell the social media vision to the highest levels of business leadership**. At some point, the C level of the organization

will need to at the very least be made aware of the team's social media plans. After all, if an organization is spending money on something and even making a hire or promotion for someone to *lead* the organization's efforts in a space, support from those highest levels is going to be critical. The executive champion needs to sell the C-suite on the importance of the social space in general and why resources allocated to it are being wisely spent.

• **Credibly take this vision to the rest of the organization.** Social media is at this point big enough and is talked about frequently enough that lots of people in the organization are going to see it as important—and if they think that it's being done poorly or that it doesn't fit with the rest of the organization's communications, marketing, or customer service strategy, they'll revolt. The executive champion needs to not only have credibly established leadership but also routinely convince his peers of the validity and strength of the program's direction. A strong executive champion will also listen to ideas and concerns from those peers in order to keep them included in the process and discourage parallel programs.

At Dell, Manish Mehta has played the role of executive champion of social media for four years. While Manish is not the face of Dell online to most people (that role falls most prominently to Richard Binhammer or Lionel Menchaca), he's been in the middle of the program behind the scenes. "Lionel does so much of the blogging, and he's one of the ones people know," says Richard, "but he's not fighting all the internal battles. That's Manish."[3] While Mehta was the first person ever to write a post for Direct2Dell (Dell's blog), he's not the most public member of Dell's social team. He just keeps things running smoothly behind the scenes. That's exactly what Richard, Lionel, and the rest of the Dell team need him to do.

Leadership Style and Needs from the Executive Champion

Once ownership of social media has been established and a budget obtained, what kind of leadership should the executive champion display? While it's true that the executive champion does not have to be directly involved in social networks, it is important that he not be wholly disinterested either. In order to be effective, the executive champion should at least occasionally be included in or briefed on strategic discussions. He should be updated regularly on how the budget is being spent and how much is left. Measurement and metrics should be shared with the executive champion regularly. After all, how can he champion the cause inside the organization if he's not being given information that solidifies his position or proves that what's being done is working?

It's also important for the executive champion to enforce consistency among social media, marketing, and communications strategies. Imagine that a brand's social media lead directs his team to execute an online-centered campaign around one of the brand's products. The event seems like a big success from a social media perspective: participation from the targeted bloggers is high, the event goes smoothly, and there are lots of positive posts about the brand. Perhaps the brand or the event being carried out even becomes a trending topic on Twitter, and the brand's Facebook page and Twitter account pick up several hundred new followers. Sounds like a win, right? But what if the campaign centers around a specific product and targets "tech-savvy twenty-something young professionals," while the target market for the product is actually "suburban mothers from upscale families"— and there's about to be a high-visibility advertising and marketing campaign aimed at reaching that audience? While it wouldn't invalidate the success the social media campaign achieves, that campaign would certainly have been "off message," wouldn't have reached the product's target audience, and wouldn't have taken any advantage of the advertising to reinforce the message. Wouldn't that feel like something of a missed opportunity or an incomplete effort? With that in mind, another very important role for an executive champion is ensuring that social efforts sync with larger communications and marketing strategies for the organization. A social media initiative that isn't in line with larger branding efforts is not just a missed opportunity. At worst, it can be counterproductive, cause inconsistency, and confuse an audience as to a brand's message or positioning.

No matter how well informed the social media lead is about an organization's overall communications and marketing strategy, the executive champion is inevitably going to be privy to more information by virtue of his access to senior leadership. It's the responsibility of both the evangelist and the executive champion to ensure that what's happening in social media reflects these larger strategies—and it's the additional responsibility of the executive champion to ensure that social media tactics are part of greater strategic planning from the outset. In the earlier example (the ad campaign targeted at twentysomething professionals), the role of the executive champion would be twofold. First, as the new ad campaign focused on those upscale moms was being developed, the executive champion should have been reminding everyone in marketing and advertising leadership to keep social media in mind as the program took shape and asking them to work with the social media evangelist in building social media into the program rather than adding it as an afterthought. Second, the executive champion should have been briefing the social media evangelist on the upcoming strategy and campaign and telling the evangelist whom to work with in marketing, advertising, or PR to learn more. At that point, it becomes the evangelist's job to actually build the social program, but the executive champion has to have made the connections and primed the pump for social media to be part of the larger program.

The Most Important Relationship in Brand Social Media

It's said so often that it's become cliché: social media is about relationships. I'd argue that within a big organization, the most important social media relationship of them all is the one between the evangelist and the champion. If these two people aren't working in sync, the social program will inevitably suffer.

Trust is key. Since the executive champion is most often going to be a communications or marketing leader rather than a social media specialist, he's unlikely to be familiar enough with the social space to know whether an initiative makes sense. The executive champion will have to trust the social media leader and her team. This is not always a natural trust—smart social tactics often make traditionalists uncomfortable—so it must be worked on as a priority. There should be frequent and two-way conversations between them—with the evangelist taking the time to share activities and to explain why each activity or program makes sense socially and the executive champion making sure that broader company strategy is clearly communicated. This would help ensure that the social media evangelist is aware of upcoming marketing or communications efforts that could be relevant to the work the social team is doing or that the social team should be working to take advantage of. Ideally, the two should have regularly scheduled conversations—informally over coffee, formally in the office, whatever works best for them. Not only will doing this keep information flowing freely and build the necessary trust between the two, but it can also guard against overreaching by either party.

Micromanagement by the champion can result in social initiatives that feel too "corporate" or "marketing-y." On the other hand, a rogue evangelist not fully integrated with the rest of the organization can be disconnected, inconsistent with the brand's larger strategy, and blind to opportunities to reinforce the brand's message or take advantage of traditional marketing efforts already in place.

It's not fair to expect an executive to champion social efforts across the organization that he has not at least been briefed on; it's also not fair to expect a social media leader to work in line with the organization's larger efforts if she's treated as little more than a community manager and is never made aware of other strategic efforts. The champion and evangelist should communicate regularly, and their relationship has to be a priority for both.

Managing Risks and Insulating Against Failures

All the hype about and emphasis on social networks in the past few years might lead people to believe that there's a definitive right way and wrong way to do it. In reality, the social media space is still emerging, and the playbook for social media is being written and rewritten as the space evolves.

In this environment, an executive champion will have to be comfortable with ambiguity and taking risks. There are going to be times when "I think so" is the best answer the evangelist will have for the question "Will this program work?" There will be times where something the evangelist thought would work instead fell flat or met resistance. There will be efforts made that will in hindsight have been mistakes and monies spent that everybody involved will wish after the fact to have back. As long as lessons are learned each time, and the same mistakes are not made repeatedly, this is part of the social media marketing process.

The executive champion must also be comfortable taking these risky programs to leadership and perhaps even be willing to report back to leadership occasionally on the lessons learned from failed initiatives. Without that kind of managerial courage from the executive champion, the social leader or team can be isolated, left out on a limb to twist when something doesn't go as planned. Future initiatives might not get the support necessary to empower the social team to take chances and innovate.

Managing Agency-Company Relationships

As social media continues to generate attention and draw the spotlight, most organizations will experience a barrage of marketing, PR, and social media consultants and agencies approaching various parts of the company and offering to run the organization's social media initiatives. Many of these are going to be good, solid agencies or consultants with lots of good ideas and experience helping clients achieve both business and social media results. In fact, I'm not aware of a single big brand that's achieved success in social media that hasn't worked with at least one agency or consultant—outside thinking and perspective is often a critical element to your effectiveness. The executive champion should work with the evangelist to identify strong potential agency or consultant partners and then help make sure necessary funding and resources are available to bring them aboard.

Unfortunately, some agencies will talk fast and drop a lot of jargon into their presentation hoping to fluster, confuse, frighten, or dazzle brands into thinking that they know the online social world better than the brand does. The social media evangelist should know the difference but will occasionally need support from the executive champion to help hold off a particularly enthusiastic marketing or communications manager who's been on the receiving end of such a presentation and is pushing to sign on with them. (The champion's moderation may be needed because the evangelist might be seen simply as "protecting her turf" when arguing against such a proposal. Having a leader back the evangelist at times like these can help avoid contracts with agencies that prove to be costly mistakes.)

Money Talks

Finally, the executive champion is going to be in the best position to provide budget for the social media program or be able to credibly and effectively go "tin-cupping" through the rest of the organization to acquire that budget—and the odds are, at least at first, the executive champion will *need* to do this. Perhaps the biggest myth around social media, at least from an organizational standpoint, is that social media is free. Let's disabuse everyone of that notion right away: *success in social media is not free.* Compared with other forms of marketing, it can be incredibly cost-efficient and give you a bigger bang for your buck, but if all you're ever able to put into social media (as a big organization, anyway) is time and conversation, you'll find limited return. Social media marketing is still marketing and, as such, requires an investment at least at some level in order to be successful. An executive champion must control a significant-enough budget to allocate resources to social media (this can include product for use in promotion)—or needs to be high enough up in the organization that he can impose upon his peers for contributions to the effort. Without at least some sort of product or financial resources available to a social media program, that program faces a much more uphill climb to social media success.

Ultimately, your executive champion is vital to ensuring open-mindedness to social media within the organization, establishing where authority rests within the organization, enforcing that authority when disputes or challenges arise, ensuring that social leaders have the opportunity to integrate with broader communications and marketing initiatives, securing or providing resources to support social efforts, and maintaining consistency and control across agency efforts. Most executive champions will not be directly involved in the development of social strategy—but they don't need to be. The right social media evangelist will play that role when the organization brings her on. But absent a champion playing this critical role behind the scenes, no evangelist can be fully successful. The job of an executive champion of social media is not to be externally visible or to be your social media visionary—it's to be the manager behind the scenes clearing the path for social media inside the organization.

CHAPTER 3

OWNING SOCIAL MEDIA

There's an age-old trick played by most children with their parents in order to get their way. I'm willing to wager that at one point during your childhood you tried it. (I'll confess that I did!) Imagine a child wants to do something like go online to play Club Penguin. The child asks one parent—say, Mom—if she can go online. Mom says no. Undeterred, the child approaches Dad with the same question, hoping that he will unwittingly give the desired answer despite Mom's denial. In the child's young mind, she's insured against punishment because she asked Dad, and Dad said yes, so how could she be disobeying?

Almost every parent, or for that matter almost anybody who was once a kid, can relate to this concept of divided authority. In family situations, the best-case scenario is that when Mom and Dad find out about the dual requests, the child in fact doesn't get what she wants and is disciplined for trying to play the parents off one another. But if parental direction and authority haven't been established and the parents don't agree on what the answer should be, the divided authority game can quickly degenerate into tension between the parents or even arguments over which parent has the final say. What started out as simply a child's desire to play Club Penguin can create unintended consequences, cause internal disputes, and perhaps make different members of the family unhappy with each other!

Not that I want to call working professionals "children," but organizations run a somewhat similar kind of risk with social media. Social media is in vogue right now, and lots of people see it as an opportunity to make their mark or establish their value to their organization. It's almost a given that more than one group inside an organization will believe that social media belongs to them. It's also pretty much a given that multiple groups inside your organization are going to start planning or even executing social media programs or initiatives independently. H&R Block's Zena Weist has observed at her own company and others that "there's stepping on toes, typically because one group doesn't know the other existed."[1]

Absent a clear and established authoritative structure that is accepted by all parties and functions, a brand or organization faces disconnected or disjointed social efforts at best. At worst, you can have not only an inconsistent social presence but also campaigns that compete with one another for the same audiences or even present conflicting messaging. You might even have two parts of the company hiring or promoting individuals for the same job function! (You laugh—but I've seen organizations in which both marketing and communications have hired a "director of social media" for the company.) Clear lines of authority and agreement on who is going to "own" social media in your organization are perhaps the most critical of all the elements we'll discuss. Without them, your program will suffer from too much chaos to present a consistent presence and voice in the social media world.

This clarity of authority isn't always easy to achieve. There are at least three business functions with legitimate claim to leadership in social media within an organization: communications, marketing, and customer service. In many organizations, each group will assume its own supremacy in the social space and resent what seems like an intrusion of others into a capability that rightly belongs to it. It's important to prevent this kind of territorialism when possible. Clear authority isn't just about heading off fights and inconsistency. It's about incorporating the best of what various parts of the business do into the social media program mix. The reality is, each function brings a different strength and a different weakness to social media activity. In an ideal situation, these strengths and functions are brought together as sort of a hybrid function operating together and directing the rest of the business.

Before getting into how to establish an agreed-upon authority and getting the acceptance of everyone in the organization of this authority, let's explore the claims to social media leadership of various parts of the business and identify what each brings to the table.

Public Relations/Communications

In many of the organizations that have done social media well, public relations or communications hold the reins. That's not to say that other departments can't do this well—my friend and competitor at Ford, Scott Monty, famously resides within Ford's marketing department—but most frequently, you find communications at the helm of successful social media programs.

This isn't an accident. The social Web is interactive by nature, and a community not only expects two-way dialogue but also frequently controls the subject and tone of the conversations. This situation is ideally matched to the expertise of a PR pro who is used to responding to questions with the right answers to represent the brand and convey the information the organization wants people to know. Public relations people, because of the nature of their job, also are more used to taking into consideration how an audience is going to react to a message or action and then building a strategy around it. Additionally, PR professionals are much more used to skepticism about a brand's messages than marketing people tend to be—many of us have spent countless hours on the phone trying to sway recalcitrant reporters or fending off critical questions during press events. For this reason, the sometimes intense criticism and negative aspects of conversations that occur online may not faze a PR person as much as someone in marketing (who may be more used to crafting a message and then identifying the best channels through which to distribute that message). The ability to think quickly on one's feet and to address the concerns of a critic while remaining "on message" is critical to being a solid PR person—and critical to success when representing a brand within social networks and online. There's something of a natural fit for PR people within social networks.

But it's not a perfect fit. Even when doing a more traditional media relations job, whom do the PR people get their key messages from? Who decides the core audiences the messages need to go to, so that the PR person can choose his target media outlets accordingly? Who knows the core attributes of the products being promoted by the PR people? In each case, the answer is almost always the same . . .

Marketing

And that's the big argument against having PR run your brand's social media presence: PR doesn't know the essence of the brand as well and doesn't have the same information and research at the ready as to target audiences, focus group reactions, or product attributes as marketing has. And while all the talk from social media pundits about "engaging" and "the conversation" and two-way dialogue is nice, ultimately your organization is not online just to talk with people; you're there to eventually affect market-place behavior (drive customer loyalty and sales in a for-profit business or generate volunteers, donations, or action in a not-for-profit organization). Isn't it better to put the social outreach in the hands of the people who know best how the brand should make people feel, who know the kind of audience a social program should be trying to reach?

Maybe. But there are problems inherent in a marketing-led social media program. For starters, many marketers are so used to pushing a message on a particular calendar that they forget that social media audiences expect actual real-time dialogue. (I've even seen marketers draw up editorial calendars for *Twitter*, for heaven's sake—trying to schedule out even their "casual" conversations by time, frequency, and subject—and ignore audience interaction altogether.) As Facebook surpasses 800 million users and Twitter approaches 200 million, it's easy to see why marketers get so excited about getting in front of all those "eyeballs." Often, though, marketers don't realize that people don't join social networks to be marketed to, and many people might not *want* to be marketed to on social networks, at least in the traditional sense. If PR-driven social media can sometimes seem purposeless or like conversation for conversation's sake, marketing-driven social programs can seem *devoid* of conversation or interaction—just like the same old marketing tricks and techniques that audiences have been increasingly rejecting over the past few years. Social media isn't supposed to be about messages, after all—it's supposed to be about the customer, right? The defining difference between social media and traditional media is that in traditional channels we broadcast messages *at* an audience that has little to no opportunity to reply to or challenge us, while in social channels, the customer's voice is equal to that of the brand or organization. In social media, the *customer* sets the tone, and brands and marketers try to earn their way into a trusted conversation with customers. And that brings us to . . .

Customer Service

Perhaps overlooked in the rush to market or promote, your customer service department has in some ways the most natural claim to social media leadership in your organization. After all, customers today are less likely than ever to send you a nasty letter if they're displeased with your product or the service they've received from you. Often, they don't even pick up the phone to let you know they (or you) have a problem—they take to their keyboard and let their networks within Facebook and Twitter know about it. Bad news can travel even farther if a customer maintains a popular blog or creates a social site dedicated to highlighting the negative experience. (Just ask Alaska Airlines, which was famously accused in November 2010 of "hating kids" after declining to hold a flight for a couple who were changing their baby's diaper.[2] Or United Airlines, skewered relentlessly on YouTube by singer David Carroll with his song "United Breaks Guitars" after he had a particularly bad experience with baggage handlers at Chicago's O'Hare Airport.[3]) Social networks in general represent an amazing opportunity to listen to customers "in their natural habitat" talking about your brand, your products, and the services you provide. Best of all, helping a customer through social networks allows everyone in both the customer's network and your organization's to see the interaction—thus enhancing your reputation as a company that cares about its customers.

One of the companies most frequently held up as an example of a brand truly "getting" social media is Zappos. It's built its social presence centrally on the premise of using social channels to provide uniquely extensive customer service—in fact, every employee, no matter what the role, is considered a customer service specialist and is encouraged to use Twitter and other social networking platforms to reach out to customers and provide exemplary service, making sure not only that problems are solved but also that the customer is feeling cared about and develops a connection with the brand.

If it worked so well for Zappos, why would it not for your brand? If online audiences are ultimately customers and potential customers, who better than customer service to lead the outreach to them? Right?

The problem with customer service leading your social presence is that customer service agents and departments are usually set up to do two things: solve problems for customers who have them and keep happy the customers who don't have them. That's great, but what about the members of the audience who aren't your customers yet? Unless you're thrilled with your market share and don't feel the need to grow or increase your revenue from new customers, your organization is going to need to do some sort of promotional outreach. You need to have some mechanism for sharing information about your products and services, and you need to be able to raise awareness of new products and services when you launch them. Customer service professionals and departments are perhaps better suited than anyone else in your organization to handle the sometimes testy or harshly critical conversations that can happen online—they're often used to hearing from unhappy people and not only know how to solve problems for customers but also are specifically empowered to take the steps to do so (something PR and marketing people often are not). But they're not usually exceptionally skilled at the kind of promotion and proactive relationship building that is needed for a brand to excel in social media—and having a social presence that centers around solving problems for current customers seems just too big a missed opportunity to reach out to new ones.

Those are three functions of the business with legitimate claims to social media leadership. But I've heard arguments that at least two other business functions should be involved in social media programs, so let's explore them before moving on.

Human Resources

The claim to leadership (or at least inclusion) here usually involves pointing out that whenever you put employees online interacting with the public, there is risk—for both the employee and the company. Well-meant product advice gone bad could be grounds for a lawsuit if it results in a customer's product breaking or causing damage. Employees could inadvertently reveal confidential or proprietary information if not properly trained. An unhappy employee could in theory use social channels to air dirty laundry or criticize the company. An employee involved in a personal conversation in a social network might say something controversial or perceived as insensitive to a particular group—which could reflect negatively on the company as well as the individual, not to mention potentially making the organization liable for the fallout if the employee was engaging from work. Can you imagine the potential PR headache for your brand if an employee who is associated with your brand decides to engage in a debate in social networks on, say, the Arizona immigration law or gay marriage? (It's happened, you know. In May 2011, for example, Canadian hockey announcer Damian Goddard was fired by Rogers Sportsnet in Toronto after wading into the gay marriage debate via his Twitter account. Goddard was in fact reacting to comments by New York Rangers tough guy Sean Avery and hockey agent Todd Reynolds on the same subject.[4])

And, there's always the argument that social media is a time-suck, that employees spending time talking with online audiences aren't doing their work. (To that argument, I say this: when a company reinstitutes the nine-to-five workday with set and strictly adhered-to hours, and when the company promises that the only time an employee will work is when she's at the office or facility . . . that will be the day it will be OK to be worried about employees spending moderate amounts of time online at work. But while work hours continue to extend well into what used to be considered personal time, and when the proliferation of devices and wireless access points means that you're increasingly *never* out of touch, companies and organizations are going to have to learn to accept a mild amount of social networking or other online activity.)

All these arguments are good reasons for HR to be involved in some aspects of social media programs—especially developing the social media policy and helping get as many employees informed and educated about social media as possible. But HR is not an outward-facing function. Because much of social media involves significant interaction with the external world, HR is not equipped to lead a social media initiative (while I've never heard anyone argue that it should lead on its own, I have heard it argued—most often by HR people—that it should have a guiding say in the program's development). In addition, HR exists in part to protect employees and can have a risk-averse instinct as a result—also not a trait that lends itself well to social media leadership. So while HR has a legitimate role to play in the behind-the-scenes elements of a social program, it's not the right fit to lead in this space.

Information Technology/Web Development

The tools we're talking about all involve technology, don't they? Whether online or mobile, all the networks and conversations we want access to rely on technology for their existence. If we're going to have a team accessing these tools from the office, it is IT that makes that access happen. Opening Facebook or YouTube to an employee base could theoretically create demand for the IT department to have to manage. Mobile apps and access certainly involve IT—and in some cases, the knowhow to develop new mobile apps for your organization may rest with someone in the IT or Web department. Many of the early adopters of new platforms or technologies are going to be the people who work with, invent, and get geeked about new or emergent technologies. Often the people in your IT department, along with their peers and friends in their community, will discover the next big thing and be flagging it for the attention of the marketing and communications departments before it would ever have shown up on the radars of those groups. Wouldn't it make sense, then, to have IT leading the charge in social, since these media are at their heart digital and technological?

Well, no. As we've discussed, social media is not about technology. Technology is merely the enabler of a bigger dynamic, which is the changing manner in which consumers get information, the changing networks through which they take it in, and the new sources they'll trust for that information. Social is still largely an outward-facing medium, and in most organizations, IT is still largely an internal-facing support function with little experience with customer service or interacting with the public. In an environment where a slight misstep can be pounced on and spread virally before you even have time to realize someone's upset with you, do you really want to have a group unused to public interaction in charge of your online presence? I know several organizations where social media is led out of the Web development team, and I've been in organizations where the IT department has argued rather strenuously that social media is a matter of technology adoption and incorporation and thus should be led and directed by the technology team. I couldn't disagree more adamantly. IT has a role to play in supporting implementation of social tools, especially internally, but should not be running your social media presence. The skills needed to build social platforms may reside with your technology team, but the skills needed to use them to great effect externally do not.

Ideal Conditions for Winning

So where does that leave us? Obviously, there are many functions within an organization that at the very least touch social media—

and several with legitimate claim to take the lead on social media initiatives. Ideally, you'll have some sort of consensus within the organization—and a hybrid group assembled of public relations/ communications, marketing, and customer service, with some input from HR and IT, making decisions together on social initiatives and operating in a sort of dotted-line reporting structure to each of these functions. But even within this group, someone's got to have the end responsibility for making final decisions, setting direction, and settling differences of opinion. To draw a baseball analogy, not every pitcher can start for you and be on the mound for Game 7 of the World Series; no matter how good your rotation may be, only one pitcher is your ace and gets the call to start your biggest games. For social media, which function is the "ace"? Who should "own" social?

The two-way interaction demanded by social media audiences is too important to your long-term success—and most marketing departments (at least the ones I've been exposed to and heard about from other leaders in the social media space) just don't "get" how to interact *with* people without messaging *at* them. Giving ultimate control of social media to marketing in most cases means your efforts will lack the shift in tactics and mindset necessary to win. Ironically, while the social media industry increasingly refers to what it does as "marketing," most of the strongest practitioners have communications backgrounds, and most of the most decorated or praised corporate programs are led by communications and PR departments.

The Importance of Collaboration

That's not to reject the validity of the contributions and perspectives of the other groups—and it's incumbent on the communications team to develop and maintain social media programs that incorporate the strengths and needs of the other functions, especially marketing. Unilateral action or too much arrogance from communications doesn't utilize all the resources available to your company for social media—and in many cases, it can lead to unnecessary and unproductive internal battles.

At IBM, when we started planning our social media program, we began by putting a wiki together behind the firewall and having the 25 or so people inside the company with the most active blogs and most extensive knowledge of the space collaborate on the guidelines we would eventually propose. This dynamic set the tone early, and social—while nominally led through communications—was always seen as something of a collaborative process and function. There were fewer "turf wars" as the program evolved, largely as a result of the team-oriented or collective way things were initiated.

Dell experienced similar collective evolution. Richard Binhammer says that while the initial team doing online outreach sat with tech support, the company realized quickly a greater opportunity existed than simply doing tech support online. "There were corporate reputation issues to address," he remembers, "explaining the transformation of our business, clarifying Michael Dell's role after his return as CEO. There were questions about sustainability and our green program, questions about our evolving business model. This was about more than just tech support."[5] The company brought together members of the technical support team already interacting with customers, members of the communications team, and Binhammer from public affairs to be the new social media team. Richard reports very few "turf wars" as the social media program has evolved over the past four years at Dell—and just like at IBM, he ascribes this to the culture of the company adopting social media as a *business* tool applicable across the entire organization rather than as a marketing tool, communications tool, or customer service tool.

Unfortunately, "ideally" doesn't always happen. In many organizations, one group usually takes the lead—either by design or by accident—and moves ahead of the others. Despite the best or well-meant efforts of the people tasked with running the show, turf wars can often develop—especially when the organization begins to see success from its social efforts.

This is especially true if the company is undergoing changes unrelated to social media. At General Motors, we launched our social media program while going through the paroxysms of radical restructuring, bankruptcy, and the pressure of rebuilding the company and our brands. People were losing their jobs, leaving those left in the company scrambling to prove their worth or find something that made them more valuable to keep at the company. Social media was achieving greater prominence and getting a lot of attention in both the mainstream media and the marketing and PR trade press, and in some minds it represented job security, so many people in the organization gravitated to it as something to make their own.

In hindsight, while I was and remain proud to have been hired by the communications department and to have led GM's social media program from the PR side of the house, I wish I had done a better job of reaching out to and including marketing earlier in the development of the program. We could have been more effective and could have avoided some of the internal squabbles over control that sometimes affected our program even into 2010 and 2011. (In fact, GM's marketing department hired its own social media agency in late 2010 and began developing its own social programs—first independent of the established program and then superseding it. While there were lots of reasons that this occurred, and it might well have happened no matter what we'd done on the communications side, I can't help but wonder now if we could have avoided some of the duplication and uncertainty if I'd worked more closely with marketing, perhaps lessening perceptions they might have had that our program wasn't inclusive of their needs.)

Leading Inclusively

If you're starting from zero in your organization, how should you go about establishing clarity of purpose and where the lines of authority should run? First and foremost, you should start not with an action but with a mind-set: by seeing social media as tools for the *entire business*, not just a marketing, PR, or customer service tool. When you begin building a program with the entire organization's benefit in mind, you have a better chance of being inclusive of the entire organization's needs and objectives for a social media presence—which will decrease the likelihood of parallel efforts or turf wars later on, because in this scenario, no group should feel left out of the process or that its needs aren't being met.

Second, no matter which group is hiring the social media lead or department, that group ought to reach out proactively to every other group we've discussed in this chapter. (It's a relatively safe assumption that the executive champion will be leading the hiring or driving the initiative, so he will likely be the one doing the outreach.) Let the rest of the organization know you're hiring. See if there are any debates or disagreements about that group's "right" to hire a lead. Whatever turf wars there are to be fought should be fought *now* by the executive champion and his peers, before the department or program is established and before a lead is hired. (This could be a test of the executive champion's ability to successfully defend his vision and establish himself in the role of social media champion within the executive ranks.) Without agreement on this most basic start, your organization is setting itself up for internal battles and discord down the road, when your energy will be better expended on external audiences and customers.

In smaller organizations, there may not be turf wars or disagreements over leadership—perhaps only relief that someone else is willing to take it on. Even so, those initiating the program should take care to get buy-in from as much of the rest of the organization as possible. Even if fewer people think they want to take social media on for themselves, it's still important to include the interests and needs of their role in the program you're building. At nonprofits, I suspect this is even more important—with resources (both people and money) being scarcer, collaboration and buy-in from all arms of the organization are vital to supporting successful social media program development.

When leadership is on board and in agreement, you can move on to establishing a structure that ensures all parts of the business are represented in the social media program no matter who is leading the way. At General Motors, we established what we called "Social Club"—so named because we felt a more formal name would turn people off, and if folks thought there might be alcohol or fun involved, they'd be more likely to show up. Social Club was a regular weekly meeting among all the brand (Chevrolet, Buick, GMC, Cadillac) PR and marketing reps who touched social media as part of their responsibilities, with additional representation from legal, customer service, IT, and occasionally some of our partner agencies. Within Social Club, we did everything from share best practices to solicit assistance from one another on upcoming programs or initiatives to make each other aware of emerging platforms, technologies, or opportunities. For example, in late 2008, Phil Colley—then working as our lead social media person for the Chevrolet Volt—came to Social Club to show off a new chat technology he'd learned of and begun to use in Volt social efforts, CoveritLive. We were all impressed with its capabilities, and within weeks, many of us in Social Club were using CoveritLive to conduct live chats between our executives and consumer audiences. During the weeks around the bankruptcy filing, we used this tool to conduct frequent chats featuring senior leadership (including then-CEO Fritz Henderson)—a remarkable openness during an obviously challenging and important time for the company and for American taxpayers, and something we were able to do simply, quickly, and inexpensively. These chats were a cornerstone of our communication strategy during the bankruptcy period, and we found the tool that made them possible through the Social Club structure. This was just one example of something that first surfaced at Social Club and was adopted throughout GM's social media practice.

It's important not to overformalize this structure or turn it into yet another interminable organizational meeting. You'll lose enthusiasm and participation rather quickly—or you'll find your organization unconsciously structuring the social program and removing the spontaneity that will make you successful. Consider holding the meeting outside of regular conference space (at GM, we held several of our earliest meetings in the bar area of a restaurant then located on the first floor of the Renaissance Center—not for the alcohol, but because the bar featured fantastic views of the Detroit River and the skyline of Windsor, Ontario, that inspired us and added to the "not just another meeting" feel we were aiming for). Keep some semblance of structure—know what you're going to discuss ahead of each meeting—but also encourage spontaneity, and don't be afraid of unscheduled brainstorming. Just like in social media in general, there is a delicate balance between discipline and creativity that you have to find.

And don't give in to usual corporate culture—in this meeting, not everyone *has* to speak or provide a report. You're not aiming for a "check the social media box" atmosphere. Just make sure you're giving everyone in the organization who touches social media a chance to access the same information and new tools, and encourage people to share the programs or initiatives they're preparing. Lessons learned are also important items to share—including what *didn't* work or what *not* to do. The leader of this meeting has to cultivate an environment in which no one is afraid to report "failure"—because in an emerging space like social media, there are going to be missteps or things you won't do again. These aren't failures or underperformances; they're valuable opportunities to refine what you're doing—and you have to promote a culture in this group that rewards the sharing of what hasn't worked as much as what has.

Ultimately, what you're trying to do is make sure that the entire business is integrating social media into what each function does, that each function's needs or objectives are being met by social initiatives, and that information is being shared freely among all parts of the organization.

The role of the executive champion continues to be vitally important here. It's inevitable that disagreements will arise even among your core "social club" group. Most often, they'll be solvable by consensus or discussion, and in most other cases, the social media lead should be able to make a command decision that is respected and accepted by the rest of the organization. But on a few occasions, there will be a debate that can't be settled or an answer that a particular part of the business will not be willing to accept. In these cases, the executive champion will need to be prepared to step in to either defend the social media lead's decision and enforce it if necessary or make a final decision that the rest of the organization must adhere to. Absent that hammer from the executive champion, you're risking anarchy and a lack of cohesion among the parts of the business involved. This core group should meet regularly and frequently. The social Web changes rapidly, and the group must be able to help the organization adjust when a new platform emerges or Facebook announces yet another change in its service. Frequent meetings also encourage a quick, coordinated response should your organization need it. Given the immediate nature of social networks and audience expectations of almost instantaneous response to situations as they arise, you're going to be agile and organized should you be faced with a social Web or business crisis. Richard Binhammer recalls that at Dell, as tech support, communications, marketing, and public affairs came together to build the company's social program in 2006 and 2007, "We realized later that what we achieved in those first days was establishing a coordinated rapid response team. We didn't know at the time that that's what we were doing, but that's exactly what we did."[6] You're not going to have time in a crisis to try to assemble a group of relevant or interested players unless it already exists; this coordinating body will serve as your rapid response and crisis management team.

By this point (I hope), there's agreement at the senior leadership level of an organization that social media is a tool for the whole business and that social efforts should be inclusive of all parts of the business. An established and acknowledged executive champion has pushed through his vision as to which part of the business should be leading the others (or what the leadership structure will look like if he's creating a hybrid body to direct social initiatives) and clarified to the rest of the organization who has final authority on adjudicating disagreements or internal dissension about the direction of a social initiative or program. There are arrangements for a regular body or group to keep each other informed and coordinated under specific leadership—and in doing all this, perhaps fend off turf wars or internal battles before they start. The organization is now ready to take the biggest step: hiring or promoting the person who will be the biggest face and voice of the brand in the social Web and the most visible and vocal champion of social media inside the firewall. The next piece of the puzzle is a social media evangelist.

CHAPTER 4

THE SOCIAL MEDIA EVANGELIST

W hen most people think of social media at big brands, let's face it: the social media evangelist is usually who comes to mind. The work of Richard Binhammer and Lionel Menchaca at Dell, Paula Berg's work at Southwest Airlines, Scott Monty's at Ford, and Frank Eliason's at Comcast are often what comes to mind whenever people think of "social media at big brands." (Maybe, if I'm lucky, you even thought of me and my work at GM and IBM. Since you're reading my book, I kind of hope so!)

It can seem like a glamorous position. Those who represent a big brand within the social Web get to be the "human face" of a large organization to millions of people online. Their Twitter responses are much coveted, thousands (or tens or even hundreds of thousands) of people read their blogs, and they are invited to speak at social media conferences around the world.

I'll admit that the flashier elements of being a company's social media lead are pretty exciting. But the exciting stuff is not even half of the job—and sometimes, the job isn't very fun at all. If you're the social media lead at a company that does something unpopular with the public, online audiences will turn to *you*, whether you had anything to do with the activity or not. (In fact, your role is sometimes to publicly defend an action or decision that you specifically advised *against* in the behind-the-scenes meetings.) And the public part of the job is only a small piece of the role of social media leader; you'll spend more time in meeting rooms than on conference floors, talk more frequently to your in-house colleagues than to online influencers, and have your greatest victories and defeats inside the walls of the company where none of the social media in-crowd and no marketing publications will ever see or know much about what you accomplished. Still think it sounds glamorous?

Big brands, too, suffer from organizational misperceptions when it comes to the role and job of a social media leader. It's not quite as simple as hiring someone to write a few blog entries on the company website or putting a customer service agent on Facebook. It's not even as simple as finding someone to create great videos or content and push it into social networks. You can't just put any old marketing or communications person into the social Web and think it's going to make your brand a leader in the space. There's a unique set of skills that goes into being a great social media leader within a big brand, a combination of business savvy, a common touch, marketing sense, common sense, and a little bit of geek—ideally all in the same package and absent an overdeveloped ego.

A successful social media leader inside a big organization is much, much more than just a community manager. It's more than having a quick wit, displaying a magnetic personality, and being more fun than people expected for someone who works for a big company—though personality is critical to success, because the social media leader's role is still significantly about evangelizing. To audiences outside the company, the evangelist is winning converts to your brand—in an environment and through channels that can be hostile to the presence of brands in general and most definitely do not want to be marketed or sold to (at least in traditional ways).

To audiences *inside* the company, the evangelist wins converts to the idea that these channels matter, that they should be taken seriously, that a positive hit in Mashable can sometimes be as valuable as one in the *Wall Street Journal,* and that the organization should invest as much time in winning over an Indiana mom with a blog as a reporter for the local paper, or spend as much money in reaching an audience of "Internet geeks" as it spends reaching television viewers or magazine readers. Make no mistake: the most important job of a social media leader is sales—the selling of new ideas and new ways of perceiving a brand or its products or services. That's why it's still safe to call this person an "evangelist" inside your organization, even if a social media presence has long since been established there.

All the same, it's important for everyone to remember that the evangelist and her personality are *not* in and of themselves a brand's presence in social media—at least they shouldn't be. The brand—and the evangelist herself—must maintain proper perspective on that person, her job, and the role the brand needs her to play. Having a "social media rock star" on board might well be a great start if the person's a fit for the brand. But she should not be the beginning, middle, and end of what the brand does in social.

Employing someone who's very good at social media is not the same as having a very good social media program. This is an important distinction that too often is missed by brands and organizations until it's too late—when they watch most of their relationships and social media equity walk away when their rock star takes a new job with another brand. You're not looking for a social media rock star as much as a business leader who is equally adroit inside your walls as outside—someone with the brand not just to represent it online but also to build social media into a business practice *within* that company. If that person happens to *become* well known and well respected in the industry as a result of her work, that's OK—but it's the work and not the renown that is most important.

That said, the person charged with being a brand's social media evangelist is going to be the most important person in its program. She's likely going to be the person most associated with the brand within social networks, the person whom influencers within the social Web reach out to with opportunities for the brand, and the one most often representing the brand at social media conferences and events. Most important, however, she will be the person helping the company or organization effectively blend the social Web into its marketing, communications, and customer service strategies. She will be the one setting the direction from behind the curtain, teaching the rest of the organization how to do social media well and ensuring that its efforts make both social media sense and sense for the business.

We'll spend the rest of this chapter going through some of the characteristics a good social media leader or evangelist needs to possess and the roles or responsibilities she should have or be given if she is to make your brand successful. You might recognize yourself in this description if you aspire to represent a big brand; you might recognize someone in your organization if you're thinking you need to hire one. Or, you might see someone you're interviewing or hoping to interview. If you're applying to be a brand's social media lead, you should know what your prospective employers should be looking for from you. If you're hiring, this section will give you a better sense of what characteristics distinguish a strong candidate from weaker ones.

The Great Lead Is *Actively Involved* in Networks

That active involvement in networks is necessary might sound obvious. After all, you wouldn't put someone in charge of your broadcast strategy who doesn't even own a TV, right? But you'd be surprised how many companies look at social media as simply another channel to market in and turn the keys of their program over to marketers or PR people who barely use their Facebook page, have a protected Twitter account (if they have one at all), and wouldn't have the slightest idea how to start a blog. If a company's social media leader isn't active in online communities, the company will never understand the community dynamics so vital to social media success. How do you know what online audiences want from your brand if you're not talking with them regularly? How do you know if people didn't like something you did if you're not in the networks listening to them? How can you expect to have credibility with online audiences if the person calling the shots isn't even active online? How will your social media evangelist have a sense of what's coming "next" and what your brand should be exploring and experimenting with—would you rather have her hearing it from conversations she has with influencers and members of the online community who know her or hearing it second-, third-, or fourthhand from an agency or underling?

There's another reason having your social lead active in the networks is so important: accountability. Hopefully, your efforts in social media will be well received and appreciated by the communities you reach out to. But on the occasions when you do something that the online audience doesn't like, they're going to let you know about it—and the people responsible for the idea ought to be the ones to hear the feedback. As David Puner puts it, "If you did it, you have to be the one out there to take the heat for it."[1]

It's not fair to put a community manager out there to bear the brunt of a community's frustration or disapproval with something conceived by someone else. More important, online audiences *expect* that kind of accountability from brands. It's a basic issue of credibility to have the person or people formulating your social media strategy involved in these networks and interacting frequently with the communities they're attempting to reach.

But a social media leader needs other skills too—so your brand's evangelist doesn't always have to *come* from the social media world in order to be effective. It's entirely possible for someone in the corporate or organizational house to build a winning program—

if he is willing to take some chances, listen to audiences, and adjust his thinking where necessary. At the end of the day, organizational success in social media is about skills and instincts, not whether you came to the table as an outsider or an insider.

There are people who just "get" people, who understand how to relate to others—not as "an audience" or "a consumer group" to be pandered to, talked down to, or sold to but as fellow human beings deserving of respect and as peers within a conversation. These people are the ones being sought out at conferences, being paid handsomely by organizations to consult with them, who acquire followings on Twitter and within Facebook, and whose blogs and books are read by hundreds of thousands (or even millions). But they don't have some alchemist's formula for turning pixels into gold or possess a mystical secret knowledge that turns them into prophets or maharishis. They just have a skill set that has become the most critical in today's environment and a talent for sharing what comes naturally to them.

Many of the people with these skills can be found within large companies, corporations, and organizations, often somewhere in the communications and marketing departments. They went into these professions because they're extroverts, they enjoy interactions with people, and they could be rewarded for their ability to be persuasive. They're not called "social media experts," because they don't present themselves as such or ply their trade as a free agent working for whoever is willing to pay for what they know. But they possess the same talents and have the same ability to transform an organization if given the chance.

Take Lindsay Lebresco's situation at Graco. Lindsay built up a strong following within the online parenting community and earned a great deal of customer loyalty and affinity for Graco during her two-year stint as its social media leader. But she didn't come into Graco from the outside as a rebel determined to shake up the corporate culture; she already worked for Graco when the company launched its social program.

In the summer of 2007, Graco started making plans for the upcoming year. Lindsay was the public relations manager at the time. She recalls, "Who would manage 'social media' was up in the air, being tossed between myself and a woman working on the e-marketing team. Some believed it should be handled within the online marketing department because after all, this thing that was being called 'social media' was done online. But I fought for the position truly believing that this was a communications initiative versus an online marketing initiative—after all, this job would entail speaking on behalf of the company directly to our consumers. Who was best trained to do that job, and who could best connect to consumers?"[2]

At Dell, Richard Binhammer was working in the public affairs department when he got the call to help lead Dell's emerging social media program—much to his surprise. "This was not a job I asked for," he remembers. "I had to go to Wikipedia to look up what social media even was."[3] Five years later, Dell's program is commonly cited among the best brand social media programs going, and Richard is in high demand as a speaker on his company's experiences and perspective.

Age and Wisdom > Youth and Inexperience

I'm assuming that if you're reading this book, no matter where you sit in your company—or if you work at an agency supporting a client inside a big organization, how high up the chain your client sits—your organization takes social media seriously enough to want to do it right. So why, why, *why* would you put an intern or junior employee in the lead of the program or as the primary online presence? When the organization built its other significant practices and functions—marketing, communications, HR, legal, finance—did you put an intern in charge? Would you have a rookie with a few weeks' experience calling the *New York Times* to pitch a story about your CEO? Both those scenarios seem so ridiculous that you probably dismissed them as exaggerations— but hundreds of organizations still act as if social media is either a "young person's thing" or not serious business, and they make the Facebook page or Twitter account an intern's summer project.

But think about how visible that role is and how quickly word can spread when a mistake is made online. (I'll talk more about that in Chapter 12 when we discuss Kenneth Cole and other notable social media screwups.) Do you really want to put an intern or someone junior whose professional judgment is still developing into a role in which a bad decision, uninformed comment, or flippant response could have seriously negative ramifications for your brand?

Social media, and particularly community management, is not a job to just dismissively pawn off to the "kids" in the office. It's true that many very good brand representatives in the social space are, relatively speaking, junior in their organizations and in the early stages of their careers. But that doesn't mean that every program should automatically be turned over to the Gen Y-er in the cube down the hall. Your online representative is going to have a significant impact on how your brand is perceived and respected by sizable portions of your audience and potentially millions of your customers. Recognize the importance of that role when you're choosing to assign it, or your choice will come back to bite you.

But an organization's social media evangelist is not just its community manager. The role of the social media evangelist is much more than just representing the brand or organization online. In fact, in many ways, the public part of the job is the less important aspect of the evangelist's role.

Having a Business Outlook Is Critical

I emphasize having a business *outlook*. That doesn't always mean having a business *background*, though having some experience in business obviously contributes to someone's ability to see things through a business prism. But whether she comes from the social world or from business, the person setting a brand's social media strategy has to act as a businessperson utilizing social media rather than a social media person using social tactics first and retrofitting the business part. An evangelist needs to set goals for the program that reflect the goals of the business, beyond the nebulous metrics of creating "buzz," acquiring Facebook fans, and generating Twitter followers. That means developing social programs with more in mind than the social media buzzwords of "engaging" and "joining the conversation" and thinking more about what happens *after* you've gotten engaged and what you want from the conversations you're having.

Social media should not be about fluffy, feel-good, high-minded talk about how we can all connect to one another and how we can humanize our brands. That's a table-setter, yes—humanizing your brand is one of the main goals of a social engagement program. But the whole point of doing so is to build better relationships with *customers* or potential customers. Businesses hope that through this engagement, people come to feel better about being their customers—so the evangelist is still ultimately there to drive sales.

In the real world, if a guy gets engaged but never follows through with an actual marriage, the girl is going to get tired of waiting and will give him his ring back and go find someone else. Never forget that the purpose of having a business in the social Web is to go *beyond* engagement to an actual marriage of some sort—positive buzz is nice, but ultimately buzz doesn't pay the bills.

Aren't you looking to see a purchase (or a donation or specific action if you're a nonprofit) made by someone after either seeing you or talking with you online or by someone who read something written by an influencer you've built a relationship with? How does the buzz a company generates translate to business results? A brand evangelist must have some sort of an eye toward those goals and must be able to set up metrics of success that measure both online buzz *and* any impact on sales or actions resulting from that buzz. Get engaged, but do so with that eventual marriage in mind.

An evangelist will need to be able to make decisions based on what makes sense for the business as opposed to just what makes sense in social media. For example, there are dozens of social media–related conferences and online community gatherings that happen every year—and once word gets out that an organization is actively involved in the social space, it will likely be peppered with requests for support, to sponsor individuals to attend conferences, for its products at the event, and even to sponsor conferences or events themselves.

In itself, this isn't bad—smart involvement in events and with bloggers helps get word out within social communities about a company's program and begins to establish the brand among the leaders in the social space. But in the wrong hands or without business strategies in mind, it's easy to fall into the trap of getting involved with social media events, conferences, or influencers for the sake of generating social media buzz or attention, accumulating follower counts, and ratcheting up your Klout score rather than driving your business goals. It's true that a smart, well-executed PR or marketing activation or program at a social media event can get a brand and its products coverage in Mashable or might even make the brand a trending topic on Twitter. But unless you've reached the target market for your product or brand and somehow affected their attitudes or behavior, online buzz is just buzz. If you haven't got a map for what that buzz will get you or how you're going to build on it with your core audience, it's a wasted opportunity—and the impact of the program won't be nearly as strong as it might look on the surface thanks to all those impressive-sounding numbers.

It's better to say no to a few good conferences or bloggers in favor or focusing on the events that best fit your target demographic and the audience for your product. This might mean a handful fewer speaking opportunities for your evangelist or fewer mentions online of your brand as a superstar brand within social media circles. But when weighing the costs of social engagement, what's worse: a couple of small potential opportunities missed because you were trying to be deliberate in your social involvement or exhausting your limited social media resources on misaligned opportunities of debatable benefit to your brand and running low on budget or product when something really solid comes along? A good social media brand evangelist will have the strategic mindset, foresight, and fortitude to recognize that success isn't just about saying yes. It's also about saying no at the right times.

Business savvy doesn't just come into play when you're considering external efforts, however. Ideally, the social media evangelist will demonstrate enough communications or marketing expertise to be seen as a legitimate counsel for non-social media efforts as well. Whether sitting in communications or marketing, the social media evangelist should be respected as a knowing and able practitioner whose instincts are as solid in traditional communications or marketing work as in the newer social networks. The head of communications, marketing, customer service, or any other function must have confidence in the social evangelist's instincts—and the evangelist can earn this by providing solid advice or input into broader discussions. (Admittedly, this assumes the evangelist was given the chance to provide such advice or input.)

Showing Some Online Skin

I'm of course not suggesting that the way to be an effective brand representative online is to literally show skin. But a successful brand evangelist in social media will need to be comfortable revealing some personal details about herself. This involves talking to online audiences about subjects of mutual interest, sharing experiences that make her relatable to real people, and winning people within social networks over by being more than just a brand rep but a friendly figure with whom they have something in common. The really good brand representatives aren't just "comfortable" with expressing some personality while doing their jobs—they *thrive* on it.

Lindsay Lebresco, reminiscing about her time at Graco, recalls that "part of the reason I loved my job so much was that I could simply be myself—a new mom with two children under two years old. I talked about being a mom, I connected with Graco's consumers over talks about our sleepless nights, breast-feeding discussions, teething questions—and oh yeah, product discussions. Because I used them too—I needed a swing to soothe my fussy baby just like they did."[4] Lindsay was certainly an effective representative for her brand—no one was unaware of whom she represented or that she was joining communities as Graco's social media person. But she earned that effectiveness by not just talking about her products or company but by being relatable and being herself, and talking about the things her intended audience was also interested in.

This openness and the dropping of the professional "shield" can make some employers nervous. There's still a mind-set out there that "professionalism" dictates that there are things you don't talk about with customers. You're going to have to get over that if you want your organization to have an effective presence in social networks. Frankly, audiences can get commercials and straight-up brand messaging in lots of other channels. They're in social networks *specifically* for the personal aspect. A skilled evangelist will be able to artfully blend those brand messages into her online conversations without losing that personal touch—but it's that personal touch that usually ends up helping the brand!

Of course, it's not just employers who can get uncomfortable with employees sharing personal stories or details of their personalities; many people prefer to keep some distance between their "real" lives and professional acquaintances. That's fine for most professional roles—but not for a social media brand evangelist. The reality and demands of this kind of a position require a comfort level with sharing pieces of yourself with total strangers online—for the benefit of the brand that's employing you. Anyone uncomfortable with that is not in the right line of business.

Walking the Line

All that said, there is a boundary—not necessarily for what gets shared, but for how much personal ownership can be claimed of a brand's presence online. A brand social media evangelist and strategist is by definition in a very odd and challenging position. On one hand, they are asked to use their personality as a selling tool for the brand—to put themselves online and into social networks and communities as the face of the brand, helping to humanize the company to customers and potential customers. On the other, while their most valuable asset is their own personality, evangelists can never forget that they are in these networks for the benefit of the *brand*, not for their own personal reputation. This means having to understand and walk an undefined line between revealing enough of themselves and their personality to be effective but keeping in mind that their goal is still to promote the brand. In other words, you need someone in this position who's not susceptible to being overcome by her own ego and who isn't likely to start reading too much of her own press.

Zena Weist of H&R Block defines it nicely. "The most important characteristic of the brand's social media leader is to think like a renter," she says. "Do not have any ownership issues. Do not try to build a social media empire that you claim yourself emperor of. It will fail. Realize that what is being built is for the brand, its customers, and all stakeholders. If you try to own social media, the empire will come a-tumbling down . . . on you, poof!"[5]

Despite building the brand's presence in social networks in part on her own personality, the evangelist does not define the brand online. Forgetting this can doom your evangelist's effectiveness for your brand. One of the tricks to choosing a great social brand evangelist is finding an individual who is willing to use her personality to win fans for your brands but is also able to do so without investing so much of her own ego into it that she begins to see the effort as *hers* instead of the brand's. If you have aspirations of being in one of those corporate social evangelist jobs, you have to accept that when the program goes well, the brand should get the credit—but if things go south, it's on you and not the brand. Still think it's a glamorous job?

Willingness to Place Equal Focus on the Internal Part of the Role

As I said at the beginning of this chapter, being the social media lead for a big brand is more than being a good community manager. In many ways, the most important elements of the job happen *internally*. Many brands haven't really fully embraced social media with much fervor yet. As much work as an evangelist has on the outside of the company in social networks trying to win hearts and minds for a brand, she has just as much to do *inside* the organization. She must persuade employees—not to mention managers, executives, and even the CEO—not only to get involved in social media but also to do it the *right way.*

In some organizations, there may still be resistance to engaging in social media. That's certainly the popular conception, anyway—the intrepid social media visionary forging ahead against internal resistance in order to make things happen or trying to talk reluctant leadership into embracing the new world. Some of that is still around, and even when leadership hires an evangelist and empowers that person to start doing social media well, there will still be pockets of the organization that don't want to acknowledge the importance of online influencers.

But these skeptics are increasingly an endangered species. These days, all but the most hardened disbelievers have been forced to acknowledge social media's staying power and influence. As we discussed in the last chapter, the greater challenge is that now that social media has achieved greater acceptance in the business world, multiple people inside multiple functions will think they know how to do it. And that's where the social evangelist's job inside the company becomes critical—she serves as a linchpin, keeping consistency, maintaining order, and herding the cats. A successful social media evangelist is adept at convincing marketing and communications peers that the evangelist's vision is strong, addresses the needs of the business, and will work when given the chance.

Knows How—and Is Willing—to Delegate

A social media evangelist has to be a little bit of a manager as well, because no matter how good a person might be, no one person can go it alone or be up 24 hours a day. To successfully lead a social media initiative at a big brand, a social media lead needs to be comfortable turning over at least some of the community management to others. It might be tough for some to do, but a social media evangelist needs to accept that her value to her organization comes as much from her *administrative* ability as her *creativity*.

I'll be the first one to confess that I've occasionally struggled with that reality. As is true of most people who've achieved some success in social media, being out in the middle of all the action—out in the communities we're trying to reach, interacting with real people, unleashing some creativity, and rolling our sleeves up to execute a program and get stuff done—is what I like best about having a social media job. That, after all, is the most fun part of social media and of being a brand's social media evangelist. It's the glamorous part that most people think of when they think of someone serving as a brand's human face within the online world.

But anyone spending all her time with external communities is neglecting the very real responsibilities of actually building a program. If, as a social media lead, you want to be seen as more than a community manager by your superiors and fellow employees, you need to do more than just manage your brand's presence in online communities. If you expect to actually win support for social media initiatives and get them adequately resourced to execute them to their fullest potential, you cannot overlook the processes and organizational politics that are needed behind the scenes—where no one is watching and that no one writes articles or blog posts about.

The bulk of the work of a social media leader within an organization will be spent in conference rooms and on conference calls. This isn't really unique to social media, especially at a large organization. Your head of communications delegates much of the media relations activities to the rest of the communications team and spends much of her time working with senior leadership and setting the communications strategy for the organization, and your head of marketing doesn't spend most of his days writing the creative for a new campaign—he has a team of people developing it for his approval after giving them a sense of the direction he wants it to go. A good deal of a business leader's time is also spent administering the function, grooming underlings for future promotion and success, ensuring that each part of the business is on board and informed as to the strategic direction the leader has set, and mediating any disputes or disagreements that arise.

So it's only natural that, as social media matures as a legitimate business function and profession, its top people will spend increasing amounts of time *off-line*. Social media purists might decry this as a bastardization of the original promise of social, but I disagree. It's actually a sign of the maturity of social that leading it requires someone equally adept at administration and mastering internal politics as interacting online or building relationships with people in social networks. Think about spending

all that time in meetings with the brand marketing teams to identify brand target audiences, reviewing core messaging, meeting
with legal to discuss proposed changes to the social media policy,
persuading reluctant leadership to sign off on an idea that makes
them uncomfortable and that they find too risky . . . or even trying to flesh out such an idea with a cadre of collaborators. It may
not sound as exciting or fun as being online and interacting with
people on Twitter, going to conferences to speak on behalf of
your brand, or running a program at a major social media conference, but it's an increasingly vital part of social media leadership.
All those core characteristics of other marketing and communications leaders are needed in social media leaders, too. If social
is to be treated seriously as a practice within your organization,
its leader must behave as other leaders do: focusing as much on
internal structures as external, as much on paperwork and process as on interacting with the outside world.

(Please note that this emphatically does *not* mean that a brand's
social media leaders can remove themselves—or be removed—
from external networks altogether. As I said at the beginning
of the chapter, it's critically important that they retain regular
touch points and interaction with online communities. It just
can't be the whole of their job—nor really even the majority of it
as the program matures.)

Ultimately, the person placed as the leading social media
voice in any organization is the most critical element of all when
determining whether its social initiatives will succeed or fail and
whether they will be considered innovative or mediocre. She'll
be the most visible online face a brand has—and the most visible
in-house representative of social media it has as well. If the person selected is someone who has too much of a focus on external
communities, the brand risks building a social media program
centered too much on one personality and one person's presence.
Its social program will be little more than community management. Choose someone who has too great a focus on internal
process and procedures and syncing too closely to traditional

marketing or communications, and the company risks building a social media program that is little more than an extension of its traditional marketing or communications—a program that is not truly social, only digital. Social implies two-way interaction and relationship building; *digital* is simply taking content and putting it online or into social networks in an effort to "get your message out."

But if the brand chooses wisely, hiring someone with the right mix of social and business savvy—someone who can charm and wow a crowd at a social event, disarm an online critic with wit and empathy, teach others inside the organization, and elevate both the company's and her own visibility online while remaining a smart business strategist who always keeps business goals and the bottom line in mind—it'll have a winner.

It might sound like a tall order, but the right people are out there. If you're the business, finding one is the most important decision you'll make as your program develops. If you're the evangelist, your job is to be that person and find the right balance between social and digital, external and internal, strategy and tactics, relationships and business goals. If you're successful, you'll win converts—external converts to your brand and internal converts to your vision for social media success.

Can I get an Amen?

CHAPTER 5

DEAL BREAKERS

On the hit TV show "30 Rock," Tina Fey's character, Liz Lemon, doles out relationship advice on TV shows and even lands a book deal around a single catchphrase: "That's a deal breaker!" The phrase is used to highlight a trait or behavior that is so significant that it outweighs any positive aspects of a relationship or friendship and requires ending things or cutting things off. "If your boyfriend is over 30 and still wears a name tag to work—that's a deal breaker." "If your man has to sneak you into his house at night to avoid his mother—that's a deal breaker." "Your man leaves in boxers but comes home in briefs—that's a deal breaker." Fey's dry, nononsense delivery of the line "Deal breaker!" made for big laughs and propelled the catchphrase into the cultural vernacular.

Within the context of social media, we might use the phrase in the same way. The relationship between a big brand and its social media lead might well be seen as a marriage of sorts. Despite the fact that the other party seems like a perfect match, there is still an overriding trait or behavior that should serve as the proverbial deal breaker. Just as in "30 Rock," there are a few telltale signs or situations that represent trouble down the line. The reasons vary depending on your perspective and which side you're on, but they're there if you look for them. We'll start by looking at it from the organization's point of view when assessing a candidate aspiring to be its social media evangelist. Then we'll reverse things and zoom in on the company or brand, looking at red flags an individual might look for that would be warning signs to proceed carefully or not to take the job.

If You Are Hiring a Social Media Lead

Deal breaker 1: Overemphasizing personal brand. As we've discussed, an individual's reputation and online savvy can draw credibility to a brand's social media efforts. There is value in the personality of a social media evangelist. But if a candidate spends too much time during the interview talking about the value of his "personal brand" and how it can help your organization, watch out.

So many marketers—not to mention many would-be social media practitioners—have focused so heavily on "personal branding" and becoming an invaluable social media resource that they've started elevating their personal brand over what they bring to the table for a potential employer. The personal branding cottage industry has become a monument to big egos and self-importance, and in the minds of many critics—Geoff Livingston, Olivier Blanchard, David Binkowski, and quite a number of others—it is emblematic of what's wrong with social media: an overemphasis on individuals with an inflated sense of their own value, too much focus on what people think of the person as opposed to the employing brand, and conflicting loyalties when it comes to bottom-line goals.

You don't want someone who's going to overemphasize the external element of the social media leader's job at the expense of her internal responsibilities. You also don't want someone in that role who will be more about her own "brand" than yours. If she is already talking during the interview about how much her brand can help yours, how confident can you be that she's going to place your brand first at all times once she gets online for you?

Conversations during an interview should revolve around strategies for making the *brand* more prominent online—and nothing else. Talking too much about how someone's personal brand will help your brand . . . deal breaker.

Deal breaker 2: No formal marketing or PR background. You don't have to come from PR or marketing in order to be generally successful in social media. Plenty of people who aren't from these fields have developed widely read blogs, achieved hundreds of thousands of Twitter followers and Facebook fans, and get invited to speak at conferences based on their followings and insights. But we're not talking about general social media success. We're talking about representing and promoting a *brand* within social media. This task requires at least some sort of understanding of an organization's goals, branding across other media, maintaining consistency in brand identity, handling critical questions about a brand or company, and other tricks of the PR and marketing trades.

A manager would never consider putting an employee with no formal communications or marketing training on television or letting him speak to a reporter unsupervised. In fact, many companies have policies specifically prohibiting noncommunications personnel from talking with the media at all. Given the speed at which gaffes can spread through the social Web, it would be twice as crazy to put an untrained or inexperienced employee into the fray as your social media lead. If a candidate for social media lead lacks at least some experience marketing or representing a brand, that's a deal breaker.

Deal breaker 3: Not enough homework. You're not necessarily looking to hire an expert in your industry or on your company and its products. (Hell, I still couldn't tell you the details of how an internal combustion engine works, even after having been at GM for four years.) But you do want someone who at least understands the basics. After all, he's going to be representing you within social networks and online.

This isn't unique to social media roles. Regardless of the position you're hiring for, companies generally look for candidates who've done their homework and who know at least a little bit about the organization and its products or services. Social media is relatively new and still intimidates some companies. Some may be tempted to overlook a candidate's lack of basic research in order to land a "social media expert." Don't fall victim to that temptation. Your candidate need not be an expert—you can teach him about your business once he's on board—but he needs to be able to talk with you about your business. Failing to do the research doesn't just show that he didn't prepare for the interview. It telegraphs that he may similarly fail to prepare for other programs or engagements while representing you. If your candidate seems to know a whole lot about social media but hasn't bothered to do much research about your business or industry . . . that's a deal breaker.

Deal breaker 4: Social media–speak. If social media isn't your day-to-day work, you're not going to necessarily know every last detail about the latest social network, nor will you be up on the slang and etiquette on every possible platform. In an interview with a potential social media lead, the candidate will probably use some terms you're not familiar with. Obviously, you've got to talk about social media. And some words are used with good intent and for good reason; for example, *influencer* in and of itself is a decent catchall descriptor of someone whose opinion carries disproportionate weight. (It only becomes a problematic word when it's overused or when it's applied to oneself.) But beware the candidate who spends all her time talking about the importance of "authentically and transparently engaging your audience in the conversation" or who promises to develop a content strategy to create and deliver viral marketing or video without actually addressing your business, targets, and goals or setting tangible measurements for results. Simply put, an overreliance on jargon or buzzwords should be a red flag.

Don't fall prey to someone who uses jargon or technical terms to obscure a lack of knowledge or business savvy. If the candidate can't be clear and jargon-free with you during a job interview, how clear is she going to be when talking with the skeptics in your organization? If she can't clearly articulate for you her vision for your program without jargon or frequent use of buzzwords . . . that's a deal breaker.

Deal breaker 5: Does he have a catchphrase? This one's simple, and related to deal breakers 1 and 4. If upon researching your candidate's online public record, you discover frequent use of a catchphrase or slogan, your candidate is not only investing far too much time in promoting himself or his "brand" but also doing it via a gimmick—which not only is cheesy but also usually has an expiration date. Your social lead will be interacting with your customers online and should leave them with positive feelings about your brand. That's not going to happen if banal catchphrases are dropped at the end of every post or tweet. If your candidate has a recurring phrase he uses for effect or to punctuate his posts, theories, or outlook on social media . . . deal breaker.

Deal breaker 6: Professional immaturity. Related to deal breakers 1, 4, and 5. In some circles in the social media world, it's become vogue to refer to oneself as a social media "ninja," "Jedi," or "guru." Supposedly, this is meant to convey not only levels of expertise and skill that exceed that of the average professional but also a superior grade of hipsterism and nonconformity. In reality, these self-granted titles scream immaturity and don't have anything to do with the job you're hiring for. (Unless you're really looking for an actual assassin or intergalactic quasi-religious warrior, that is—in which case, the winning candidate likely won't leave business cards.) Calling oneself a ninja, Jedi, guru, rock star, etc., reveals the candidate to be far more concerned with image than results, style over substance. No one who wishes to be taken seriously as a professional should use the same business title as a bunch of cartoon turtles with a fondness for pizza. And any business that wants its social media leader—and by extension its social media program—taken seriously both externally and internally will reject this kind of silliness. If the candidate refers to himself with cartoonishly self-aggrandizing titles . . . that's a deal breaker.

Deal breaker 7: Bottom lines. As mentioned in Chapter 1, companies and big organizations don't just get into social networks for the sake of "the conversation." Sure, a company may use social media to improve customer service, extend the relationship with customers beyond their purchase, or promote products or services via conversations, relationships, and events. But at the end of the day, a company does social media for the same reason it does other kinds of marketing: to drive business.

A good social media program is designed around a company's business goals and objectives, and a social media evangelist should understand those goals but also how to build a program and online presence around them. When evaluating a candidate for social media lead, look for tangible results that she has generated—signs that she knows how to deliver against a bottom line and contribute to someone else's revenue growth, not just her own.

When you ask the candidate for her results, does she give you something concrete? A list of endorsements of her book or referrals from people who've heard her speak is not enough, unless those referrals and endorsements are accompanied by real results achieved for a client. Alternately, if you're looking to promote somebody from the inside, you'll want to look at the results she's achieved for you rather than just picking an employee with a popular blog. Did she deliver against the objectives set out for her in your business environment? Has she shown an ability to work across multiple parts of the organization and build bridges rather than taken a scorched-earth approach to teamwork? Has she been rated highly more often than not in yearly reviews? Do the people who work with her most directly feel comfortable that she would represent the entire organization well in social networks? There's a lot more to the job than just being able to write blog posts that draw in an active community.

You're looking to turn the keys of your program over to this person, so you'd better make sure that she actually knows how to deliver the goods for someone other than herself. If book endorsements, speaking referrals, and Twitter followers are all you get when you ask for results . . . that's a deal breaker.

If You Are Applying for a Social Media Leadership Position

When it comes to social media, there are two sides to the interviewing coin. A candidate for the job should also be on the lookout for warning signs. Companies and big organizations can screw up social media no matter how good the evangelist is, and there are several indications that the company or brand may not be "the One."

Deal breaker 8: Lack of clarity in the organization as to authority for social. Who's hiring you? Which department has determined that it can bring you on board? Do the rest of the functions inside the business recognize this department's authority for social media? Or will you be brought on only to spend much of your time fighting turf wars with other departments that believe *they* have responsibility for social media or that might even go as far as hiring their own social media lead? Will your authority to lead social media be recognized inside the organization—leaving you free to focus on figuring out how to build your program or winning online initiatives?

You *have* to ask your prospective employers these questions during the interview process. You must be assured that you really are being brought in to build a program rather than to be one department's foot forward in a jump ball for social media leadership. Winning in this space is hard enough without having to get bloodied before you get out the door. If the company or organization can't tell you with certainty that *you* are the man (or woman) and that all divisions or functions in the company are on board with that . . . that's a deal breaker.

Deal breaker 9: No clear champion for social media or for you. We've already discussed the importance of an executive champion, someone in senior leadership who will carry the ball for social media to her peers and who will mediate or settle any disputes. This isn't just vital to the company's social media success; it's critical to yours as the social media evangelist. As social media continues to draw audiences and attention, there *will* be differences of opinion internally about its implementation. Some opportunities and ideas won't have enough internal support to get off the ground. Even if everyone in the organization agrees at the outset that authority to lead social media efforts rests with you, there *will* eventually be challenges to that authority from inside, perhaps even by those who agreed to your authority at one point. And try as you might, you *will* make mistakes.

When these challenges arise, you're going to need to know who's got your back. Who will stand up among leadership and endorse what you're doing? Who will help you fend off efforts to do social media the "wrong" way? Who will help you tin-cup for budget or other resources if you end up short, or otherwise support you when the going gets rough?

Of course, internal politics can shift, leaders move on, some fall out of favor, and even your most ardent supporter can withdraw that support if you repeatedly fail to justify it. Just because someone's your champion at the interview doesn't mean he'll always be around to have your back. But there needs to be someone committed to you at the beginning. If no one in the organization is appointed or willing to be the one to have your back and advocate for you during the internal political battles that lie ahead . . . deal breaker.

Deal breaker 10: No commitment of resources. It's worth repeating: the biggest myth about social media is that it's free. Social media may have lower costs than traditional forms of marketing, promotion, or communications, but it's definitely *not* free. Your program may involve bringing online influencers to your events, providing your product or services to online influencers for review, hosting contests, or sponsoring social media events—everything from smaller, local events like those put on by Social Fresh to one of the big social media gatherings like SXSW, BlogWorld, or BlogHer. You might want to explore partnerships or applications with emerging platforms or networks (a Gowalla or Foursquare badge, for example). You will also need monitoring tools such as Radian6 or Trucast (among others) in order to measure results, glean insight, and eventually justify your department's existence. All of these things take money.

Even at the biggest organization or company, no director ever has "enough" money to do everything he wants. As a social media evangelist, you'll need to make value judgments as to how to allocate your limited resources.

Still, the organization must make some sort of financial commitment to the program. You can't be expected to pull results out of your hat through a handful of conversations online or a few good blog posts. Before you accept a position as social media lead at a large organization, try to get an idea of what you'll have to work with. It's much easier to keep your commitment to certain accomplishments if you have a sense of the limitations involved. How can you promise that your brand will have the most effective social media promotion at SXSW or that you'll reach 500 environmental bloggers this year if you don't have the resources to make it happen?

Resources aren't all financial, either. The most important investment in social media success will always be time—yours, and if you're fortunate, the time of others. Will you have a team helping you execute social media programs and initiatives? If a team doesn't currently exist, is there a decent possibility of getting head count or approval to hire someone a little further down the line? Or will you be a one-person shop, making things happen for your employer solely through your own efforts? (That's not a deal breaker in and of itself, by the way. Several of the more well-respected corporate social media programs are largely the work of one person. It just helps to have as full an understanding as possible of the environment you'll be taking on.)

A potential employer should be able to give you at least an approximate answer on the anticipated budget and a candid reply on the staffing question. If the employer cannot give you a budget estimate or refuses to commit to providing resources for your program . . . deal breaker.

Deal breaker 11: Failure to understand the basic currency of social media. Engagement and interaction are the basic currency of social media. Two-way dialogue between organizations and people—both customers and potential customers—is expected by social network audiences. This interaction and engagement is what distinguishes "social media" from other channels or media. So it's critical that the company have a grasp of this dynamic and a willingness to embrace it.

Unfortunately, this isn't always the case. Sometimes, a company's marketing or communications leadership still looks at social media as little more than a series of alternate channels in which to deploy traditional tactics. Producing content specifically for the social Web is a great idea—in fact, as we'll see later, if you're not doing it, you're missing a huge opportunity—but it can't be the whole of a social strategy. Placing commercials on YouTube or having a one-way Twitter account that just pushes links to your content without ever answering anyone back or letting the community control the conversation at times isn't social media; it's just placing digital assets into social networks.

Part of your role as a big brand's social media evangelist will be to create or commission content that online audiences want to see and share. But if that's all the company wants to do, it doesn't recognize the full value or scope of social media. Great content is supported and enhanced through the conversations you have about it and the relationships built through those conversations. If the company wants you to simply push marketing or advertising content or PR messages into the social Web . . . deal breaker.

Deal breaker 12: Social media is pushed to the kids' table. As we saw in Chapter 2, one of the most critical elements within a brand context is integration with the rest of the company's marketing and communications efforts. Social media initiatives that happen independently of marketing campaigns, desired brand positioning, a brand's target demographic, or company news and announcements are of limited value. They may generate some decent conversations and build a few solid relationships, but what good does that do the brand if the message the audience receives doesn't represent what the brand is supposed to stand for?

Social media should be taken into account from the very beginning of campaign and announcement planning. The social media evangelist—or her delegates—*must* have a seat at the strategic table; she has to be in on the discussion as marketing and PR campaigns are conceived and planned. Building an entire campaign and then bringing in the social media tactics at the very end as an add-on or afterthought greatly reduces the effectiveness of social media in that campaign. In many cases, the social evangelist or team with knowledge about the plan from the beginning can devise or conceive ways to extend its reach and more effectively spread it across social networks. They might also be able to suggest online influencers who should be briefed on or included in the campaign or initiative. The social evangelist could also collaborate with the rest of the teams involved in the marketing or communications initiative to identify ways to make content being developed more social Web–friendly.

As someone directly interacting with the public on a daily basis, the social media strategist is attuned to what audiences will expect, appreciate, or reject from the brand. If a campaign or message is falling flat with an audience, he will likely be one of the very first people to hear about it. He might even be able to float a trial balloon in private with a few trusted influencers to gauge their reaction. Companies spend millions of dollars every year on focus groups designed to predict the impact of major marketing efforts; why not take advantage of the social media lead's unique insight?

If the choice of evangelist is made wisely, he will have a strong marketing or communications mind-set and a good track record as a successful and smart marketer or communications professional. He's earning his position—and he is going to be trusted with the brand's reputation online—because he knows what he's doing and has good instincts. Those talents warrant inclusion in strategic and confidential internal conversations.

The brands doing social media most effectively—in the automotive industry, the IT industry, and the airline industry, among others—all include their social evangelist in higher-level marketing and communications planning. Ask whether, if hired, you would be included in strategic discussions beyond social media and whether social media could be considered from the outset of communications or marketing campaign development. If the answer is no, you as that brand's evangelist will nearly always be playing catch-up with the rest of the organization's efforts; your ability to be as effective as possible will be hamstrung. If social media isn't seen as a critical enough element of marketing and communications to afford the evangelist a seat at the strategic table . . . deal breaker.

In any successful marriage, there has to be a lot of common ground. Sure, there is room for individual needs, hobbies, and interests—but for the relationship to work long-term, there must be consensus more often than divergent views. The two parties need to see eye to eye on priorities and values, or there's more likely to be a somewhat turbulent relationship in the future, and the odds of things working out decline significantly. Similarly, for a marriage between brand and social media evangelist to succeed, you need common ground—the brand and the individual have to see eye to eye on everything from the extent of the role the individual's personality should play in the brand's presence, to the authority of the individual to set direction in social media, to the amount of resources needed for success. Just like in a marriage, if there isn't agreement from the outset about values and priorities, the relationship is likely doomed to a premature and unhappy end.

Of course, to determine whether the relationship is working, you first have to decide how you'll define what success in social media looks like to both the brand and the evangelist. And once you've defined success, the next critical step is determining how you can measure your progress against that goal and establish whether you're getting your money's worth for your efforts.

CHAPTER 6

ROI AND MEASUREMENT

One of the quickest ways to initiate an animated discussion in America these days is to bring up politics. Even in the politest of company, the rules of civility can go out the door whenever the subject rears its head. People who had been laughing together in camaraderie only minutes before can become quickly entrenched in heated debate. In social media circles, you might well achieve the same effect by bringing up the subject of measurement and return on investment.

One school of thought within the social media world is that the ROI of an active social media program is self-evident. Companies have paid big money for years for focus groups to tell them what customers think about their brand, products, or marketing campaigns. Now that the social Web makes it possible for us to get the same information for free by simply taking part in online conversations with customers and potential customers, the ROI is pretty clear. Talking to customers, this argument goes, should not be something considered of questionable value. People want to buy from people they know, like, and trust—and the tools of social media help an organization develop these relationships more effectively and humanly than ever before.

Scott Stratten, author of *UnMarketing*, is fond of joking, "Every time someone asks about the ROI of social media, a kitten dies. And a unicorn."[1] The dismissive nature of the statement is Scott's way of reinforcing the argument that not all investment is financial, that not all return should be measured in terms of revenue, and that business today (from the consumer's perspective, anyway) is based on a brand's willingness to spend time building those relationships and earning that trust.

Of course, anyone who's been in a business environment knows that there will *always* be an expectation of demonstrable return on any investment. There's another school of thought that argues that it doesn't make any sense for a big organization to engage in an activity that doesn't deliver a demonstrable return and pay-off—be it in revenue or sales for a corporation or donations or volunteerism for a nonprofit. Why would any organization for which revenue generation is the *raison d'être* continue an activity that does not contribute to that goal? What good do thousands of unique visitors to your blog, tens of thousands of Twitter followers, and hundreds of thousands of Facebook fans do you if they're not generating revenue?

Resources in any organization are limited, and they need to be applied to activities that reliably return the investment in them. Olivier Blanchard, author of *Social Media ROI*, argues that non-financial impact—while valuable—is not ROI and that unless social media programs are tied to actual business performance, they're not viable in the long term within a business environment.[2] (As an aside, I greatly respect Olivier's work and suggest that you might want to check his book out too.)

As with most debates, the truth probably lies somewhere in the middle. I'll confess, I fall closer to the side of those who argue that social media should be tied to business performance and goals and should be measured accordingly. There is room for the nonfinancial elements—to a point. But ultimately they still need to be means to an end. Think of it this way: in a traditional sales environment, sales don't happen in one meeting. They are a series of relationships and earned trust—the salesperson walks into the client's office and makes a presentation, then perhaps takes the client to dinner. They go back to the office in another week or so and present to a few more people, including the client's boss. Then they might go golfing or out to a ball game. Then there's another presentation and another dinner . . . eventually, the sale is made—although often the client is buying the salesperson as much as the product, so great is the trust and so strong is the relationship established. Rarely does a good sales manager look at her sales team and ask, "What was the ROI on that golf game? On the dinner you are expensing?" She knows, as all successful salespeople know, that selling is a process and that the building of relationships is an essential part of that process.

But note that in that analogy the process ended in a *sale*. The ROI of individual relationship-building activities isn't in question as long as the sale is eventually reached. Remove that end achievement, and we have a whole other story. A salesperson who is constantly taking potential clients out to dinner or golfing or to ball games but who never closes a deal is going to have some serious questions to answer about what he's spending on and why—and without a sale or two in short order, he'd probably be looking for a new job. All the nonfinancial-impact stuff (as Olivier calls it) in the world is only valuable if it results in the desired end goal. If you can show that and increase in sales, revenue, or the meeting of business goals results in that end from the strategy, the individual tactics are called less into question.

Now, not all business goals are specifically financial. Not everyone in the business will always understand this, especially those without marketing or PR backgrounds. As Geoff Livingston, cofounder of Zoetica consulting and a prominent social media influencer in his own right, reminds us, "Many executives do not understand the difference between a desired outcome and literal ROI."[3] But that difference can be crucial to judging a social media campaign's success or that of the overall social media program. If leadership is expecting a program that will demonstrably result in revenue generation, you'd better develop one designed to do that which includes measurement tools and strategies designed to track to those goals. If nonfinancial impact is an accepted goal of a campaign or program (i.e., product awareness, brand reputation, "buzz," online mentions, etc.), design your program to achieve those goals and have a measurement system ready to back it up once it's completed.

ROI questions, of course, are not unique to social media. Proving the value of something not designed to be directly tied to sales or revenue generation can be challenging in traditional PR and marketing efforts as well. What is the worth of a fantastic story in the *Wall Street Journal* or *USA Today*, or of a glowing review (in GM's case) in *Motor Trend*? How do you prove the value of a PR hit or campaign? How do you prove that a marketing campaign is responsible for a purchase by a customer?

While these questions still do exist within the social Web, the technologies of the Internet do offer perhaps a better opportunity than ever to directly answer them. Through the use of short links, for example, it's possible to know not only where a click to your site is coming from but also, in many cases, where the short link was accessed. You can get a sense of which outlets or individuals are driving traffic for you.

Four Questions

Before beginning a social media program and trying to measure its success, there are four fundamental questions to ask:

1. What data will we be collecting? (Which metrics do we believe are the most important?)
2. How will we be collecting it? (Which tools do we believe or find to be most effective in acquiring the data we've chosen?)

3. What kind of analysis will we apply to it? (Will we report just raw numbers? What kind of insights are we hoping to get from the data once it's collected, and how will we derive them from this data?)
4. How will we report it? (Through what mechanisms will we distribute what we learn to the rest of the organization?)

Once the answers to these four questions are understood, measurement becomes much less mystical, and ROI seems far less abstract.

I'm going to spend this chapter focusing on the answers to question 1 regarding the metrics that truly matter in social media and what information you should be collecting. Answering question 2 would involve my endorsing specific tools or platforms—and while I am a fan of some in particular, it's for each organization to decide among Radian6, Converseon, Looking Glass, Google Analytics, CoTweet, Collective Intellect, Attensity360, Cymfony, BuzzLogic, Visible Technologies, or any of the myriad other tools available to big brands. Each has its strengths and its shortcomings; I've used several different listening and metrics platforms and will use more of them in the future. I can't tell anyone which brand to use any more than I could use this book to tell you which make of car to drive, which airline to fly, or what brand of toothpaste to use. But once an organization has identified the metrics and data it finds most important, suffice it to say that there are now more than a dozen strong options, companies that specialize in collecting that data and reporting it back to the client. Monitoring and assessing the social Web isn't as overwhelming a proposition anymore as it used to be.

Question 3 is simply a question of intellectual capital. Whether the brand's team or agency partners are analyzing the information that comes in, someone has to be making sense of the numbers and what they mean. If an organization has decided that "number of mentions" on Twitter is a key metric for it, someone has to take the report of how often the brand is mentioned on Twitter and apply insight to it: What was the effect of being mentioned 1,789 times on Twitter yesterday? Did it drive traffic to our website? Did sales via our site increase after the Twitter campaign because? If the brand is a retail outlet, did foot traffic in stores increase after the campaign began? Someone has to tie all the numbers together and determine what they mean. And the answer to the fourth question, reporting, is going to be different for each organization. Will findings be reported via e-mail? Via a password-protected website behind the company firewall? Through PowerPoint presentations at meetings attended by only relevant parties? And who will have access to these reports—only the department that commissioned the measurement? Executives within marketing and communications or customer service? Business leadership? Thought must be given in advance to the questions of how the analysis of collected data will be distributed, and to whom.

We're going to spend the rest of this chapter talking about which metrics truly matter in social media and which reflect true success. But before you start thinking about how you're going to measure your program and which metrics you'll use, there's a more important foundational issue you need to address. It stands as the first step in determining the ROI of your social media program.

Identify What Success Will Look Like *Before* Identifying Tactics or Platforms

One of the biggest mistakes an organization can make is establishing a social media presence that's there for the sake of being there, without rhyme or reason. "Because everyone has a page" is not a good answer to the question "Why do you want to be on Facebook?" You have to know what you're looking to do and what senior leadership wants to see as a result.

If an organization begins with the platform—e.g., "We need a Twitter account," or "Let's get a Facebook page"—without knowing what it wants from the tool, the result is usually a cluttered, purposeless, and undirected social program. Many will experience a disjointed "mission creep" as social presences are built around sub-brands, product lines, or even marketing campaigns. Would you consider buying TV time without having a product and a desired outcome in mind? Of course not—all media buys have a great deal of thought behind them. You should consider similar levels of planning for social media.

Clearly identify what success will look like and what leadership's expectations are for the program. Are you looking to draw people to your blog, Facebook page, YouTube channel, or Twitter feed? Are you looking to just spread your content across as many channels as possible and get the message out as broadly as you can? Are you looking to directly impact sales? The answer matters.

- If you're ready to claim success because 151 blogs have posted your video on their sites, but management was looking for new subscribers to your YouTube channel and there are only 14 of those, you have a disconnect about what constitutes success.
- If you're aiming to generate 50,000 new fans for your Facebook page but only attract 9,000—but at the same time generate 10,000 mentions on Twitter in less than a week, is that an unexpected success, or does it represent an unacceptable failure?
- Does "buzz" equal success? Do numbers? Do sales?
- Whatever the answer, do you have mechanisms in place to measure whether you're hitting that target? Are you monitoring online conversations to even know how much "buzz" you're generating?

- Do you have anything in place to track whether visits to some of your specific Web pages are increasing during the campaign or to know which links they're coming from?
- If you're expecting sales results, do you have anything in place that will demonstrably show that sales are increasing due to the people reached in this social campaign?

Unless you have an idea going in of what you're looking to do and what success would look like—qualitatively and quantitatively—you're never going to know whether you've really achieved a return on your investment.

Know Your Zero Point

To know whether you're having an effect, you have to know where you're starting. How will you be able to tell whether your social media efforts are having a demonstrable ROI if you haven't identified a baseline?

If your goal is "buzz," then you should begin any effort by doing a sweep to identify how often your brand is mentioned in social networks *before* one of your campaigns begins. That way you'll be able to demonstrate more effectively that mentions or buzz increased as a result of your efforts. There are multiple tools you can use—from Google Analytics to SEOmoz to Radian6 to Converseon—to monitor various social networks and platforms in order to identify the frequency and sentiment of mentions of your brand and establish a baseline of the ratio of positive, neutral, and negative sentiment toward your brand to compare with the sentiments after your campaign has run. Whatever tool you use, it should help you measure not just volume or reach: "How often are we mentioned?" "How many followers/fans do we have?" It should also look at things like authority (how often your content is being shared by others into their networks, signifying that you're seen as a trustworthy source of information), responsiveness (how often your community is choosing to engage or inter-act back with you and what percentage of your reach is active with you, indicating that people are actually absorbing the infor-mation you've put out rather than either ignoring it or passively observing it), and influence (what percentage of your content is shared or distributed by others as opposed to sitting on your sites or pages alone). After all, a big part of what you're aiming for is for your content to be shared through social networks, so shouldn't you know how often your stuff is being shared? Being on YouTube or Facebook isn't "winning" at social media; you'll never achieve millions of views of a video by trying to attract all those people to *your* site or channel. If you want the big view counts, you're going to need people to share and distribute that video for you. So shouldn't you have a sense of whether you're creating the kind of content people want to share by checking to see how often your audience is influenced to share what you're putting out there?

But no matter which measures you're looking at, you still need to know your starting point if you want to really understand the impact of what you're doing. If you're defining success as driving visits to your website or Facebook page, shouldn't you know how many visitors you get in an average day or week before your cam-paign begins? Can you track where any additional visitors are coming from, via short links or IP analysis? Can you prove that it's your campaign or initiative driving that traffic? If you can, you're going to find it much easier to stand in front of the bosses and report on your program's success and justify whatever bud-get and resources you've spent. If you're going to define success by actual sales or increases in revenue, you need to establish the baseline of where sales are at the start of the campaign or initia-tive so that you can determine whether there's a tangible impact.

The bottom line is, quite possibly the most important element in measuring the effectiveness of your social media efforts is knowing your starting point, making prework and preparation vital to your ability to demonstrate results. This is another reason not to just jump into Facebook or Twitter figuring that you'll learn as you go and experiment along the way. Experimenting and taking risks is good and necessary in social media, but there has to be purpose to your efforts, and you have to know what you're trying to achieve in order to know what success looks like.

Once you've decided what you're hoping to accomplish with your social program and determined your baseline against which you'll measure success and actual return on your investment, the next steps are incorporating the metrics and measurements you'll use in assessing and reporting that success.

Lies, Klout Scores, and Statistics

With the explosive growth of social media and networks in the past few years has come, at least superficially, a more tangible measure of someone's influence and import: numbers. Whether they're Facebook fans, Twitter followers, Klout scores, or Technorati rankings, these numbers may seem in the digital environment to be what a thick Rolodex was in the eras of "Mad Men" or *Wall Street*: measures of someone's connectedness and value as an entry point to any number of spheres of influence or communities. And unlike Rolodexes, it seems that you can see those connections *before* you hire or retain someone, just by checking the person's fan/follower counts or Klout scores.

Conscious of the seeming value of these numbers, over the past few years, a mind-set has developed around the importance of increasing yours. Services like Klout purport to measure an individual's connections, networks, and activity within them across multiple social platforms—and even reward the individuals with higher scores. It's common at social media conferences to hear an audience member asking a speaker how to increase follower or fan counts quickly—often because the questioner has been given precisely that direction or assignment by someone in marketing or communications at his organization.

Numbers are universal, and because they're so prevalent in business, they provide a level of comfort and familiarity that can make the "new" digital environment feel less scary to traditional marketers or communications people who are used to numbers being objective—and measuring their own effectiveness through numbers. It's easy to be lulled into an overemphasis on them. But this obsession isn't healthy or wise; numbers are like the golden calf of social media—the false god that serves as an easy, lazy interpretation of the benefits or effectiveness of social media engagement. In lieu of the harder work of deeper and more accurate measurement, all too often companies play a pure numbers game: quick but misleading interpretations of the benefit or claims of success that don't always stand up to scrutiny. For example, Twitter follower counts can be misleading because, according to an Experian Hitwise survey cited by *Fortune* in a cover story about Twitter in spring 2011, up to 47 percent of those with Twitter accounts are no longer active on the platform.[4] So if someone you're targeting for outreach has 10,000 listed followers, how do you know how many of those are still actively engaging the service and reading your target's tweets? Is it all 10,000? Closer to 5,300? Somewhere in between?

Whether you're deciding if your own efforts can be considered successful or trying to determine whom to approach externally for a program or initiative, don't get caught up in looking purely at numbers in the social Web. It's a little like getting excited about the Home Run Derby contest during the Major League Baseball All-Star Game festivities: those massive power shots off of batting practice pitches look impressive, and they thrill and wow the crowd, but they're kind of for show; hits don't really count until there's an actual game going on. The fact that someone can hit a monster shot during practice is great, but how will he do during a real game?

For generations, marketing and PR practitioners were evaluated in numbers—specifically, eyeballs and impressions. How many people saw this article? What is that publication's circulation? How many people saw that commercial? What are the ratings? Beyond the number of readers or viewers, PR practitioners were also measured in terms of number of stories placed: the thicker the clip report, the happier your bosses were.

Even when the social Web emerged, we still employed numbers as a primary arbiter or measurement of the value of our interactions. How many unique monthly visitors does a particular blog have? What is its Technorati ranking? Where does its author fall on the Ad Age Power 150? Give me its Quantcast and Compete and SEOmoz scores! We try to quantify the success of organizational websites through numbers as well: how many page views did that feature get on the corporate website? How much time are visitors spending on the site? How many comments does a particular post on our company blog get?

When other social channels sprouted, marketers' collective use of numbers reached obsessive heights. With the explosion of YouTube, companies became so consumed with the idea of numbers of views that they began churning out what they foolishly christened "viral" videos—content designed from its conception with the specific, primary goal of generating millions of views.

There are two problems with this approach. First, worrying about the number of views a video is going to get before it's even created is a distraction from crafting your story effectively. But more important, designating a video "viral" from the outset displays a ridiculously arrogant belief that we in corporate marketing can dictate to the online audience what it will find worthy of sharing. Corporate marketing departments and digital PR agencies do *not* decide what goes "viral"; audiences do. If an agency or consultant pitches you on "creating a viral video," politely but firmly show him the door and go find yourself someone who will focus on the story you want to tell rather than looking at the desired result first and promising the unpromisable.

When Twitter emerged, the cycle began all over again. Both marketers and individuals began a blind chase for followers, believing that number of followers was the best measure of influence within the new network. Brands got another number to use in determining whether to interact with a particular person: "How many Twitter followers does he or she have?" In many companies, it's somewhat common, when encountering a negative tweet or critical customer, to hear company representatives ask the "followers" question before they even ask the nature of the criticism or complaint—as if the criticism is less valid or the complaint less troubling if the person issuing it has only a few followers!

But it's not just brands who've fallen victim to the mind-set that numbers equals influence in Twitter. Within the social media world, we grant the greatest stature and respect to whoever is able to accumulate the most followers. The Twitter community got all caught up in the race between Ashton Kutcher and CNN to get to one million followers first.[5] At some social media conferences, a high number of Twitter followers is enough to get you invited to speak, whether or not you've actually achieved anything or you provide anything of value to those followers. Many judge brands' forays into Twitter more by the number of followers the brand has than by the quality of what the brand shares and the nature of the dialogue it has with followers. This emphasis on followers and the mad scramble to acquire them was partly to blame for the birth of the ubiquitous "get more followers" spam (both tweets and sites)—which reached proportions previously attained only by spam for male enhancement, which is perhaps fitting. As HARO founder and social media influencer Peter Shankman famously cracked, "Twitter followers is the new penis envy."[6]

There are two great examples from the entertainment world as to why pure numbers do not always equate to "influence." Social networking indexing site Klout ranks individuals on social networks for their influence based on number of Twitter followers, "likes" on Facebook, connections on LinkedIn, people mentioning them in Facebook status updates, Google mentions, and several other factors. In January 2011, a flurry of media disbelief and incredulity resulted from the revelation that in Klout's rankings, teen idol Justin Bieber was more influential than the Dalai Lama or President Obama.[7] While Klout was quick to acknowledge that its algorithms weren't perfect and could be improved, this demonstrates the danger of looking at numbers as a pure indicator of influence. (I hasten to add that while I find Klout flawed, it is one of the first serious attempts to scientifically measure online influence and shouldn't be dismissed out of hand just yet. It's trying to do something important; it just hasn't perfected it.)

The second example came in early March 2011. Actor Charlie Sheen famously went through a bizarre public meltdown that involved drug incidents, stays in rehab, and a series of almost surreal media interviews in which he blasted the producers of his television show and made grandiose, almost messianic statements about himself. On Tuesday, March 1, he started his Twitter account, @charliesheen. In just over 25 hours, Sheen reached one million followers, setting a Guinness World Record.[8] While some of those followers undeniably were there just to observe the train wreck in progress, the sheer number of Sheen's followers dwarfed longtime social media influencers like Chris Brogan and Jason Falls as well as major brands well established on Twitter, like Disney and Best Buy. In less than a week, Sheen even achieved two million followers—25 percent more followers than Starbucks![9]

No one would legitimately argue that Charlie Sheen—especially mid-meltdown—is more influential than Chris Brogan or Jason Falls or that he can affect more people's behavior online than a Disney, Best Buy, or Starbucks. Yet an assessment of simply follower numbers would seem to indicate that with more than two million followers, Sheen is orders of magnitude more influential than those other individuals or companies or has more influence on people's behavior or what they do online. If a company had commissioned a list for outreach based on those numbers, we can see how flawed the result might be. No one in her right mind would argue that Justin Bieber is more influential on real-world behavior than President Obama—and that's the rub: you're not just trying to drive online behavior, are you? Ultimately, you want to affect real-world behavior too.

Five-hundred-foot towering home runs in the Home Run Derby look great, but the hitter who's crushing them is only valuable to his team if he can do it during a real game of a pitcher throwing real heat, along with being able to advance a runner, hit to the opposite field when necessary, not strike out 170 times, and play defense as well. Piling up statistics in a meaningless exhibition doesn't help your team win. In social media, the numbers do matter, but in and of themselves, they do not constitute ROI. "Impressions" are nice and might constitute a measure of the effectiveness of a social media campaign, but unless there's a more specific tie-back to business objectives, social media is going to still be looked at with a skeptical eye by the bean counters—and quite a few others in the organization.

In the real world, the companies considered most successful at social—and that have the most support at an organizational level for their programs—are the ones looking at social media as a means to an end, not an end in itself. They use social media as one tactic in an arsenal designed to hit real business objectives.

At H&R Block, Zena Weist says, "In order to be a big kid at the ROI and metrics table, you have to talk the company metrics talk."[10] Some of the "big kid" metrics Zena shared with me that H&R Block uses to measure its social media initiatives: acquisition online (appointments made and digital software units sold); cost avoidance (call deflection and first-contact resolution); and client resolution metrics (resolved issues, customer service surveys, and "saves").

Nowhere in this list do you see "acquire X number of followers on Twitter," "attract X thousand fans to our Facebook page," or even "engage in X number of conversations within social networks each week." Social media helps H&R Block achieve real business objectives, rather than being an objective all by itself. If we had time or space to list the goals and objectives of the social programs at other companies successful in social media—Dell, Southwest Airlines, IBM, Coca-Cola, and many others—we'd see that this pattern is replicated. A key characteristic of successful social programs is to actually tie them to business goals and measure for results against those goals.

- Is traffic to your own sites or pages up as a result of your activity on social networks? (Are all those followers actually interested in learning more about you due to the conversations or content you have?)
- How often are your followers sharing your content or information with their own networks? Surely 25,000 passive followers don't do you as much good as 5,000 who actively share your stuff.
- Is whatever the "desired result"—be it website visits, requests for product or service information, appointments set, or even sales or purchases—of your program happening, in at least measurably higher numbers? If not, then how can you argue that your program is working? If so, have you eliminated other factors in order to definitively conclude that social media was the driver of those results?
- How many of your followers or fans are actively interacting with your brand within these networks? Do they ask you questions often? If so, how quickly do you answer them?
- Are customer service response times reduced because of your customer service team's involvement in social networks? Are customer satisfaction rates increasing? If so, are they higher within social networks or increasing at faster rates than for your traditional customer service?

My point isn't that you shouldn't seek out followers or be excited when you reach a milestone number of fans. You just have to have a sense of what you want to do with all those fans once they like your Facebook page or follow you on Twitter or visit your blog. You have to have a reason to have gotten involved in social media in the first place. The numbers aren't the goal in and of themselves; they merely indicate how big your opportunity is, assuming your plan and program are solid.

If you build a program designed to draw people to your Facebook page as fans, don't just stop with attracting them. Have a "part two" ready to go and know what you're going to do with all those fans when they get there and like your page.

- Given that most Facebook users click a "like" button only eight times a month, including liking a friend's status update or photo, how will you cut through the clutter and attract them in the first place?[11] Don't think that people will like your page just because your brand is loved or has a following; there are tens of thousands of brands on Facebook, almost all of them backed by marketers who are just as *sure* that their brand is loved and that people will want to follow them. Whether it's placing ads on Facebook or putting your Facebook URL on some of your other marketing material, you'll need to do something to break through the noise and grab their attention.
- More important, how will you engage them once they've arrived and keep them from leaving or keep them coming back to view your pages regularly? What incentive will they have to *stay* with you once you've gotten their attention? Think of it this way: what if someone invited you to a party, and it sounded as if it was going to be hopping, so you decided to cancel other plans and show up . . . but when you showed up, nothing was happening, no one was talking, and there wasn't any music or food or anything to drink, just a bunch of people standing around listening to one person talk. How long would you stay? You're the host of this party on your Facebook page. Never forget that getting people to show up is the easy part, and the real aim is getting them to not only stay but also participate in your community.
- If you generate more followers on Twitter, what is your strategy to engage them—or, how much leeway have you given

your community managers to do so? Are you ready to go past "content calendars" for your Twitter feed and actually pursue conversations and topics you didn't initiate? When people start following you, will they get anything more out of the experience than a pipeline of information they could have gotten somewhere else? Why would a customer choose to follow your brand on Twitter instead of going to your website or Facebook page, or even just reading the paper or news websites or watching the TV news?

• Do you have anything in place to measure the effectiveness of specific campaigns—a short link to specific Web pages, or a code that your community can use to get a discount on your product, admission to your facility, or access to special, exclusive content? How will you know that those extra Twitter followers are taking any action as a result of your engagement with them?

• If you draw more visitors to your blog, what do you want them to do once they start reading? How will you enable, empower, or entice them to do that? It's critical to your success to plan from the beginning what will happen once you've attracted the attention and fans you hope to attract.

Understanding what you want to achieve or get out of social media is critical to determining whether you've received a sufficient return on your investment. A clear definition of success helps you determine what you need to be measuring. And by looking beyond surface numbers to measure true effectiveness against those objectives, you avoid the trap of executing programs designed to win online popularity contests rather than to achieve your business or organizational goals.

7

THE FIRST THING WE DO . . . LET'S WORK WITH THE LAWYERS

"The first thing we do, let's kill all the lawyers." That line, uttered by the otherwise forgettable character of Dick the Butcher in William Shakespeare's *Henry VI, Part 2*, has been referenced so often that it's become a cliché unto itself—a blanket denunciation usually intended to dismiss the entire legal profession as a negative and damaging influence on society.

It's a common enough sentiment, isn't it? Even in the corporate and organizational world—or perhaps *especially* in the corporate and organizational world—meeting with lawyers is usually grounds for grumbling, concern, or at the very least a significant dose of caffeine!

When social media and legal collide, the complaints usually hit the stratosphere. The uncontrolled and perceived "free-for-all" nature of conversations within social networks, along with the fact that any employee can theoretically engage in conversations about the brand or even purport to represent the brand, tends to make lots of legal departments plenty uncomfortable. Lindsay Lebresco remembers about her time at Graco, "The 'hows' of social media sometimes made legal nervous. After all, they didn't use Facebook, they'd never heard of Twitter and Flickr, and this 'blogging' thing seemed strange to them too."[1] Graco's attorneys were hardly unique; we had the same situation at General Motors, and I'm willing to bet that you'll have it at your organization too. While your legal department is likely aware of social media, it is equally likely to not understand it—and in many cases, your lawyers may see it as a threat.

That said, you have to remember that lawyers are not the only ones reacting to social media in the "same old" fashion. (Marketers who see Facebook as a collection of 750 million eyeballs to whom one-way "messaging" can be sent come to mind.)

In turn, the caution of an organization's attorneys is usually received by social media types as surefire proof that legal "doesn't get it" and just wants to get in the way of progress. Legal's job is to protect the company from risk and exposure, reducing or eliminating it when possible. A smart social media strategy specifically *requires* you to embrace a lack of control and *rewards* you for taking some risks. It would seem, at the surface anyway, that legal and social media might be an oil-and-water mix.

Whether a natural mix or a forced one, however, social media and legal departments are increasingly required to not only coexist but also in many cases cooperate. Zena Weist of H&R Block is quite matter-of-fact about this: "Legal needs to be at the table, roped in from the get."[2] Given the importance of getting social media right and the consequences of getting it wrong—and the seemingly opposite directions from which legal and social media might be approaching the same idea—frequent communication between the two groups is critical to an organization's social media success. The rapid development of social media platforms and networks might have initially overtaken legal's ability to restrain it, but this is rapidly changing—especially as cases involving social media begin to hit the courts and precedent is established. Just as in matters of traditional marketing or PR, legal and the social media team must increasingly work together.

This isn't always a marriage easily understood from the outside. Sometimes, the "right" thing in social media is dangerous territory for corporations or large organizations. Anyone who's ever worked inside a big company understands this reality. Yet acting in ways that protect a company's self-interest can seem antisocial or antithetical to social media audiences accustomed to hearing the gospel of transparency.

For example, while at GM, I once found myself taken to task by some of the audience of the FastLane blog because during a UAW strike against GM, we weren't posting the company's negotiating position or explaining what specific elements of GM's proposal the UAW was rejecting. To me, it stretched credibility to think that anyone associated with the blog would even be informed on the state of labor talks, much less discuss details in public while negotiations were ongoing and risk upsetting a potential settlement over something said in the post. But to many in the audience, our refusal to discuss details of the negotiations or go beyond an acknowledgment that there was a strike signified an incomplete commitment to transparency and openness and, in their eyes, cost us credibility in the social space. (Thankfully, most of the FastLane community sided with us on that one, but the dissent was common enough to draw out the conversation on the site for a day or two.) For many members of online communities (and more than a few self-proclaimed social media "experts"), transparency can seem a zero-sum game.

This is, I think, one of the major reasons for the disconnect that sometimes occurs between social media audiences and large organizations. The concept of self-protection seems so very "corporate" that audiences can forget that there are legitimate reasons in our litigious society for an organization to take steps to protect itself, even at the expense of open communication. This is also a big reason so many social media consultants and "gurus" aren't taken as seriously as they think they should be within organizational walls and their messages don't always resonate with employees of those organizations. It's not that companies "don't get it" or don't want to engage with audiences; it's that they recognize the limitations and exposures of answering every question that might be of interest to an audience. To those used to corporate structure and legal oversight, constant exhortations to be "authentic" and to "engage" can often seem naive or simplistic. Most social media "gurus" haven't worked inside a truly big organization, and no matter how smart they are, this inexperience often shows; the same principles that may work well for individuals in social media can be quite impractical in a corporate setting. Corporate lawyers—and those trying to engage in social media from inside those corporations—understand this. Many who have never worked inside a big organization do not. That's why so often the leading thinkers in social media find the actions of big companies in the social Web to be so frustrating.

That said, the advancement of social networking and technologies has led us to something of a Mexican standoff, with legal departments and social media practitioners warily eyeing one another, perhaps not trusting the other's intentions but each hoping to survive with its concerns intact. Caught in the middle, perhaps, are the online audiences hoping to interact with the brands they care about.

In any such standoff, the participants have to be willing to drop their guns in order to survive. Even though much about social media makes many lawyers uncomfortable, and even recognizing that the need for protective measures is still present, legal departments are increasingly realizing that the businesses they work for have to be present in the social Web in order to remain relevant to a growing generation of customers.

On the other side, there is at least one compelling reason that brand social media representatives are increasingly involving their legal teams in the brand's social media activities: because the lawyers are going to find out about them whether they were originally included or not. Perhaps even a couple of years ago it was possible to "just do it" without legal's catching on because legal wasn't paying attention to the space yet. But those days are *long* gone. Even if your organization hasn't really jumped into social media yet, I can assure you that your attorneys are giving it a close eye and watching for developments in the space. Social media is as big and hot a topic in the organizational law field as it is in marketing and PR circles. And while most attorneys are reasonable enough to work with you when you've given them the chance to do so, they're not going to be so forgiving if they're being brought in after the fact to "clean up your mess" or try to apply company standards to something after the fact. Bringing lawyers into your effort from the very beginning, even if it means that you can't do something you really wanted to do, saves lots of cycles of work, saves aggravation, and helps both sides get it right the first time. It also helps you build relationships with your legal team, getting you seen as a willing partner rather than a threat.

So whether social media thought leaders like it or not, big organizations cannot behave quite as openly as they might wish. Whether audiences like it or not, big companies and organizations cannot be as openly communicative—or just accede to every proposal we receive—as they think we should be. Whether social media leads inside big organizations like it or not, they can't just go off executing social media programs without buy-in from the lawyers. And whether legal likes it or not, social media exists, and your company will increasingly be losing opportunities if it is not involved in it.

So, since we're all kind of stuck with each other, shouldn't we figure out some way to make this work?

What Legal Brings to the Implementation Strategy

Let's start by examining why a legal team can be the brand's social media lead's best quiet ally when it comes to implementing organizational social media. Here are a few things that legal can do for you:

1. **Ensure understanding of FTC regulation and compliance.** In October 2009, the Federal Trade Commission actively inserted itself into social media, issuing guidelines regarding "endorsements" offered by bloggers and issuing organizations direction on what must be divulged to online audiences whenever they are courting bloggers' opinions. As you might imagine, there are still shades of gray around much of the interaction that takes place in social networks between brands and individuals—and with so many new platforms emerging and technologies developing as quickly as they do, those guidelines are likely to evolve in some way. Unless your social media lead also happens to be a lawyer—a rare find indeed!—no one in your organization is more qualified to fully interpret and explain those guidelines than one of your attorneys. While it's possible for your social media team to keep up on developments as to how other companies choose to enforce the FTC guidelines, your legal staff are the right people to interpret current or updated guidelines. The fact is, you *need* these guys to help keep you compliant.

2. **Research case law and legal precedent as it develops.** With as much talk as there has been over the past few years about social media, it is sometimes difficult to remember that social networks (as a mass phenomenon, anyway) haven't even been around a decade and that Miley Cyrus has been a cultural phenomenon longer than business use of social media. There hasn't really been a lot of time for case law or legal precedent to be established on various elements of social media. That doesn't mean, however, that no precedents have been set or no cases have been tried. Familiarity with the cases that have reached courts can help inform everything from your social media policy to choices you make as to which bloggers to interact with and which campaigns to run. Your legal department will be able to not only follow these cases and precedents but also understand better than the rest of your organization any contexts and histories included in relevant decisions. Having

your legal department keeping up on social media case law and precedent as it develops is a critical part of informing your social media efforts.

3. **Help develop your social media policy.** While multiple parts of the organization should be involved in developing your social media policy (we'll talk about that in the next chapter), your legal department or attorneys have a significant role to play in its creation. For starters, the legal team can point out proposed parts of the policy that could expose the organization to liability. In an environment where the line between personal and professional continues to blur, do you really want to empower *every* employee to join *any* online conversation taking place about your organization? The legal department will also have a sense of what protections *it* wants to write into the policy, which makes the policy more palatable to legal and more likely to be approved. Working with the social media lead on the policy will also familiarize an attorney with some of the challenges inherent in social media that the social lead faces every day—helping him to understand the needs of the social media team more clearly.

4. **Develop rules and guidelines for online contests and promotions.** At some point in the development of your programs and initiatives, you're most likely going to run a contest or offer some sort of incentive for your fans and followers. Perhaps you give away a product or a service that you offer; perhaps it's a contest in which the winners get to visit one of your facilities (if you're a theme park, for example); or maybe you run a promotion in which you send a lucky winner to a landmark or vacation destination. Maybe it's something as simple as giving a five-dollar gift certificate to one of your stores. If you're a nonprofit, perhaps you give away access to one of your higher-priced and most anticipated fund-raising events of the year.

Whatever it is, there are going to be rules in place—set down by either federal or state law, or by company policy—governing what you can and cannot give away, how you can go about it (random drawing? some sort of qualification?), and how you might distribute the prize. Legal has probably done this kind of thing before with other marketing programs or campaigns. Even if it hasn't, it's still probably better qualified than you to identify the requirements you must adhere to in executing your giveaway. Contests and giveaways are huge winners in social media—done well, they drive and incent interaction from the audience with your brand—and you're going to need legal to steer you through the ins and outs of executing your contests and managing the payoffs to the winners.

How to Win Friends and Influence People—Even If They're Lawyers

At this point, I'm hoping that you're agreeing that legal has a significant and important role to play in the development and ongoing existence of your social media program. It can be challenging, for the reasons outlined in the beginning of this chapter. The relationship with your organization's legal team will likely be the most difficult of the relationships your social media team needs to build and will take more effort than the others to find common ground. But believe it or not, social media teams and lawyers can work together pretty well when they try to. Here are a few tips and tricks that will help you make this relationship work.

1. **Look in the mirror—maybe the problem is *you*.** Do you consider working with legal a "necessary evil"? If so, the first step in making things work smoothly between legal and social is for you to shift your mind-set.

   Don't just recognize the importance of the role of a legal team in developing your program. Welcome it. We've all been in rooms where it's clear that the other folks at the table don't want to be there or are resentful of having to meet with us. It's not fun, and it usually results in our putting up walls or getting our guard up. Lawyers are people just like anyone else; if you make it clear that you neither want to work with them nor like having to do so, can you blame them for returning the favor?

If you're looking for an active and healthy partnership with legal, you've got to drop the attitude before anything else. The lawyers' job is to *protect* the organization; the social media team's job is to be innovative marketers and drive actual business results. Both of these goals ultimately come down to doing what's in the organization's best interests—you're not on opposing teams! Yes, there's that element of risk aversion versus occasionally needing to take risks, but those are simply two different approaches toward the same goal.

Usually there is at least one pragmatist within legal who sees things for what they are and reacts accordingly, rather than being reactionary and trying to fight an uncomfortable change. Use your powers of observation to identify that person and set him as your target. (If no such attorneys are employed by your organization, it may call for the intervention of the executive champion with the head of the legal department to ensure the cooperation of the legal team.)

Build up your relationship with that person and develop some familiarity with, if not genuine affection for, each other—to the point where your meetings with him are convivial, not combative. The more you come off as a colleague and friend rather than a member of an opposing team, the better off you're going to be. This shouldn't be all that daunting. Building relationships with individuals is at the core of doing social media well. With your legal department, it's a stronger tactic to try to deal with the same attorney and build that relationship so you earn that person's trust—even to the point where he may advocate for you to other lawyers.

2. **Make the lawyers part of the team.** Part of your job on the social team is to help your lawyers get up to levels of social media savvy similar to those that your team members have;

doing so will make the rest of your job easier. While your law-yers are most likely aware of social networking, they are almost equally unlikely to have the same level of understanding of its potential or ramifications that your social team has acquired.

You first have to convey to the lawyers that social media is not a fad, it's not going away, and it's not something that large brands and organizations can ignore or avoid. Once you've made that point clear (and in 2012, this shouldn't take too much convincing), you should move quickly on to including the legal team in your planning from the outset, not just bring them in after the fact to review an action or program they cannot change.

At GM, our Social Club meetings always included at least one representative from the legal team. While we didn't always see eye to eye, it was amazing how much smoother my team's relationship with legal became once we made a stronger effort to inform and educate them.

Doing this will help them recognize that while their prefer-ence might be to stay out of social media, it's not an option—so their job is not to say no or block programs; it's to understand the goal of a particular program or activity and then help the team find the least risky way to carry it out. At Dell, Richard Binhammer credits the legal team with being constructive in their approach. "Legal didn't drop all their concerns," he remembers, "but they came to the table with the approach of 'how do we make this work?' rather than 'how do we stop it?'"[3]

Here's the reality: every big brand I know that has been suc-cessful in social media so far has had its legal department well represented and included in the discussions about social and digital and the development of the organization's social media program. I'm not aware of any big brand that's found success while keeping its lawyers out of the loop and unaware.

3. **Create social media experts within legal.** From the legal side of the house, it's important for one attorney to be desig-nated as responsible for interacting with the social media team

and developing expertise in the legal aspects of social media. Sometimes this is someone formally assigned by the department based on various skills and interests; other times, it can be someone who emerges informally through watercooler or hallway conversations with the social team. Either way, you need to have someone in legal who is the identified go-to attorney for social media.

Once that attorney has been identified, it's critical that the social media team work directly with that attorney to help her become an expert in social media. Don't just tell her what your organization's team wants to do. Show your social media attorney how to be as smart in the social space as humanly possible. The social media evangelist in particular needs to spend a great deal of time with this attorney, educating, familiarizing, and providing as many educational resources as possible—everything from white papers to webinars to conference opportunities.

H&R Block's Zena Weist also shares this assessment. She advises, "Get your legal contact engaged in the social media industry and its nuances—through conferences, social media business councils, and private communities. I think it helps for you to be right by your legal lead's side while they are learning, so you can comanage through—and maybe you'll learn a bit more about the law around your brand along the way as well!"[4]

Consider taking your "adopted" legal sister or brother to a conference with you, having her or him attend the local Social Media Club meeting with you, or designating this person to attend a webinar or join a private community (a Facebook group? other private communities?) on the organization's behalf. Give this partner from legal a reading list of prominent influencers' blogs or books—nothing too long or overwhelming, but representing just the handful of people whose thinking influences yours or who you think are most "on the ball" when it comes to this space. Send along articles or posts that you find particularly insightful. As new networks and platforms emerge, invite your attorney friend to join those networks or get an account on those platforms so that she can learn along with you. If you've built a decent relationship with someone online whose opinion you respect, whose influence you acknowledge, or whose endorsement you covet, introduce your attorney to him. The more your organization's social media attorney knows about the space, the more she's going to be able to help you—and the smoother your relationship is going to be. If you're not making the effort to help her get educated, you can't really complain that she doesn't "get" social media, can you?

Ultimately, the idea of working with lawyers should not cause a lump in your throat or a rise in your blood pressure. Did you ever go to a theme park as a kid and spend hours working up the guts to ride the biggest roller coaster, chickening out a couple of times before finally staying on line long enough to anxiously board the ride, convinced that you'll die of fright before the end of it . . . only to find out that the ride isn't nearly as scary as you thought and that in fact having gone on it made your entire day at the theme park better? Working with legal on social media is a little like that. You can't avoid it and hope to be successful, so you might as well screw up your courage, take a deep breath, put on the seat belt, and enjoy the ride. It might even make your job easier in the long run.

CHAPTER 8

A SOLID SOCIAL MEDIA POLICY

One of the most popular comic strips of the past 20 years has been Scott Adams's *Dilbert*. A merciless skewering of corporate culture, *Dilbert* pokes fun at the mundane, contradictory, and maddening aspects of office life in America today. Just about everyone who works in the office of an organization employing more than 20 people has a favorite *Dilbert* strip clipped from the newspaper and pinned on the cube wall.

Few subjects are as *Dilbert*-worthy as policies. (In fact, one of my very favorite *Dilbert* strips refers to the need to develop a procedure for creating policies, which generates a question about the policy on creating procedures, resulting in the entire team's looking for a white paper on policies for developing procedures for creating policies.[1] Still makes me laugh every time I look at it.) Nothing quite seems to scream bureaucracy like policies and procedures—and nothing would seem to be more antithetical to the uncontrolled world of social media.

But there may be no more important element of your digital and social program than developing and regularly communicating a social media policy. Ideally, your social media policy should contain some elements of familiarity with FTC guidelines, as well as with social media or digital community etiquette, and elements of corporate or organizational policy that make it consistent with other business guidelines and policies. Without a social media policy, legal and HR may never be comfortable with having any of your employees interacting on the social Web. Your employees may never feel comfortable enough to actually go out and engage on your behalf. And social media really can be the risk many perceive it to be for your organization.

The primary reason for establishing a social media policy is protection. You're building in precautions for the organization, protection for employees, and clear rules or parameters for all involved. From an organizational standpoint, you're putting rules in place and communicating them clearly to your employees. It's no different from providing your employees with a set of rules and expectations around things like expense reporting, business ethics guidelines, and new internal IT tools. Given the speed and reach of social networks, don't you think that a more formal, more coordinated approach makes even more sense in this realm? In the era of social media, not having a formal and established social media policy is as foolish as not having business guidelines on ethics and conduct.

A solid social media policy also helps to indemnify the organization against charges of inconsistent handling of social media issues or unfair reactions to employees' social media activity. Having a policy in place as early as possible not only establishes the expectations of the organization but also can help to justify any action necessary against an employee should a violation occur.

Let's say your policy specifically states that employees are allowed to be critical of "the company" but not of individual company officials out of respect for individuals in general. If an employee writes a blog post or sends out a tweet blasting the CEO, your HR team can point back to the policy and indicate that the employee *knew* that such a post violated company policy.

Without a social media policy in place, the lines become much grayer. Was that employee just exercising her right to free speech? Did the company give its employees fair warning that such criticism would be considered outside the fair or expected bounds of employee conduct? Without a social media policy in place, your case for whatever action you might wish to take becomes at least a little more difficult.

Once your organization has decided what you're going to allow from employees in the social Web, put it in writing and clearly communicate it to your employees (we'll talk in the next chapter about how to most effectively do that).

To employees, the policy should be seen as not a tool of the organization but as similar protection against overzealous or inconsistent evaluations of or judgments about social Web activity. An established written policy should be a bulwark against those in management who "don't get" social media. Every employee has the right to expect that his employer will make the rules and expectations clear. Without a clearly communicated social media policy, an employer could potentially discipline or even terminate an employee over his social media activity, even if the employee has done nothing that strays from accepted norms or etiquette within those networks, or that was considered unacceptable at a previous employer.

Additionally, by spelling out what constitutes unacceptable behavior, an employer is in many ways protecting an employee's right to be active in social networks within those parameters. In other words, anything that's *not* prohibited or frowned upon by that policy is something you're allowed to do without fear of reprisal or harm to your career. Especially in a space evolving as rapidly as the social media environment, it's sometimes hard to have a feel for what's acceptable and what's not. Dell's Richard Binhammer puts it this way: "Our policy protects our employees so that they don't get themselves in trouble over an innocent misstep."[2]

If clear boundaries are set and you stay in bounds, there should be no penalty flags thrown at you. A social media policy shouldn't be seen as a list of things you can't do; rather, it's a guidepost for what you *can* do in social media as an employee.

Get the Right Players on the Field

The first step in developing a solid social media policy that protects the interests of both the organization and its employees is to identify all the parts of the organization with skin in the social media game—especially the stewards of company policy—and get them in the figurative room together. Human resources is a critical partner, as is the legal department, from an employee rights and company policy standpoint. You're going to want your IT department involved as well, especially if you're building or incorporating any internal social-sharing platforms—such as an employee blog or blogging platform or an internal microblogging platform like a Socialcast or a Yammer—or allowing employees to access social networking sites from work.

You should also involve the departments that are involved in social media as part of their job responsibilities. While HR, legal, and IT are needed from a policy and support perspective, communications/PR, marketing, and customer service will bring working knowledge of social media to the table. Finding the right balance between institutional understanding of social media and the folks who regularly develop and maintain policies for your organization will be critical if the policy is to be accepted and embraced by the organization, standing up under scrutiny rather than being opposed or rescinded by either camp.

Remember, it's not always the suits or the leadership who have the best understanding of social media in the organization—or the best grasp of what the culture can handle, for that matter. As Mike Wing, IBM's VP of strategic and executive communications, wisely puts it, "Understanding what the organization is ready for is not always achieved by asking *executives* what the organization is ready for."[3] Of the two dozen or so people who contributed to the original IBM blogging guidelines (which have since been updated several times), more than three-fourths were *not* executives or functional leaders. We were just IBM employees who happened to be involved in blogging on our own and thus knew something about the space. We weren't in it for money or business at the time. We all blogged because we enjoyed blogging and talking with the communities we'd developed. The guidelines that we helped create together still stand, more than six years later, as some of the industry's best and most frequently cited. The credit for this goes not only to the people who chose to get involved and worked on these guidelines but also to IBM leadership for being willing to hand over creative control to what Mike Wing calls "a handful of people who were doing it for love."[4]

That's not to say that turning the creation of the social media policy over to employees is going to work at every company. But it goes without saying that at least some employees are already active in social media, whether sanctioned or not—and that some of them might have knowledge or perspective that could inform an organization's policy-making efforts. If you're aware of employees at your company who have particularly well-read or well-respected blogs or followings online, you should consider including them in the policy-development process as well. Not only will your policy be potentially better informed, but also you could end up elevating a hidden gem of an employee who was just waiting for a chance to shine.

Bring Everyone Up to Speed

You can't draft a strong, winning policy when starting from zero. So the first step after assembling your policy team is to give them a crash course on social media. Your flash education course should include basic rules of social media etiquette, the expectations of the various audiences, famous "fails" from other organizations, and policies from other organizations that are publicly available and have perhaps won some acclaim as being strong or sensible or progressive. True, what works for a tech company may not work for a pharmaceutical company, and what works for an automaker may not work for a government agency or a nonprofit. But if you study enough of the policies that have won acclaim or are often cited as examples within the social media space, you're going to find some common threads that you should probably incorporate into your policy in some fashion, even if you have to adjust or tweak them to fit your culture or industry.

The legal team might be able to offer some additional perspective by reviewing recent cases involving social media, especially when large organizations are involved. Instances when other organizations are considered to have failed can provide "teachable moments" for your organization—not just so that you can avoid making the same perceived mistakes, but also so you can anticipate audience reactions to elements you might choose to include in your policy anyway.

Posts and interactions on blogs devoted to your industry can provide some guidance as to what online audiences expect in the way of discussion and candor from an organization in your business. Starting personal Twitter accounts and following prominent social media influencers, your competitors, or journalists who cover your organization can provide some insight as to the kinds of discussions you can expect to have on that platform and others. Almost everyone on your organization's policy team is going to have some education to contribute to this preparatory period, and everyone involved should devote themselves to soaking in as many of these perspectives, histories, and case studies as possible. The more broadly educated your policy team is before embarking on the actual drafting of your policy, the stronger the end result is going to be.

Find Middle Ground

Once everyone involved has gotten up to speed on as much of the social media world as possible, it's time to begin drafting the actual policy. There are a few things all parties need to bear in mind before getting to the actual content of the policy.

You want your social media policy to be in the informal, non-corporatespeak language that permeates the social media world. Nothing will make you look more bureaucratic, old school, and as if you just "don't get it" than a social media policy written in law-yerspeak and seeming as if it were designed as light reading for an HR managers' convention. But keep in mind that you're drafting an official corporate or organizational policy at this point, not a jaunty e-mail to a friend or the rules for a private Facebook group. For a while, it was in vogue for companies to have short, pithy social media policies seemingly designed to show how cool or "social media savvy" their organization was; one of the most famous "policies" during the nascent era of social media was the four-word admonition once given to Sun employees: "Don't do anything stupid."[5]

While it might earn style points for trusting the common sense of employees, a casual statement like that will not cut it anymore. Your policy may someday need to stand up in a courtroom or with a judge mediating a dispute between the organization and an employee. Do you want to go to court armed with "Don't do anything stupid," or "Don't do anything that you'd be afraid to have your boss find out"? No, you have to make your policy a bit more explicit, a bit more comprehensive, and more in line with other organizational policies. It might seem antithetical to social media, but it's the reality.

That said, your policy needs to be concise. Four words is too short and pithy, yes. But make it a veritable *War and Peace* of poli-cies, and none of your employees are actually going to read it. They'll skim over it long enough to be able to click a little button on the intranet or sign a piece of paper affirming that they read it, but they won't really bother to take it all in. And that won't be their fault. Your company's employees are very busy and have a lot of demands on their time, and they're not going to take much time out of their day or let something else drop in order to read a policy. As you start drafting your policy, aim for something that can be read in a just a few minutes—something that spells out everything the company needs to yet stays basic enough to not be a chore to read. Think in terms of putting it in a page or two—or, if it must be longer, at least drafting a one-page Cliffs Notes version that distills the policy into something employees can peruse and digest quickly.

Finally, you must accept before you start that no one on your policy team is going to be 100 percent happy with your policy when it is completed. This is normal. The social media experts among the group (probably PR, marketing, or CRM folks) are likely going to believe that the policy is far too restrictive, is out of character with the spirit of social media, and doesn't give employees enough freedom to truly impact external perspectives of your brand or organization. The organizational support teams (probably HR and legal, mostly) are likely going to be uncomfortable, feeling that the policy is too liberal and grants employees permissions that expose the organization to risk. Each "side," as it were, is going to look at the end result and find things it wishes would be changed. This isn't because your organization is particularly dysfunctional (though it might be tempting to believe that anyway!) but is because the nature of social media and organizations pretty much invites this conflict. It is not unexpected and doesn't represent a failure.

This was one of the hardest lessons I had to learn when General Motors updated its social media policy during most of 2010, a process spearheaded by Mary Henige in corporate communications. When I first read the final policy that was approved after months of discussion, I was dismayed and thought it was far too strict—but I quickly realized that the policy represented a compromise and a lot of willingness to meet in the middle by all sides. A policy as indulgent as what I as a social media person would have liked would never have met approval from the rest of the organization. This is one of the realities of working with a large organization and is something that a social media leader has to accept and understand when taking on the role of leading the social media program at such an organization.

Since it's understood going in that no one is going to be completely happy with the final policy that results, all parties must accept that perfect can never be the enemy of good when it comes to social media policies. It's better to have something in place and adjust or amend it as necessary than to delay the implementation and release of a good policy because the team is waiting until everyone involved thinks the policy is fantastic and is comfortable with every aspect of it. If you do that, your organization will never have a social media policy.

Now, the "Easy" Part: Writing the Policy

Finally, you're ready to draft the policy. Start by asking the toughest legal- and HR-related questions. Here are some examples:

1. Which actions or statements by an employee within a social network or on a blog would constitute a fireable offense? This may include the following:
   - **Revealing company confidential or legal information.** This should be self-evident; the Internet is no place for talking about upcoming product releases or updates. It's not just a question of inadvertently tipping a product launch; such slips or leaks could in an extreme circumstance end up even affecting stock price if the product or news is significant enough. Other information leaked or posted online could impact pending litigation or expose the company to legal liability. Start with specifically prescribing into the policy the kinds of disclosures that will constitute a fireable offense.

You should also probably prepare some sort of review process to build into the details of your policy for identifying whether a leak was inadvertent versus being a case of carelessness or deliberate intent.

- **Libeling a competitor or an individual.** Any criticism or trash-talking of either a competitor or an individual in a social community would be bad form anyway. But when the smack talk crosses the line into untrue assertions or libel, that's something your organization can be held legally responsible for—so you have to make clear that not only will an employee face legal repercussions for libeling someone but she'll also lose her job.

- **Promoting hate speech.** This is a no-brainer but should be spelled out anyway. There is a fine line between freedom of expression and promoting hatred of or danger to others. That's a debate for a different book perhaps, but when an employee engages in such talk, it reflects on your organization and can cause you all kinds of headaches. Work with your HR department to develop the right language around what kinds of expression your organization prohibits, and make sure it's clearly part of your policy.

- **Financially compensating an external blogger for positive discussion of the organization or its products.** This problem tends to arise not in initial phases of social media programs but in organizations where social initiatives are decentralized or informal—as social media begins to gain traction and employees or departments occasionally develop programs or efforts on their own. While advertising with bloggers or on their sites is a perfectly valid model, crossing the line into the editorial side—where compensation is exchanged for positive writing—puts your organization in an ethically compromised position the ramifications of which can last and hurt your reputation well into the future. If your organization is of the mind-set that you're going to keep advertising and editorial as separate in the social media as you do with traditional media, you've got to spell out in your policy and make clear to all your employees that you don't pay in exchange for content or positive mentions.

2. What actions would not get an employee fired but would initiate disciplinary action? For example:

- **Overtly and publicly criticizing a competitor.** Even when commentary doesn't become libelous, it is still bad form and reflects poorly on your brand to have your employees bashing or overtly criticizing your competition. It's unbecoming, and it makes your organization look insecure and defensive. (Not to mention it invites potential retaliation from the competitor who's been bashed, and a social media spitting match involving your brand is a distraction with no benefit to you.) Make sure your employees know it's not acceptable to aggressively pick fights with a competitor.

- **Unauthorized use of company time or computers to access social networks.** This is a little touchy, because you are after all in at least some sense encouraging employees to engage in social networks. But not everyone in the company is going to be empowered to engage in social media from work—and every company will have varying opinions about what level of social activity is "acceptable" from employees not working directly in social media. Whatever your organization's perspective is about accessing social networks from work, make sure you've made it clear in your policy.

- **Allowing social media interaction to interfere with job duties.** Related to the previous item, while you do want your employees engaging in social networks, you don't want them doing so at the expense of their "day jobs." Remind your employees of the need to be responsible with their use of these networks—and that permission to engage does not mean allowing other duties to slip.

- **Presenting oneself as officially representing the company's or organization's position if not authorized to do so.** This is an important element because of how quickly word or rumors can spread over the Internet. If your employee isn't specifically empowered to officially speak on behalf of your organization, he needs to make clear that his thoughts, tweets, and writing are his own and don't represent company policy or official statements. And you need to make clear in your policy that employees need this kind of a disclaimer.

3. Which actions by an employee might not constitute disciplinary violations of the policy but would be frowned upon? These will vary by organization and thus are harder to prescribe, but areas of concern might include:

- **Politics.** Cultures might have different impressions about how active or vocal employees should be in politics or political discussions, for example, and thus your policy might include language prescribing conduct or interaction on political sites or subjects.

- **Customer service issues.** A company might want all its customer service inquiries and issues to route through its customer service department, so its policy should instruct employees to route any customer service issues they encounter in social networks to a specific destination or group.

Each organization will have unique expectations and cultural aspects that determine the conduct it will accept from its employees in social networks. Whatever your organization's specific rules, just be sure that they are included in the policy. You can't ask people to adhere to guidelines or rules they've never been apprised of.

Start the process by identifying the most egregious and obvious transgressions that you want to protect the organization against and have them defined and ready to be incorporated into the policy once you start crafting it. It's not always good to start developing a policy based on what people *can't* do as opposed to what they *can*—but because social media is such an emergent space and the list of what's possible seems to grow every day, in this instance, you're probably best off starting from what you're absolutely not going to allow.

Next, look at the legal aspects specific to social media and identify how you're going to build adherence with those elements into your policy. How will you ensure compliance with FTC social media guidelines—by having only those specifically empowered by the organization interact with influencers on behalf of the organization and carefully managing your "influencer" lists? By embarking on a training program to make as many employees as possible familiar with the FTC's expectations? Since the FTC will be watching your program, you need to determine how you're making sure it won't see anything it doesn't like.

Also, depending on your industry, you may have specific legal or regulatory requirements within the customer service sphere that will need to be incorporated into your policy. For example, General Motors is obviously in the automotive business. Automakers are bound in the United States by the Transportation Recall Enhancement, Accountability, and Documentation (TREAD) Act—which among other things requires manufacturers to report to the National Highway Traffic Safety Administration (NHTSA) information related to defects in their products or reports of injuries or death related to their products.[6] TREAD compliance is obviously very important to GM and all automakers in the United States, so when we started expanding into the social media world, we had a lot of discussion as to what our TREAD responsibilities were within the social Web.

We addressed the issue by making TREAD awareness part of the social media education module that all employees receive, building deeper explanations of GM's TREAD responsibilities into the training for employees who might be expected to engage in social media as part of their job responsibilities, and instructed *all employees* to direct anyone they observed raising an issue about one of our vehicles straight to GM customer service—either within social networks, by e-mail, or by phone. GM customer service representatives are specifically trained in TREAD compliance as part of their jobs, and we wanted to ensure that customer service and TREAD reporting was handled by the expert team members who knew how to process such reports.

Your organization may or may not be bound by regulatory requirements like this, depending on your industry or business. Or, you may have specific customer service procedures that it is your policy to follow whenever you become aware of an issue. Whatever those requirements or procedures are, you're going to want to have them explicitly and especially built into your social media policy in order to make sure they're followed by any of your employees who become active in the social Web.

Of course, the social media policy should remain consistent with your organization's other conduct and ethics guidelines. The next step in putting together your social policy is to review the larger conduct policy and incorporate any elements that might have ramifications in the online world.

First Things First: Policy Before Etiquette

One of the biggest mistakes I think I made at General Motors was that the first policy I drew up upon arriving in 2007—besides being largely a solo project that I brought to the rest of the organization after having written it—was more focused on social media etiquette issues than on being a solid and lasting "policy." I was trying to write the next corporate social policy that the social media world would love, respect, and cite often—and I didn't draw up an actual *policy* that would work for my organization so much as a social media etiquette guide, full of reminders about the importance of transparency and stating that as a representative of GM, employees should always take the high road in Internet discussions no matter how much they might be goaded or how anyone else was behaving and emphasizing the need to make valuable contributions to conversations rather than simply pushing GM messaging or products. Can you imagine that kind of a document holding up in court if an employee had ever been terminated due to conduct in social networks?

The rules of "social media society" are important to those in your organization who will interact regularly on the social Web, but you can cover many of these in your training programs. Policy planning is the time to discuss the things that the organization will consider violations so egregious that they could warrant punitive action.

What to Include

Among the elements common to many organizations' social media policies are these:

- A statement that employees are expected to follow company ethics guidelines
- A reminder that all employees will be held individually responsible for their posts and actions in the social Web and that if they violate the law online, they and not the organization are accountable
- That employees should not represent that they are officially speaking on the company's or organization's behalf and should make clear that their thoughts are their own
- That employees should strive for transparency in interaction and are thus expected to divulge their employment with the organization when discussing it
- A statement that employees should respect all copyright and fair-use laws
- That employees are not to divulge information that is proprietary or confidential to the organization, including and especially financial information
- A reminder that because they are employees of the organization, their conduct reflects on the organization—so disre-

spectful conduct like ethnic slurs, insults, or hate speech will not be tolerated

- A privacy reminder that the Internet is forever and that whatever gets posted is usually searchable and findable by someone, so employees should exercise discretion in what they post

What to Put in a Usage Guide Instead of the Policy

Only after you've addressed prohibitions and legal or regulatory compliance as well as ensured consistency with your other conduct policies should you turn to matters of "social media etiquette." "Do unto others" might be a great philosophy to live by, but it's kind of tough to write that into law. In the same sense, it's good to share with your employees the things that will go over well in the social Web and help your organization avoid criticism or turning off social audiences—but many of these items have no legal ramifications at all and don't belong in a legal policy. Instead, consider putting them into a usage guide or some sort of "tips and tricks" document ancillary to the official policy. This guide should contain some of the "unwritten" rules of the social world, adherence to which will make entry or ongoing participation a lot less daunting for employees—and may save your organization some headaches along the way. Among these rules might be the following:

- **Acknowledge any mistakes you realize you've made, and correct them before anyone calls you out for it.** Don't hope a mistake escapes notice and simply push it off the front page with further updates before anyone sees it. Admit it and fix it.
- **Don't delete any posts or factual errors, under almost any circumstance.** Deleting a post that you find after the

fact to be embarrassing or controversial only highlights its nature and makes you look far less trustworthy or transparent. If the post or comment has offended, issue an apology and admit to having learned a lesson. If it has generated controversy, acknowledge the controversy even if you opt not to make additional comments on it. Only in circumstances in which proprietary or confidential information has inadvertently been revealed would deleting the post be understandable—and even then you should acknowledge that you've removed a post and why. (A word of warning: even if you've deleted something, people can usually still access it through caching or sites like Waybackmachine.org; deleting a post rarely makes it wholly inaccessible.)

- **Be respectful of others even when respect isn't being shown to you.** People will get unruly and occasionally insulting or downright vicious online—especially if they've got the chance to engage with you anonymously. It's an unfortunate side effect of the Internet. But as a brand representative, you can never win if you allow yourself to get dragged into a spitting match or if you start treating people disrespectfully. When you do, you reflect poorly on your brand and turn the other party into the victim of an arrogant big company. No matter how challenging someone gets, you have to take the high road as a brand representative.

- **Link back often to others' posts.** Show a little "link love" when someone makes you think or writes something you want to share, especially if it's good about your brand. The currency of social networks is connections and sharing. You will be more relevant and trusted the more often you share what others are saying rather than just saying what you have to say.

A usage guide makes a great addendum or corollary to your official policy and will in many cases make your employees feel more comfortable plunging into the social Web than a formal policy. Just be sure to understand what kind of counsel is appropriate to each, and then assign it accordingly.

Prepare—Then Share

Your policy's been written, pored over, and reviewed a dozen times by everyone involved in its drafting. So you're done, right?

Not yet. First, go back and rewrite as much of the corporate-speak and bureaucratic language as possible into plain, everyday English. That's not an easy task, because you need to preserve the intent and meaning of the policy. But social media is a casual platform used by real people, and to the extent possible, the concepts and prescriptions in your policy should be written in the informal way that people talk. This doesn't mean that we go back to "Don't do anything stupid"; the goal is just that we don't sound like a bunch of lawyers.

Once this is done, run the policy past your executive champion to get the imprimatur of one of the senior leaders of the organization. Next, run it by anyone else who needs to approve it before it becomes organizational law.

Finally, when the organization has signed off on the policy, share your policy externally. Put it on your corporate website; link to it from the organizational Facebook page; share it on the company blog.

You do this for three reasons. First, you want to take in and listen to as much feedback as you can, from your employees, customers, investors, and donors. If there's something too strict, too lenient, or too vague, you'll hear about it. Second, this keeps with the expectation of transparency in social media. You want to let the world know you have a policy and what it can expect from your people when interacting with your company. Third, if your policy is really solid and well thought-out, publishing it gives the social media influencer class the opportunity to see it and talk about it, potentially. (This happens a little less often now than it did when organizations were first getting into the social Web, but policies do still occasionally provide fodder for blog posts.) If you're just getting into the social Web, a smart policy can help to announce your presence or arrival.

Your other step is to communicate the policy clearly and effectively to your employees, either by itself or as part of a broader social media education or training effort. Having a solid social media policy is only half the battle. You also have to make sure everybody in the organization knows about it and has the opportunity to learn about engaging in the social Web. Your internal education initiative can be the make-or-break element of your social media program. Get it right, and you kick-start creative thinking and help to create some emerging leaders from your organization. Get it wrong, and you've hamstrung your own efforts and perhaps choked the life from your fledgling program before it has the chance to take off.

In the next chapter, we'll talk about building an effective program to educate your employees on not only your policy but also social media engagement as a whole.

CHAPTER 9

TEACHING THE ORGANIZATION TO FISH

You know the old philosophical question, if a tree falls in the forest but no one is there to hear it, does it make a sound? I'd like to offer my own adaptation of that saying: if an organization builds a great social media policy and program but doesn't involve its employees, is that organization really involved in social media?

Not every organization or company will empower *all* of its employees to engage in social networks. All the same, it's a good idea to build a social media education program for all employees anyway. Given the pervasiveness of the social Web, the odds are strong that at least some of your employees are already active in a network or two; maybe they even maintain active blogs. A basic level of instruction or guidance for all of your employees is the minimum you should offer, if for no other reason than to familiarize everyone in the organization with the social media policy you've developed.

But what if you want to go further? What if your organization is aiming higher? What if you want to build social media capability into your organization's DNA—to the point that rather than having just a social media specialist or two, your organization naturally integrates social media into every program, plan, and campaign? How should the company's education program change in order to achieve that end, and what things should it include?

An organization can do plenty of interesting or even great things in the social space without an employee education initiative, but engineering the culture change often necessary for the full embrace of social media—and by extension making social media an integrated and instinctive part of what an organization does—requires going beyond having a center of expertise, a handful of experts, or even a social media rock star on staff. Organizations have to educate employees across the company broadly and give them the information they'll need to effectively engage in the social Web.

One Shoe, Many Sizes

The first step in developing a social media education program is recognizing that one size does not fit all. Not everyone in the company will use the information or get involved—and depending on what your policy dictates, everyone may not be allowed to. But some will begin interacting in social networks. Others will touch social media occasionally in the course of their jobs. Still others may have social media as a direct part of their official responsibilities.

Each of these "tiers" has different needs, and a good social media education program will have to be varied enough to accommodate them. Your organization shouldn't try to develop a mandatory expert-level webinar series or certification exam for every employee. The majority of your employees will not be called upon to use social tools regularly as part of their jobs. Exposing them to more than they'll ever need to know for their jobs or for how they'll use social (if at all)—or any other extraneous subject, for that matter—only heightens the risk that they'll tune out and go back to focusing on subjects more germane to their roles.

People should be experts in the role for which you pay them, but it's not necessary for someone in finance or engineering to become an expert social marketer—and he has enough to think about without adding another topic to master. You're giving your employees who don't use social media professionally enough information so that they don't make a really bad mistake that reflects on you when they use it in a personal capacity.

Some of your employees, however, will be tasked with regularly using social media in their jobs—and still others will be called on to be your experts and community managers. You can't offer basic policy familiarity and nothing else to the people who are going to be your faces and ears in the social world. A company has to arm its designated experts with information and training at a level that will help make them experts.

Level One: Undergraduate

The base level for all employees, regardless of whether they'll ever touch social media for their jobs, should be familiarization with the organization's social media policy. Even if an employee isn't blogging or tweeting on behalf of your organization, she may well be active in the social Web on her own—and thus is still subject to your social media policy and guidelines. You need to build a basic instructional module just as you would for expense rules or business conduct guidelines and make sure that *every* employee takes the course. It doesn't have to be expansive, but it does have to cover the core of what employees are and are not allowed to do in the social Web.

For example, consider what H&R Block has implemented. Zena Weist explains: "We have over 100,000 employees, and there's a lot of chatter going on out there [in the social Web]. How do we keep their work talk on brand? In order to respond in one brand voice, we educate our associates on our online communication policy, which is tied to our code of conduct. We include our online communication policy in all our partner and vendor agreements so everyone that is speaking on our brand's behalf is speaking with our brand promise and the customer's expectations in mind."[1]

H&R Block's approach reflects a solid understanding of the environment. It recognizes that employees and associates are going to be active in the social Web and that trying to restrict or control all of their conversations is futile—not to mention limiting their potential effectiveness. To protect its brand and ensure consistency, H&R Block educates *everyone* at the company on its online communication (social media) policy—to the extent of even including that policy in vendor and partner agreements. It's a savvy acknowledgment that its associates, partners, and vendors—in order to serve its customers who are also there—will potentially have at least some exposure to the social Web. Its effort to familiarize its policy to as many people as possible with an affiliation with H&R Block not only promises greater consistency in customer interactions but also protects both H&R Block and its associates by making sure that everyone knows the ground rules.

So what should be included in a basic instructional-level education module?

• **Review of the organization's social media policy.** Start by making sure employees are aware that the organization *has* a social media policy and covering its basic tenets. Before a teenager actually gets behind the wheel to learn how to drive, he first spends weeks in the classroom learning the rules of the road—so that when he does actually get out on the road, he has at least a basic idea of what to do. There's no substitute for experience, but knowing the rules better prepares someone to actually do it. Social media within a corporation is much the same. Teach everyone the company's rules before getting them out on the road.

• **Basic familiarization with some of the most popular platforms in the social media universe.** This includes Twitter, Facebook, Foursquare, and Gowalla, how blogs work, social bookmarking, RSS, Google Alerts, Quora, and others as they emerge. (They'll keep emerging; Google+ launched in June 2011 and promptly attracted more than 20 million users in its first month, even while still in beta.) You don't have to get too deep into the weeds; just make sure that people know the ABCs—what the platform is, how it works, how you sign up for an account, and the basics of how to interact on it. Videos are often a great vehicle for getting the basic ideas across. At GM, we licensed several installments of the Common Craft "In Plain English" series by Lee LeFever. The videos are simple, as well as entertaining, and make clear the benefit of the platform or tool being discussed. They're a very useful set of tools for quick instruction, and I recommend them.

• **A beginner's etiquette or "tips and tricks" guide to the most common platforms used in the social Web.** Ideally, employees involved in social media will be familiar with the basic rules of the road for common social networks. They should know to link back to posts, blogs, or sites, for example, or that a first comment on someone's blog should not include a hard-sell pitch for the brand represented. You'll want them to know that using hashtags on Twitter will help not only to keep track of conversations but also to draw new viewers to your feed—or that it's not a good idea to check in "at home" on a location-based network, because then every time you check in someplace else, the entire network will know that you're not at home, which means you're potentially risking burglary or break-ins. Your purpose in these deeper dives is to decrease the likelihood that an employee commits an unintentional faux pas or breach of etiquette likely to reflect poorly on the organization—as well as to protect your employees from unwittingly exposing themselves to potential legal or reputational ramifications off-line.

• **A resource guide for people looking to learn more.** Which sites have particularly useful information and features on the social media industry? Where might employees read or hear about "the next big thing"? Whose blogs should they add to their reader? Who are particularly good or influential people for them to follow on Twitter—either from the "social media" space or within your industry? Try to help employees get as smart as they want to be on social media, and give them as many resources for continued learning as possible. Let's face it, your training module will be outdated at least to an extent within a few weeks of your rolling it out. These resources will help your employees stay up on what's emerged or developed *after* the training was built.

• **Points of contact within the organization for further questions about social media.** Who will be your employees' go-to person or people with information and perspective to help them if and when they want to know more, want some clarification on something in the policy, or find themselves in a jam? Who should be advising them on matters that go beyond what's covered in the training module? The bigger your organization, the less likely that everyone will know each other or recognize who the social media leaders are (the evangelist might have a profile internally, but what about the rest of your team?)—so make sure everyone knows who the points of contact are.

The basic module isn't a "nice to have" or an optional program that makes you forward-thinking in the realm of social media. This is, in the social media era, a simple and smart "meets minimum" for any company whether it has a social program or not.

Everyone in the organization must be aware of what activities are permissible, the basic code of conduct expected should anyone be involved in social, and what things will generate disciplinary action or even termination.

Level Two: Graduate Instruction

The second level or tier of education should be for everyone who works in the functions most likely to brush up against social media in some fashion—communications, marketing, and customer service. Whether or not social is a part of their official description right now, the odds are high that at some point in their career, people in these fields are going to have to do some social media–related tactical planning or be active in a social network as part of a campaign. These employees will need more than the official policy. A survey-level introduction to social media platforms, history, tools, and etiquette is better here.

Responsibilities of Representing a Brand Within Social Media

Just because someone knows how to engage in social networks—and has maybe even built up a following—that doesn't mean she's fully aware of all that comes with representing a brand in those networks. The way an individual conducts herself in the social Web isn't always the right way to conduct herself when she's associated with a brand.

One of my Detroit automotive counterparts, Chrysler, learned this the hard way in March 2011. One of the young people working for its social media agency—and who had access to the official company Twitter account—was frustrated at a slow morning rush-hour drive in Detroit and tweeted his disapproval: "I find it ironic that Detroit is known as the #motorcity and yet no one here knows how to f—— drive."

Only the tweet didn't go out from the young man's personal account. He accidentally sent it from the @ChryslerAutos account.[2]

It wasn't a Chrysler-only situation. That kind of accident could happen to many companies. But the resulting controversy not only cost the young man his job with his agency but also cost the agency its contract with Chrysler.

The problem as I saw it wasn't really that the accident happened. It was that apparently no one had instructed employees—whether Chrysler's or the agency's—that when you represent a brand, there's a different standard you're held to, and there are certain things you shouldn't ever do (like drop f-bombs in your tweets). Even when, as someone associated with a big brand, you're tweeting from your own account or writing your own blog, you're *still associated with the brand.* Yes, people knew that I wasn't working 24 hours a day when I was at GM, but even when I tweeted from @cbarger or wrote my own stuff, everyone still knew me as "the GM guy." My using profanity or being crude or deliberately controversial or offering my opinion on controversial subjects would have reflected on General Motors just as surely as if I'd done it while writing on GM's FastLane blog or tweeted from @GMBlogs. And so I had to behave differently—as does *anyone* in your organization given the responsibility to man the company's social accounts. Even if the employee's name isn't supposed to be widely known, that responsibility still exists. People will eventually make that connection. So make sure that any employee who's going to officially engage for your brand knows the following:

- Don't use profanity in social networks, even when you think you're on your own account.
- Don't insert yourself into political or religious discussions that could, in today's polarized climate, reflect on the brand or end up offending or turning off potential customers based on politics. No one disputes that employees don't give up

their right to free speech when taking on a social media job, but getting into political discussions rarely reflects well on the brand. Let it go and save the political argument for the bar or the gym.

- Don't join in on sexually charged banter or anything that might offend someone with a different sense of what's "proper" from yours.

This may sound as if I'm advocating a brand representative sublimate his entire personality when taking on a social media job. Not necessarily—but I am saying that representing a brand calls for a different standard, and if someone is uncomfortable with that standard, he perhaps shouldn't aspire to represent a brand in social networks. I once had a conversation with a woman employed by a large tech company after I'd spoken on this subject. She angrily informed me that "I'm me, I'm who I am, and I talk the way I talk. If they don't like who I am, they shouldn't ask me to do stuff on their behalf." All I could think was, "So you want the visibility that comes with being a brand rep, and you think it entitles you to additional compensation or advancement (she made that clear), but you don't want to act responsibly enough to be trusted with the brand's name?"

Case Study Reviews

Select several case studies, both some that are well known and those that are less so, that are considered examples of companies "getting it right" and of companies committing social media "fails." Explore them at length. Some will be cases of strong execution of a social media plan, others of poor implementation. Discuss at length what was good or bad about each of them and how the lessons from these case studies might be applied to your organization. (There are several specific examples coming up in Chapter 12 that you may find useful.)

Scenario Planning and "War Games"

Break into small group teams, each moderated by the evangelist or one of your other social media experts, and run through sets of unfolding scenarios in which the team will have to react in "real time" to events occurring at or about the company or brand. Theory and "book learning" is all well and good, but until someone has had to react in social media time and develop something of a "gut" for this kind of work, it's just not the same. So the purpose of this kind of an exercise is to acclimate a team to the pace and quick changes in the social networking world.

While the purpose of the first tier of training is to provide as many of a brand's employees as possible a basic understanding of social media and how the company wants to conduct its program, the goal of this second training tier is to begin to develop expertise among a smaller group of professionals within the organization who can easily take on social media responsibilities and even represent the brand in social networks without causing headaches or being too risky.

Level Three: Doctorate Instruction

The top-tier educational program is for those employees whose daily duties or job description include social media responsibilities, *especially* the ones responsible for running the official corporate or organizationally branded accounts. The people you're looking at for this level of instruction should have either completed the first two levels of instruction or gained enough experience running social programs or accounts that they won't need to take them.

For this group, you should consider bringing in outside speakers or authors from the social media world. Yes, I know that I've said that the premise of this book is that the outside consultants or social media experts many times do not understand or have a full grasp of the challenges faced when you're representing a brand rather than yourself online. I stand by that premise (I obviously have to, right?), but fresh, out-of-the-organization thinking can be invigorating, and every industry or business needs to be pushed a little from the outside, particularly when it gets too comfortable or set in its ways. At General Motors, we brought in outside thinkers and authors like Joseph Jaffe, Jason Falls, Chris Brogan, and David Meerman Scott to speak to members of our extended social media team—sometimes in small group sessions, other times in groups of up to 50. Each of these sessions proved extremely beneficial, not just because of the perspective that these individuals brought to us but also because of the bursts of imagination and creativity they sparked in our own people, who began brainstorming and thinking in different directions afterward.

There's another reason to bring in an outside voice to talk with your team. It is an unfortunate reality of human and organizational nature that we ascribe more credibility to outside voices than organizational ones. A social media evangelist or an extended social media team can lecture or drill until they're blue in the face, and there may still be people inside the organization who resist the message or remain skeptical. But an outside voice, especially one who's written a book or achieved an eye-catching following online, can convert skeptics to believers—even if he's saying the exact same thing you did. It's wise for the social team to acknowledge this reality, however frustrating, and take advantage of whatever relationships they've built with external influencers to reinforce good ideas. Ultimately, it shouldn't matter whom the organization credits with an idea or whom the team listens to; as long as the wisdom is accepted, the cause is furthered. (Of course, this puts the onus on the social leads to vet their outside sources wisely. Bringing in an outside influence whose perspective veers dramatically from what you want your people to understand is obviously counterproductive!)

One last consideration, hardly unique to social media but worth mentioning just the same: don't make the mistake of believing that all of your employee education will take place within your walls. Your "level three" employees need to get out and hear what others are doing, see emerging beta technologies, or just interact with professionals who have similar challenges and goals. Relationships are especially important in social media, and face-to-face interaction with influencers and peers is perhaps even more important than in other practices or functions. So it's worth your organization's time to identify good conferences and webinars for your most involved employees to attend. Visibility and participation in the social media conference circuit is also very important in getting the social media "echo chamber" to recognize that your organization is active and has a program that may be worth observation.

Making It Happen: Doing the Training

Once an organization has decided what it's going to teach to each tier of employee, it of course has to actually *conduct* or distribute this training. I've seen it done via Web modules over company intranets—in fact, we had our basic, entry-level training at General Motors done in this way. Obviously you can reach more people through these technologies, and you have a mechanism to track who's completed the training and signed off on it. (You also have the option of updating the training or doing something like a yearly recertification as the space continues to evolve.)

But for the second group we've talked about, you really ought to consider an in-person, dedicated series of sessions to get everyone up to speed. You can help these employees get signed on to Twitter if they're not already, walk them through how many of the platforms and tools are used, and do some scenario planning and case study assessments. You can go much more in depth with an in-person class session. Yes, it takes more time and resources, and not everyone has the ability or people to lead a training session like this. But if you can make it work, it gives your people far greater knowledge and deeper understanding. A few hours of time invested now can make a big difference down the line.

Another option to consider—though it takes a commitment of time and resources—is to build a mechanism for your employees to train and inform each other. This was one of our most effective tactics back when I was at IBM. As we rolled out our blogging guidelines in early 2005, the company also built an internal blogging platform (creatively enough, we called it "Blog Central") on which any employee could start up an internal blog viewable by any other employee in the company. The purpose was to enable and empower group learning and information sharing, whether about various parts of IBM's business or about the emergence of blogging or about sites or platforms different IBMers were discovering. Within just a year, more than 3,000 IBMers maintained blogs on Blog Central. Some were obviously more popular than others—but the good thing was that some new thought leaders surfaced, people whose knowledge was deemed valuable by the employee community and whose personal stock rose as the organization was able to see what they knew and the respect the employee base had for them. The blogs were searchable by keyword, the top five most popular blogs of the day and week were listed for reference, and information was shared freely across the organization and among employees. While it made some of the lessons less "centralized" or "approved," that wasn't always a bad thing—the learning was more organic, sometimes had more credibility with our employees because it came from "*us*" and not "them" in management, and was no longer the sole responsibility of the core social media team. (I did, as "blogger-in-chief," have the responsibility of looking over the content on Blog Central to make sure that nothing counterproductive or incorrect was being passed around, but that was the extent to which we tried to control it. You'd be amazed at how much your employee community knows and how quickly bad information gets corrected or self-policed.)

Again, not every organization is going to have the IT or financial resources to put up an internal blogging platform (although microblogging tools like Socialcast or Yammer provide similar functionality without the hassle of maintaining a separate internal infrastructure), but it can be a fantastic tool for community self-education and knowledge sharing.

Building a tiered education system can go a long way toward increasing the knowledge base and understanding your PR, marketing, and customer service teams have of social media platforms, networks, tools, and audience expectations. But there is no substitute for actual experience—either for your individual people or for your program as a whole. Only experience can instill a systematic, organization-wide commitment to social media as a business practice. That's why we developed a philosophy at General Motors designed not just to build winning social media campaigns and earn respect in social media circles but also to build a permanent capability for the company that would truly integrate social media into the way GM does business. In the next section, I'll argue that all employees should have some exposure to social media. I'll also discuss ways to build that exposure into your organizational framework.

Immerse and Disperse

A core team of social media experts can definitely make for a winning program—but that program will always be centered on that small core, vulnerable to individual departures and dependent on that team's internal influence. A program that exposes as many people as possible inside the organization to real-life social media campaigns can extend social media acumen and expertise throughout an organization—and in doing so, hasten the adoption of social media across the entire business.

It can be tempting, when building a social program, to try to either build a social media rock star from within or attract one from the outside to be the face of the program. It's easy to see the appeal: a social media rock star draws attention, carries name recognition for your brand or organization, and gives audiences a specific face, name, and personality to identify with a brand. If the whole point of interacting in the social Web is to humanize your brand and make you more than just a logo, why not go all out and personify your brand through that individual?

There are a few problems with this approach, the first and most obvious being that an organization is extremely vulnerable to an individual's departure. If I had built General Motors' program entirely around my own persona, the company would have had to start its social media position from scratch after I left in March 2011. (Fortunately, the department housed dozens of people, including a significant handful who'd developed solid followings of their own; as a result, my departure did nothing to harm GM's presence in the social Web.)

Additionally, having social media expertise sitting in the hands of only a core team somewhat diminishes the purpose of having a social media program. When you're not integrating social practices and tactics into every campaign from its inception, you're counting on someone in your organization to tap into the core team's knowledge and expertise—or even be aware of that individual's or small group's existence and role—in order to get social into larger strategies. If you want to make social media truly part of what your organization inherently does, you have to distribute the knowledge as broadly as you can.

A more significant problem with the "core team" approach is a simple matter of scale. No matter how prolific I may be, there is no human way for me to carry on conversations with more than a few dozen or a hundred customers or potential customers every day. Even if I'm persuading many of the people I engage with to buy something from the company I represent, I'm sure the impact of my individual efforts would be relatively minimal every month or quarter. No one person can possibly talk to everyone who wants attention or answers from a large global brand. This is the challenge inherent in organizational social media from the outset and the hardest one to overcome: social media effectiveness is crafted from the building of relationships, and that is very difficult to scale.

Worse still, credibility in the social space comes from being able to walk the walk as well as talk the talk within communities of interest. And no matter how much a social media representative studies or how hard she may work, it would be incredibly difficult for her to present herself as an expert who can speak knowledgeably about all the different subjects relevant to her business. Imagine a social media director at a retail chain. Is he going to be an expert on every product its stores carry, *and* the company's marketing strategy, *and* the business performance questions investors may ask, *and* the organization's supply chain, *and* the local activities of individual stores, *and* the company's charitable giving and social responsibility efforts? At some point, the image of "jack of all trades, master of none" is going to bleed through, because nobody is able to maintain credible expertise in every subject that touches a big brand or organization.

Wouldn't it be better to train and empower people within relevant parts of the business to engage with the communities that care about their areas of expertise? Wouldn't it be better to have not one or two "social media faces" of a company, but six or ten or twelve or twenty or even more? After all, if one person can carry on 50 conversations a day, then five could carry on 250, ten could talk to 500, fifteen could talk to 750, and so on. The way to address scale in the social media world is not just to distribute the knowledge of social media among your employees but also to convey the *authority* to enter communities and engage in conversations on the company's behalf. Unless your organization does this, you will always find yourself confronting the challenge of scale.

At General Motors, we tackled this challenge by developing a philosophy I call "immerse and disperse." This philosophy was the backbone of our program and is the reason that GM's program grew to the extent that it has. The core concept is simple: rather than have a permanent team of social media experts or rock stars recognized by the outside world, we built a sort of "revolving door" social media team, designed to move people through the system and get them plugged back into other parts of the organization as experts in their own right.

Here's how immerse and disperse works: once an evangelist or social media lead is in place, make her the only permanent member of the social team. Other employees—sometimes new hires, other times people you already have—are drafted into the team for a short-term assignment. Some organizations might choose six or nine months, while others could opt for eighteen-month stints; at GM, we mandated terms of approximately one year.

For the length of that term, the assigned employees are immersed completely in social media—it is their major or only responsibility. Give them a baptism by fire, as it were. There is no substitute for actual experience, no matter what business specialty someone wants to learn—so the immersion is designed to provide that experience. These employees spend that year becoming an expert by doing the following:

- Manning the brand's social accounts—updating the brand's Facebook pages, managing the community on the company blog, or interacting on the company Twitter feed
- Being assigned responsibility to learn about new or emerging social platforms and reporting back to the evangelist or the rest of the team on their potential uses by the brand
- Running specific social campaigns or programs around a product, coordinating the brand's presence at important social media shows, or targeting a specific online community (moms or environmentalists, for example)
- Attending social media conferences and seminars to not only learn about what other companies are doing and what the "next big thing" might be but also build relationships of their

own with other practitioners, with bloggers, and with social media influencers
- When they are ready, speaking at smaller social media conferences representing the brand, raising awareness of the brand's program and efforts, and building their own profile with external audiences as an expert

At the end of their designated term, move the employees on to other parts of the company—other branches of marketing or communications, working with sub-brands if the organization has any (for example, GM had Chevrolet, Buick, etc.), product development, business planning, or even finance and accounting or HR. As soon as employees are a credible subject-matter expert in social media, *disperse* them to other parts of the business where they can serve as embedded social media experts, teaching others what they know and spreading social media knowledge—and the practice of social media—across the entire organization.

Immerse and disperse not only helps speed adoption and institutional understanding of social media throughout your company or organization but also addresses that number one challenge of social media effectiveness: scale. It creates and develops more touch points for audiences to interact with a brand—and each of those individuals in turn can then train his colleagues in how to effectively engage in social media. None of them may individually approach the reach or following of some of the rock stars in the space, but collectively they will have not only similar reach but also perhaps more personal, regular, and relevant interactions with various online communities. Perhaps equally important, by distributing the online and social presence of the company to a range of equally qualified individuals, immerse and disperse insures the company against the impact of any individual's leaving.

Keep Teaching

As is the case with most careers and in life itself, the key to success isn't just the initial amounts of education one acquires; it's in the continued and evolving education and learning one is prepared to undertake. Social media as a phenomenon is still in its childhood, with much maturing and development to come. New technologies and platforms break out every few months. No social media education initiative will ever be completely comprehensive or all-inclusive; no individual within your organization will ever know everything that's current or "right" with social media. So plan on revising and updating your education module at least once a year, if not more often. Here are a few ways to learn or decide what to put in the updated versions:

- Make sure your evangelist and (hopefully) a few others in the organization are attending social media conferences regularly to learn about the newest trends or developments.
- Make sure that whoever is building the training remains active in social networks and isn't spending most of her time in meetings or focused on internal dynamics. The atmosphere shifts quickly online, and what "worked" or made for good brand interaction six months ago may not work as well today. Constant and regular interaction is the best way to keep current.
- Assign regular reading to your team of various social media and marketing sites (Mashable, Adrants, ReadWriteWeb, Ad Age, and any number of social media blogs). While it's important to learn to take hype with a grain of salt in social media, these are still good places to get ideas and learn about emerging platforms or technologies. Have your people occasionally send articles around. Better yet, have them analyze the content a little for perspective or potential application inside the organization.

- Attend at least a couple of social media conferences each year—not just for the programmed content but also for the hallway and reception conversations that happen with other attendees, which are often the most valuable parts of a conference.

Have your employees, even the most experienced ones, refresh their training and understanding often. Recognize that the pace of change in social media punishes complacency and that practices that a year ago made you cutting edge are now so commonplace as to be unremarkable. If you want to be a leader in this space, you constantly have to be revamping what you know, what you do, and how you do it. Just like in life, an education in social media never truly ends.

Teaching an organization to fish is the most effective way to scale social media initiatives and make social network interaction part of what *the organization as a whole* does, not just a specialty that a select few practice. The true goal when building a brand's social media program is to embed social media expertise and practice deep into the organizational DNA, as much a part of the brand as traditional marketing, advertising, or PR. When an organization's employee base is trained in the basics, and a cadre of employees has been created to serve as knowledgeable practitioners who will ensure that social strategies and tactics are part of every marketing and communications program or initiative, that's when the brand truly embraces social media and has a program that stands out among its competitors and in the industry.

CHAPTER 10

WORKING WITH
BLOGGERS

In the endearing 1990 film *Kindergarten Cop*, Arnold Schwarzenegger plays Detective John Kimble, a man working undercover as a kindergarten teacher in order to catch a criminal. At first, Kimble grossly underestimates the nature of his job and the challenges presented by his new audience. "They're six-year-olds," he tells his partner. "How much trouble can they be?" But after a disastrous first day of class in which the kindergarteners' out-of-control behavior runs him ragged, he changes his tune. "They're horrible," Kimble mumbles after collapsing in exhaustion on the bed in his hotel room. "They're like little terrorists!"

There's a parallel between Schwarzenegger's character and most big organizations when it comes to dealing with the social Web. At first, many organizations may treat bloggers or other online influencers no differently from traditional media. After getting beaten up online for "spam-pitching" a blogger with a standard "Dear Journalist" press release or some other violation of the unwritten rules of social media, however, many of these same companies return to their rooms, collapse in a heap on their beds, and mumble, "They're horrible!" into the bedspread.

Working with bloggers doesn't have to be scary, and the chaotic energy of the blogosphere doesn't have to be exhausting. In fact, working with bloggers and online influencers can be more rewarding and enjoyable than working with traditional media. (I've certainly never had more fun doing a PR guy's job than when working with online influencers.) In this chapter, I'll share a few standard practices that will make things much easier for you, for the bloggers you're working with, and for everyone watching your interactions—from the blogs' readers to the FTC.

Online Interactions

The first interaction between an organization and any blogger or social influencer usually happens online. A social media practitioner may notice a blogger's high Quantcast rating or Klout score and decide that he needs to be in front of the blogger's audience. Or a blogger might comment on your site or reach out to a community manager via Twitter or Facebook. Sometimes the interaction will generate from a shared connection or the blogger's initiative, but quite often brand representatives approach a blogger "cold," with no prior interaction. Whatever its genesis, your working relationship with bloggers and online influencers will get off to a smoother start and have a more promising future if you adhere to some core rules of etiquette.

Remember That You're Not as Important as You Think You Are

Most bloggers are not as accustomed as journalists to being approached by big brands. This doesn't mean, however, that bloggers are going to be so overcome or impressed by your company logo or the fact that a Big Corporation or its representative has noticed them that they get the vapors and write whatever message you want. They will not be so flattered by the attention that they overlook ham-handed tactics or approaches. And your new product or announcement will not be the most important e-mail they receive all week.

Bloggers who've built enough of an audience that they're attracting your interest did so *without your content*. They don't need you, and your news won't interest their audience just because you're BigBrandCo and sell to their demographic. "Dear Blogger" notes and attached press releases are as likely to find the round file as with journalists, if not more so. (In fact, such blanket approaches are even riskier than with journalists, because some bloggers will post about your cookie-cutter, fill-in-the-blank, poorly researched pitch and publicly shame you for it.) Your bosses may believe that your press release about version 2.3 of your SuperWidget might be the most important news item of the week, but most bloggers and their audiences will not agree.

It's PR 101, but anyone pitching a story to a blogger must find an angle that actually fits the blog, its subject matter, and its audience. And even when you do that, the blogger or his community may still decide that your company news just isn't that interesting. Don't get flustered, upset, or indignant. Don't take an attitude because your stuff didn't get run, and don't automatically assume that the blogger likes one of your competitors better. Focus instead on doing a better job of being relevant to him.

Read Their Blogs First

I don't just mean "see a blog with a high Quantcast rating and give the most recent two or three posts a cursory skimming so that you can refer to them in your pitch." Bloggers are smart enough to know when you're not really familiar with their interests, style, or community—in fact, it's in some ways even more insulting to have a superficial familiarity with a blog than to profess no knowledge of it whatsoever!

If you're considering reaching out to a blogger—whether to offer her a chance to review your product, ask her opinion about a campaign you're running, or invite her to an event you're putting on—you must *really* read her site first. Watch what she does for a week or longer. Don't just read her posts, but also observe how she interacts with her community in the comments sections. Pore through her archives to get a sense not only of what she writes about regularly but her style too. Has she done product reviews before? Has she written about being approached by other big organizations? If so, did it go well or badly? Did she say why?

This seemingly simple, do-your-homework step is unfortunately not taken by an alarming number of PR and marketing professionals who try to reach out to bloggers. Doing your homework takes a lot of time. Familiarizing oneself with a blogger's content or his community's interest can feel to some like straying from the brand message. And with as many blogs and sites emerging as there are, many marketers and PR people only peripherally familiar with social media can feel pressured to reach as many as possible as quickly as possible. All those "eyeballs" in communities online and so little time, right? But don't fall victim to the temptation to take shortcuts or send out blanket pitches full of key messages. The blogosphere is full of "PR People Suck" posts written in frustration after the blogger has received a particularly bad or poorly researched pitch—and you're not trying to make enemies; you're trying to earn the trust of the blogger and his audience. So take the time, as work-intensive as it may seem. Doing so will make you stand out. The savvier bloggers will appreciate that you did your background research and took the time to approach them properly, while those unused to being approached by a big brand are more likely to feel flattered that you took the time to actually *read* their stuff.

You might recall that I said earlier that bloggers are unlikely to be impressed that a brand has noticed them. There's a difference between being noticed and being *researched*. Anyone can check a Quantcast, Compete, or Klout score, or an Alexa rating (tools for measuring a site's or individual's readership, reach, and influence); not everyone bothers to actually become genuinely familiar with a writer's preferences, style, content, and community. The former can take as little as two minutes, but the latter requires genuine effort—and *that* is what generates a positive reaction from your "target."

This advance reading does not only make for a better-informed, more knowledgeable pitch. It also prepares you better for the result of your interaction. Is this writer sarcastic, with a style that places at least as much value on entertaining as informing? Better warn the bosses that there might be some snark in the post that you get. Does the blog seem antiauthoritarian or anticorporate? If so, the blogger may make some disparaging comments or backhanded compliments even if he likes your product (not necessarily a bad thing, so long as your company's leadership can handle a spoonful of slap with their pats on the back). Is the blogger witty, but profane? Does he make frequent off-color jokes or sexual references that would make your leadership blush—or worse, make them cringe if they were to see such language in the same post as your product or brand? If so, you might want to avoid reaching out to that blogger entirely. It's not worth the potential trouble or risk, and asking a blogger to not be himself is neither realistic nor fair.

Knowing your target is a basic PR rule even when approaching traditional journalists. But somehow, this step is often overlooked when companies are preparing to approach an online influencer. Don't let it be; always do your homework. Make sure whoever is researching your targets understands the parameters you're looking for. Be able to "rank order" which bloggers you're reaching out to for a given initiative, and be prepared to explain to communications or marketing leadership why they're in the order they're in. And keep track of what you've already learned. Maintain some sort of a central database that allows your full team to know what bloggers write about which subjects, whether you've ever pitched them or invited them to an event before, and how they reacted. That way, your full team is better equipped to build relationships with social influencers and their audiences. In some cases, if a blog is smaller or run by one individual, you might assign one person on your team to manage that relationship exclusively; more often—with bigger blogs having multiple authors, with blogs that focus on your specific industry, or with significant influencers who are likely to be interested in multiple facets of your company—you'll have multiple employees occasionally contacting bloggers and maintaining relationships with them. That just makes it all the more important to keep track of how recently someone with your company approached an individual blogger—you don't want to bombard anyone with numerous calls and e-mails from several contacts at your company all at once.

This isn't much different from what PR teams do with traditional media. You're not reinventing the wheel; you're just doing basic PR.

When Possible, Try Not to Make Your First Interaction All About You

I'll be the first to acknowledge that it isn't always possible to lay the groundwork. If you've been given 24 hours by leadership to put together a list of potential targets for a social media outreach program, you may not have the luxury of populating the list with only those you've previously engaged. But when you can, it's always better etiquette to reach out to a potential new target blogger *before* you need her.

Think about it: how do you prefer to be approached when someone wants to sell you something? When you walk into a store at the mall, you prefer to be at least greeted first, don't you? (Companies like Wal-Mart have turned "greeting" into a job description, not just an action one takes.) Even if it's a short, cursory conversation—"Hi, how are you today?" or "Welcome to Acme!"—we always react a little more pleasantly if we've been greeted or had our humanity acknowledged, rather than just being treated like a walking wallet. And when associates do approach you in a store, don't you prefer it if they start their approach with something like "Is there anything I can help you find?" rather than "Just wanted to let you know that we have sweaters 20 percent off today, and socks are buy two, get the third free"? You want to at least have the illusion that store personnel want to help *you* find what *you* are looking for, rather than just wanting to sell you whatever it is they're incented to sell that day.

It's much the same in the social Web. Most bloggers know that if the representative of a brand comments on one of their posts or responds to them on Twitter, a pitch is probably not far behind. It's not only nice to go through the courtesy anyway but also strategically savvy—because people want to have their humanity acknowledged, to have attention paid to their blogs, and to be recognized as more than just a "lead," *before* the "sell" begins. So do what you can to start a relationship with your targets before your actual pitch or outreach begins. Leave a comment on a post or two on their site. Respond to something they say on Twitter. Do *something* that indicates that you've taken a little bit of time to acknowledge them as a writer and as a person rather than just as a blogger whose audience you covet.

Talk About Things Outside of Your Product or Brand

If the only thing a blogger or her community hears you talk about is your product or how great your brand is, no one will pay much attention to you for very long. If you never comment on anything else she writes, she and her community will get bored with you pretty quickly; you'll be that guy at the dinner party who treats every conversation as a chance to sell to someone. You don't want to come off as the stereotypical used-car salesman. So comment every now and then about things that have nothing to do with why you originally reached out to her. You don't always have to make it a generic "me too" comment—"Great post!" or "You're so right!"—for effect, either. If you have, over time, built up a solid relationship with a blogger or her community, you can talk about everything from sports to pop culture like music and television shows all the way to serious life events—parenting issues, illnesses in the family, or a milestone in your child's life. (Some of the most touching and heartfelt conversations I've ever had online came in discussions with bloggers over the deaths of their pets. If you've ever loved a dog or cat or any animal, you know how sad it is when your pet dies; I've shared memories of my own dog and gotten into really emotional and supportive exchanges on the subject with people I've never met in person. It wouldn't seem to have anything to do with selling cars, but you'd be surprised at how many times people with whom I've had unrelated conversations ended up coming back to me later on to ask about GM vehicles.)

Often, these conversations between you and the blogger take place in the comments section of the blog. Sometimes, if you're having a particularly personal or lengthy conversation, you might want to take it off-line and converse via private e-mail. It all depends on how comfortable you are with the blogger—use your judgment when it comes to oversharing—but these non-work conversations can deepen your relationship far more than any product-related interaction you'll ever have.

It's OK, by the way, to occasionally respectfully disagree with a blogger about something he's posted. No one expects you to be an automaton or so eager to please that you never voice a differing opinion. Again, it all comes down to the relationship you have with the blogger or his community, but just as real-life relationships only work when both parties act themselves and put on no artifice, so it is with online relationships. As PR and marketing people, we sometimes make the mistake of thinking we need to stay "on message" online. But occasionally going off message makes your audience more likely to pay attention to your message when you express it.

Off-Line Interactions

Even if a blogger or online influencer has posted about your product or one of your ad campaigns, at some point, you want her meeting your people in person. Just as important, you want some of your non-social media savvy people meeting bloggers as well. (It should help them understand that bloggers aren't the Internet geeks they're stereotyped to be but are credible sources with influence in corners you don't normally reach. It's also always a good idea for any company's people—whether communications, marketing, product development, customer service, or even executive leadership—to hear perspectives from "real people" outside of the usual circles in their industry.)

It's worth noting that there's some stratification in the kinds of bloggers you'll deal with. The bloggers who write about your industry may well be professionals, paid for their work, and as knowledgeable about your industry as their counterparts who write for newspapers or magazines. Within the auto industry, for example, not only did several powerhouse online outlets emerge, but they even started hiring journalists away from the traditional media. For the most part, writers who happen to work for the major online outlets within your industry often don't, at this point, meet much resistance from their traditional counterparts. And even the ones who are unpaid or independent usually display enough knowledge and savvy that any resistance they initially meet from either the traditional media or traditionalists within your PR team will probably quickly melt away. And once you've gotten the traditional guys comfortable with their new colleagues, including social influencers from your industry in media events is relatively simple. (Automotive bloggers, for example, aren't treated like "social media" anymore at General

Motors; they're considered to be automotive media, and the PR team takes them just as seriously as they do the print and broadcast journalists.)

You'll likely encounter a second category of bloggers a little more frequently if you're a consumer brand versus a B2B company: people from outside your industry whose main focus is less about your industry and more about day-to-day life topics such as parenting, the environment, entertainment and pop culture, or social media marketing.

Inviting these social media influencers—especially if you've flown them in or paid for their travel—to a traditional media event can have more significant challenges, however, not the least of which can be resentment from traditional journalists over having to share some of their access to an organization's products and leaders. (For at least the first year and a half running blogger programs at General Motors, we would routinely hear gruff complaints along the lines of wondering how many "real" journalists didn't get to join the event in order to make room for the "amateurs.") Additionally, more of these bloggers are unlikely to have been treated like media by a brand before—they may have been approached or even given products to review, but unlike industry writers who happen to have a blog, many of these bloggers truly are "amateur" in the sense that they're not nearly as familiar with the relationship between brands and journalists, what is expected of them, or how media programs usually work.

For that reason, it's sometimes harder to just seamlessly blend these bloggers into your media program. For example, when I was at GM, we might have reached out to a travel blogger because we knew the target demographic for a new Buick model tends to enjoy travel. The odds of this travel blogger knowing the same terminology and technical details as automotive writers—or even being interested in the same facets of a car—weren't as high. Bringing this writer along for an automotive media program would probably have added an element of self-consciousness for him and extra attention for GM; it's not a fair position to put the person in. So the first rule of working with bloggers in person is to identify your opportunities wisely. Sometimes this will mean holding separate events for bloggers and social media hosted by your organization. Equally often, you should consider running programs at events bloggers are *already going to*.

Programs for Social Media–Themed Conferences and Events

It can sometimes be hard to break out of the routine that we in the communications business can fall into in our industries. We know when the big trade shows and industry events are every year, and we plan media programs for them. We know when we have new products launching, and we develop media and communications plans around those launches. It's comparatively easy to put together a program for an event we do every year, know inside and out, and have some semblance of control over.

But how often do we step out of our world and go out where people outside of our industry's cocoon, which would include most of the customers whose favor we're aiming to win, are hanging out? Social media's rise has brought about a spate of new conferences—events whose magnitude is enhanced by the fact that so many of their attendees share their experiences and knowledge online. South by Southwest, BlogWorld Expo, BlogHer, SOBCon, Type-A Mom, BlogWell, and Social Fresh are some of the biggest, but there are hundreds of social media–themed conferences now occurring that draw online audiences and influencers to gather in person. Plenty of brands from across the consumer product spectrum have begun to take notice of many of these conferences, developing programs for attendees of these events and others and, in many cases, sponsoring the conferences themselves.

When you're considering events that target social media audiences, building a consumer-driven experience is critical to a brand's success. Merely attempting to latch on to a popular social media event and hoping either to seem "trendy" by association or to generate leads or interaction with your brand as the price of entry for being there is not going to do any good for your brand. Most attendees of the big social media events are savvy enough to recognize when marketing or branding is being shoved down their throats with no real benefit to them—and somebody will probably call you out on it. Think about it: you're interacting with people at events *they've* chosen to attend. They're not there to see you or have a brand experience; they're there to have the experience the conference promises. If your brand's presence at the event is little more than a commercial shouting your marketing messages and promoting your logo, the audience members have no motivation to pay it any more attention than they would a TV commercial that happened to be running in the same room. But by helping enhance the experience *they* are there to have (as opposed to artificially building an experience that forces them to interact with a company), a brand is far more likely to make a positive impression on attendees—and to have its marketing messages eventually received rather than simply ignored or tuned out.

You're also far better off if your program helps you be part of their experience than if you try to build a coinciding, ancillary, or add-on experience that takes people away from why they are really there. In other words, you win bigger when your program *helps the audience do what they're already there to do.* Your goal should be to enhance the experience they're there to have, rather than to force them into having a secondary experience with you, your product, or your brand.

I'm not a fan of trade-show-floor presences at big social media events such as SXSW, BlogHer, and BlogWorld Expo. At the biggest events, a brand can easily disappear or be lost in the crush of sponsors who've overpaid for floor space. Constructive, interesting interactions on a trade-show floor are rare, and your organization's booth can often end up as little more than a source of swag. It's true that the visibility does help make sure that people realize that you have a social media program, and you can have some good conversations with people if they're intent on coming to see you. But for the most part, a trade-show-floor presence is really just payoff for your sponsorship, and it doesn't make you a much deeper part of the experience than if you'd just bought ad space in the program. Your relationship with the overwhelming number of people you meet at that event will begin the day the doors open and end the day everyone heads to the airport to go home. That might be effective event marketing, but it's not good in terms of social media. Remember that one of the greatest values social media provides for businesses is the ability to build ongoing and personal relationships with people. Rather than getting in front of lots of "eyeballs" and achieving as much mass awareness as possible, you're looking to build beginnings. You don't want eyeballs; you want hearts and minds. You want relationships.

If you have a limited budget, it's far more effective to spend your money on smaller but deeper relationship-building activity. Instead of building a trade-show presence that 500 people will see but will result in only a handful of good conversations or follow-ups, you're best advised to build a program that allows 25 or 35 people the chance to really get to know your product, your brand, your people, and your passion. Let those 25 or so go out and be your evangelists at the event and beyond. They'll be more effective for you than you would be for yourself anyway! Remember that the name of the game in social media is interaction and *engagement*, not visibility and eyeballs; you're looking to build relationships, not just be seen.

On Site: Now What?

Whether the event you're working is a social media event like South by Southwest, an industry event or a product launch event for your brand, or a consumer event that you've never been to before, there are a handful of rules that stay the same. Every program, every brand, and every blogger is different, but for the most part, these guidelines will make any program more successful in the long run.

1. Ask Yourself What's in It for the Bloggers and/or Their Readers

Your organization has an event going on—maybe you're launching a new product, maybe your industry's holding its biggest event of the year, and you're bringing online influencers as your guests, or maybe you're doing a targeted outreach program for online outlets with audiences that fit your key demographic. Whatever the event or reason you're inviting people to have an experience with you, you have something you're hoping to achieve: visibility, positive reviews, buzz for new products, maybe even sales. You may want people to understand that your brand takes social media seriously, or your goal may be to begin or deepen a relationship with a blogger and her community.

Please excuse me for being so blunt, but so what?

Your needs, your wishes, your *news* are important to you, obviously. But these things aren't really all that important to a blogger or the blogger's audience unless you think about the interaction from his point of view and give him a reason to have it matter to him. Frankly, I've observed too many brands approach bloggers as if they believe that "because we're BigBrandCo, they'll care."

Take your brand hat off and put your consumer hat on when planning an in-person activity, and think first of what the blogger and her audience will get out of the experience. In many cases, a blogger who doesn't make a living with her blog will have to take time off of work or arrange for child care in order to attend your event. What have you got planned that will make doing so worthwhile for her? If the situation were reversed and you were that blogger, would the event be worth using up precious vacation days or scrambling to arrange for someone to take care of your kids while you're away? You need to combine your news or product with an *experience* that the blogger will find so intriguing or interesting that she chooses to spend time with you in spite of the challenges doing so might present.

Most good bloggers will also think of their readers as well—and so should you. Remember, in order to truly influence a blogger's audience, the blogger's experience must seem at least partially transferable. You can't just offer up a once-in-a-lifetime kind of opportunity that a blogger's audience can't see themselves having and expect the audience to jump on board as your fans. In fact, an overly elaborate experience can have the opposite effect: the blogger's experience won't be as relatable, the audience will see your effort more as a PR move than they might otherwise have seen it, and some might even call the blogger out for taking freebies or junkets from a big brand.

(Look at the reaction to Peter Shankman's experience with Morton's Steakhouse in August 2011, for example. Shankman jokingly tweeted from an airplane that he was hungry and that he wished Morton's—where he is a frequent diner—would meet him at the airport with a steak when he landed. Someone at Morton's alertly noticed the tweet, and when Shankman got off his plane, a uniformed Morton's waiter was there to greet him with a steak dinner. He of course blogged and tweeted about the incident—wouldn't you?—and both he and Morton's got a ton of publicity from it.[1] But while many people were impressed with Morton's responsiveness, an equal number in the social Web pointed out that the incident was not reflective of actual customer service but more of a PR stunt—a good one, but a PR stunt nonetheless. Some wondered on their blogs or in tweets whether a customer who didn't have more than 100,000 followers would have gotten the same treatment.[2] So what initially seemed to be a no-brainer social media win received as much cynical skepticism as it did plaudits.)

So when building your programs or initiatives, make sure that even though you're offering an opportunity to an individual blogger, the experience you provide is one that most or all of his readers can relate to. At GM, for example, when we developed a drive program for new vehicles we were launching, it wasn't enough to get a blogger a driving experience in the car. Even if the blogger *loved* the car and wrote positively about it, we hadn't really brought the readers along for much of an experience. They were just reading a car review written by someone they trust a little more than an auto journalist, and it was a bit out of context compared with what readers usually saw on the site. But when we built an entire *experience* into the program—in which the car was only part of the activity—we suddenly turned a car review into a sharable story about a road trip, a food crawl, or a family vacation, for example. Readers enjoyed following along with these adventures and often were able to see themselves in the story. With such an approach, the car becomes an organic part of the story rather than artificially popping up and seeming out of place—and is desired along with the rest of the experience.

We took food bloggers on road trips to the restaurants of television chefs and on "food runs" to discover restaurants or the best pies, hot dogs, cupcakes, or pizza; provided bloggers with not only vehicles to take road trips to social media conferences but also fun and creative contests for them to take part in along the way; provided wine enthusiasts vehicles for winery tours; and took college students cramming for finals on late-night pizza runs.

Some programs were more successful than others (though all the examples I just gave were at least moderately successful). But for the most part, this approach worked. After these events, we collected pages of data and feedback from our guests suggesting that the program helped open minds toward the product and the brand. Many bloggers wrote posts that didn't just discuss GM vehicles but also cited GM's people and the kind of company we seemed to be, a critical goal particularly during our recovery from the Chapter 11 crisis of 2009. And between my team and me, we could point to dozens of bloggers who in fact had bought one of our vehicles after having first been exposed to them during one of these programs.

If you lead by considering what's in it for them, you'll eventually reap the benefits and get what's in it for you. You'll be able to measure it in not only the volume of posts that result and the tone of what's written but also the reaction of the bloggers' communities, their openness to working with you again, and how often their posts are linked to or reposted by others in their communities. It's harder to put a direct measure on goodwill, but you can more effectively see it play out in social media than in most traditional media, and there's a big difference between even a favorable product review in the traditional media and a passionate embrace of your brand by a blogger to his community.

2. Assume Nothing, and Be Direct and Clear About Your Expectations

One of the more famous dustups between brand and bloggers occurred at the BlogHer conference in 2009 in Chicago. Nikon threw an event at a bar several blocks from the McCormick Place Convention Center where the event was held, hoping to attract many of BlogHer's influential attendees from across the blogging spectrum, including those who write frequently about parenting issues (often somewhat unfortunately referred to as "mommy bloggers"). But when some of the bloggers who not only were moms but also had their babies with them tried to enter the bar, they were turned away by Nikon. The event was for adults only. At first in joking frustration and then in mounting anger, some of them began using the hashtag #nikonhatesbabies as they tweeted about the situation—and that started a frenzy. Within short order, Nikon found itself on the receiving end of an indignation storm on Twitter as the hashtag and story began to take on a life of its own. With the size and prominence of BlogHer (one of the biggest social media conferences of the year), Nikon soon became a trending topic on Twitter—but not in the good way.

There were two schools of thought around this incident. The first was that Nikon should have realized that at a conference targeted to women bloggers, many of whom happen to be moms who write about their experience with motherhood, the odds were high that there would be at least some guests who would have babies or small children with them. New mothers who were still nursing in particular comprised a significant enough portion of this event's audience that the company should have known there were likely to be babies involved and thus planned accordingly.[3] The other school of thought was that new motherhood or attendance at a conference shouldn't have clouded anyone's judgment enough to conclude that bringing a baby to a bar was appropriate, that Nikon had acted responsibly by turning these guests away, and that it was those who were angry about the situation whose planning or judgment was questionable.[4]

There was no clear-cut right or wrong, no hero or villain in this story. Nikon certainly didn't set out to infuriate some moms, and it's quite likely that no one went to that event gunning for Nikon. The breakdown occurred because there wasn't adequate communication between the brand and its desired guests as to Nikon's expectations or rules for the evening. The company appeared to assume that guests would know enough not to bring their babies (or not to attend if they had no babysitter for the evening). The entire incident highlights the importance of setting *clear* expectations for any blogger event or interaction and conveying them to your intended audience.

The rules of brand-blogger engagement you've set for your company within your social media policy might be crystal clear to you and your team. But you're a PR or marketing professional, and you do this for a living; many of the people you're dealing with in the social world do not. If you want to keep yourself out of trouble, assume nothing. Spell out everything that is going to happen during the course of the day or the length of your program. Be specific about activity or interview times and protocols you want or need followed.

We've already discussed the FTC guidelines that govern interactions between big brands and bloggers or online influencers. It's your responsibility to not only be aware of them but also make your guests aware of them, and of your expectations for what they should disclose. (Don't forget that you also have the responsibility after the event to follow up and to remind a blogger to disclose, if she did not do so in her post, facts about her interaction with you.) Before you've even brought a blogger or online influencer into your program (i.e., when you're still in the invitation phase), it's critical to make sure that you've clearly outlined what you'll need her to disclose. Be as specific as possible, even giving her suggested language if you like. "A post about this event should somewhere contains the phrase 'Disclosure: I was invited to this event by BigBrandCo, which paid for my travel and provided dinner'" might be an example. Whenever there's anything of value that you provide—airfare, hotel or lodging, food or drink, or samples of or access to your product—make sure to tell your blogger guests to divulge that you provided it. It's only fair that they know the expectations and rules ahead of time.

If you are bringing people in with the understanding that they will write a post about the experience, tell them so. (The best blog posts occur when people *want* to write about their experience with you, not when they *have* to—but if this is the expectation you have, you need to be clear about it.) Additionally, you need to be clear about what your guests can expect from you: how much access they'll have to your executives or experts, what product (if any) they will receive or have access to, what they're "allowed" to talk about versus what you're offering with an expectation of nondisclosure. The bottom line is, if there's anything (beyond a negative review, which *is* fair game) that would upset you or your organization, it's only fair of you to tell people about it up front.

Are you doing an event for parenting bloggers or taking part in a conference attended by lots of parents? Plan ahead for some of these guests to bring their small children with them—or, be clear in advance that portions of your event will be closed to children (for example, if there's alcohol involved). Few oversights can get the blogosphere's dander up like a program for parenting bloggers that turns away someone who brought his small child with him. You might think it's self-evident that a parent wouldn't bring a kid to a networking event or mixer at a bar, but many times the need for child care would have prevented the parent from coming to the event at all. As we saw in the #nikonhates-babies incident, "self-evident" can have very different meanings depending on which side of the interaction you're on.

Is there a dress code? Are your programs or events going to be formal? Or is everyone wearing jeans? Let your guests know ahead of time exactly what they should expect and what they ought to consider bringing along for the trip. I learned this one the hard way. At GM, we once invited 100 members of online communities to tour the facility where the preproduction Chevrolet Volt test vehicles were being assembled. Anyone walking the factory floor must wear pants and closed-toe shoes for safety reasons. But the event was in August. Many of those we invited dressed for comfort, in shorts, skirts, and sandals. Because we hadn't been clear enough about dress code expectations, several of our guests had to stand outside the shop-floor door while the rest of the guests took the tour. Needless to say, they weren't happy—nor should they have been. It was a bad oversight on our part. We got too caught up in our own world and forgot that what was second nature to us would not be so evident to someone who doesn't know our industry.

Making no assumptions and being as clear as possible about what bloggers should expect, what you expect from them, and the ground rules that are part of coming along on the program will reduce confusion, prevent misunderstandings, and save everyone a lot of headaches.

3. Make a Decision on Where to Draw the Line Between Paid and Earned Coverage—and Then Stick with It

Social media doesn't just represent a shift in who is considered "media" but also marks a potentially uncomfortable shift in the media model. One of the things that can make brands or big organizations uneasy with social media is the blurring of traditional lines—not just the ones between "consumer" and "media" but those between editorial and advertising within the online media business model as well. As the number and influence of blogs increase, many bloggers now make money on their sites; this isn't bad (of course!) in and of itself, but it can raise some situations that make brands very nervous.

In every other form of journalistic or informational media that's developed over time—newspapers, magazines, radio, broadcast television—one of the most sacrosanct rules has always been the separation between editorial and advertising. More closely guarded by most media than the line between church and state, having this differentiation between what its writers report and the advertising that pays them to report it is critical to the American notion of an independent press. One of the quickest ways to offend a journalist or major publication is to suggest that its coverage is in any way influenced by its advertisers.

Within the social media world, there's not always that clear delineation. Sometimes the blogger is a one-person shop and just doesn't have the resources to have a separate person or department handling advertising. Often, the blogger will not have journalistic training or won't realize that the line has ever existed. In a few cases, the blogger may argue that the concept is a bit outdated or sees nothing wrong with the idea of "advertorial" content (perhaps citing advertorial inserts in some magazines as precedent within traditional media).

Whatever the reason, a good number of bloggers will want to be compensated for their interaction with you. Some will even propose the kind of content they'll produce in exchange for specific payments. After all, some argue, this is how bloggers make their money; you wouldn't expect them to work for free, would you? (This is usually followed by stares of abject horror from the PR or social media person in whose worldview this represents an ethical breach of the highest order.)

Any brand representative has to adjust to the fact that the church-state line between advertising and editorial is often murky or even absent in the social media world—and that a blogger looking to be paid isn't necessarily wholly unethical. She's just coming into the situation with a different worldview. Organizations must come to terms with how they want to handle paid content. Either they embrace it with full disclosures or avoid that direction entirely. You can't really go halfway on this one.

Personally, I've never been comfortable with financially compensating bloggers in exchange for posts or coverage. Even with the disclosures, it's never felt right, and none of the programs I've run have done it. (This has earned some frustration from some corners of the communities that provide paid content.) But no matter what choice your organization makes regarding paid content, you have to stick with it and apply it consistently. You'll also want to make your policy clear from the beginning of conversations you have with online influencers. Set the expectations fairly up front—and be clear about what disclosures you require from influencers who do work with you.

4. Find the Right Representatives for Your Brand

The guests at your events are going to be spending anywhere from a few hours to a day or two with you and your brand. Don't make the mistake of plugging the most knowledgeable subject-matter expert you have into the program and expecting everything to go well. Success with social media isn't as simple as knowing the material.

Remember that to many (though certainly not all) of your guests, the *experience* is as important as the information you're offering. And there are certain personality types among executives that just won't give a positive impression of your brand or your company. Some executives or project managers might be dull, stiff, or obviously uncomfortable at having to interact with "the masses." Some will be on the arrogant side. Some have never mastered the art of not *sounding* like a marketer and will squawk like a walking commercial. Some are not used to being questioned or disagreed with (at least to their face). Some are just shy and introverted and won't like the "onstage" nature of interaction with media of any type. Whatever the reason, not every executive or product manager is going to be cut out for being part of a social media program—so when you're planning out dinners or activities or some sort of interaction, look for brand representatives with at least a few of the desirable characteristics:

• Extroverts make a much better impression even if they are not the most qualified spokespeople for the product or service you're promoting. That doesn't mean you should just find the most gregarious personality inside the company—the person does have to have *some* knowledge of the promotion at hand—but always lean toward your most outgoing possible representative.
• The best spokespeople for these events are able to talk like a real person. In PR and marketing, we've created some monsters. We've done so much media training and message development,

teaching spokespeople how to "bridge" and the importance of "staying on message" or "staying true to the brand," that many spokespeople have now gotten *too* good at it. They speak in sound bites. They use jargon and drop marketingspeak into virtually every conversation. They can be so focused on staying on message that they sometimes forget to read the audience's reaction to that message. The end result is that they start sounding canned, like marketers trying to sell rather than people trying to converse. This is not how to win friends and influence bloggers. You need to find a spokesperson—no matter her level within your organization—who comes off as down to earth and "real," who has mastered the art of small talk, and who simply knows how to not sound like a salesperson (even if that's what she is).

• Your ideal spokesperson should be comfortable around people who don't know your industry. The only thing worse than someone who sounds like he's selling all the time is someone who can't step out of his industry or talk without using loads of technical or industry-laden jargon. Many engineers at GM can explain how a vehicle's braking system works or how they've built greater fuel efficiency into an engine without sounding like an engineer; however, some couldn't explain this stuff to a nonengineer if their life depended on it. That's not a character flaw by any stretch—let's face it, these men and women are smarter than I'm ever going to be—but it does mean that they're probably not the best choice for me to put in front of a group of parenting, travel, or food bloggers. The ideal spokespeople will be able to explain the most complex thing your company or organization does in terms your mother or father would understand.

• They don't take themselves too seriously. In other words, they not only will be affable and at ease with your guests but also will laugh frequently with your guests—sometimes even at themselves. Mark Reuss, GM's vice president for North America, is one of the most laid-back and fun executives I've ever met. He usually manages to sneak at least one self-deprecating remark into any conversation with a blogger. That's not a "gimmick" by Mark; that's who the man is—and it goes over incredibly well. I've never had an executive responded to so positively by both automotive and nonautomotive bloggers alike—and part of the reason is that he can laugh at himself. Executives who will laugh at themselves, go along with a blogger's unorthodox but fun idea for a post or photo, or spend time beyond the allotted interview sessions just hanging out and talking will make a much stronger impression on your guests.

5. Follow Up

Following up doesn't just mean sending a cursory thank-you e-mail after your event is over. Your job as the leader of a social media program does not end when your last guest is off to the airport or has gone home for the day.

Failing to follow up or reconnect with bloggers you've just hosted is the equivalent of going on a great date, having a lovely dinner, sharing an electric good-night kiss, and then not calling the person again. As Converseon/Graco's Lindsay Lebresco puts it, "Nothing says *'I just used you'* like a fancy party followed by silence."[5] You might have made the best impression possible during your event, but if you forget that the job isn't done when the event ends, you'll undo any good you've just achieved. If you're not prepared for and dedicated to following up with your guests, you're better off not hosting anyone.

So what kind of follow-up should you do? At the very least, you need to read and comment on the blog posts that your guests write after having attended your event—if for no other reason than to verify that FTC-mandated disclosures are done. More important, however, you can learn not only whether your guests liked your product but also whether they enjoyed the event. (Truthfully, you have more control over perceptions of the event, so that knowledge is even slightly more valuable to you—in this role anyway—than their impression of the product.) Commenting on those posts and thanking the bloggers once again for joining you is simple courtesy. It's also the first step in extending the relationships beyond the event itself, which is of course what you're aiming for. Consider not stopping at one comment if a blogger's community is discussing the post. Join in the discussion; not only will you look less as if you are checking a box if you've commented more than once, but you might find yourself engaging in extended conversations with other members of the community and building relationships there as well.

In the weeks and months following your event, keep checking in and commenting on your guests' sites. You'll learn more about the bloggers and their communities every time you do so, and the communities will hopefully see that your interest extended beyond getting one post on their blogs or making one sale. Consider asking the bloggers' opinion on another program or event or something your business is doing; if you've become part of a community, you might even ask the group its collective opinion. (This shouldn't be something you always do, however, especially if the person you're working with makes her living through her blog. "I'll help you if I'm compensated for doing so" is a fair response to this kind of an outreach.) Ask a friend for advice once, and it's a favor; ask often, and it becomes an abuse of the friendship. Invite the blogger to another event of yours, or better yet, find out if he has something going on in his life or for his online community that you might be able to contribute to. Ask him if there's anyone in his community he thinks might be interested in coming to an event of yours. Build the *relationship* beyond the initial event, action, or purpose.

Working with online influencers is not the "Wild West" it's made out to be. Let commonsense rules of decency, honesty, respect, and being yourself be your guide, and you'll be just fine.

CHAPTER 11

MONEYBALL: WINNING BIG BY GOING SMALL

For baseball nuts, perhaps the seminal book of the past decade was Michael Lewis's 2003 study, *Moneyball* (the film adaptation, starring Brad Pitt, was released in 2011). Lewis documented how the small-market, small-budget Oakland A's were able to be competitive in an American League environment that favored big-market, big-budget teams like the New York Yankees. In 2002, the A's payroll was $41 million; the Yankees' payroll was more than $125 million.[1] Yet each team won 103 games while losing only 59. In a sport in which most fans and analysts assumed that spending money and boosting payroll was the key to playing winning baseball, the A's managed to be the exception to the rule, seemingly disproving the conventional wisdom. Obviously, the A's were doing something right. But what was it?

Lewis's core revelation was that the A's general manager, Billy Beane, believed that baseball's conventional wisdom was wrong. He thought clubs overpaid for players who could deliver big numbers in the traditional categories and statistics: RBI, batting average, home runs, and stolen bases for offensive players and

ERA, strikeouts, and wins/losses for pitchers. Beane believed that lesser-known statistics like on-base percentage and slugging percentage were far better indications of effectiveness and success. By focusing on undervalued players who excelled in these emerging statistical categories rather than the traditional big-money, high-attention categories, Beane built a team that was more than capable of running with its high-payroll counterparts in New York, Boston, or Los Angeles/Anaheim.

There's a similar dynamic at work in social media, especially as practiced by most big organizations—and if you heed the lessons of *Moneyball* and Billy Beane's Oakland A's, you can make your company's social media program far more effective, delivering greater return for less investment. Traditional ways of measuring effectiveness in both "traditional" media and social media reflect just as outdated a view about marketing and PR as does measuring home runs, stolen bases, and wins by a pitcher in baseball. It's not that the old methods and measures don't work (let's not forget that the Yankees also won 103 games in 2002). It's that you can find other ways to win without spending big or focusing on those traditional measures.

In social media, the big events, massive campaigns, and heavy influencers get the same attention as batting average and RBIs do in baseball; we even call a huge success a "home run." Big brands aggressively court big-name bloggers and Twitter personalities with big followings, hoping that winning their favor or impressing them with forward-thinking social media efforts will lead to greater credibility in the space. We covet not just their influence but also their reach, and we seek the "home run" campaigns that will be favorably mentioned by speakers at social media conferences around the world.

Some of these things work. I'm not here to say that you shouldn't court the big names, nor that a presence for your brand at a big event is a waste of your money, nor that you should ignore monthly unique visitor counts and Alexa ratings or SEOmoz scores. I'm not discounting the effectiveness of a big visibility campaign, like what

GM did for Chevrolet at South by Southwest (SXSW) in 2010, the Pepsi Refresh campaign, or the Ford Fiesta Movement. Big campaigns or all-out presences at the big social media events do work. They often carry with them the added benefit of drawing traditional media attention, which not only promotes your product and brand but also establishes you in the minds of the casual observer as a leading brand in the social media space.

But not every organization has the ability to do something that size. Your company might be too small to devote hundreds of thousands—or even millions—of dollars to a social media campaign. Your company might not have embraced social media enough that you can convince leadership that such a swing-for-the-fences approach is worth funding. Maybe your organization has the will and the budget, but your product doesn't quite fit at a big event. Perhaps you're a B2B company, and big consumer-facing programs don't really address your target market. Whatever the reason, an eye-catching, attention-drawing, big-money social media campaign is not realistic for many companies.

If you happen to be running social media for such a company, however, this is not the hindrance it may seem. There are ways to play moneyball in social media—to focus on the smaller, more local, less expensive programs and initiatives that are highly effective without breaking the bank or needing the digital equivalent of a $200 million payroll.

When It Comes to Conferences and Events, Size Doesn't Matter

When you're considering which events to get your brand involved with, it's tempting to look longingly at the monster social media events like SXSW, BlogWorld Expo, or BlogHer and think that you have to have a major presence there. But it just isn't so. It's true that a well-executed program at one of these events can establish your brand as a leader in almost one fell swoop or can go a long way toward reinforcing the "smart" behind your organization's social media thinking. But you're not just looking for quantity of people you reach; you're also looking for quality in the relationships you're able to build for your brand with online influencers. And in many cases, this is done as easily—if not more easily—in smaller events.

An event with thousands of attendees will be an exercise in five-minute conversations and quick-hit introductions. With that many people to connect with in just a few days, even if you're really good and your brand team spends most of the conference networking, the best you can hope for is to have short conversations with several hundred people and to follow up with them later. (SXSW usually has anywhere between 13,000 and 15,000 registered attendees for the interactive portion. GM's program there in 2010 was considered a runaway success, and yet we probably interacted with only about 20 percent of the attendees.)

At smaller events, however, you're usually competing with fewer brands for attention; there's less clutter, and it's easier for a strong, well-executed program to stand out. Not that competition for attention should daunt you or that cutting through clutter is something only experienced social brands can do—but if you can rack up some good wins and get people talking about your brand as a social media leader or innovator, why not do it?

More important, however, smaller events offer you a better opportunity to actually interact with all the attendees at the event—and more deeply and meaningfully than at many big events. An event with 50 or 80 or 200 attendees may seem "too small" by traditional marketing standards to merit much time or resources—but at an event with 500 or 800 attendees, you might likely only interact with about 200 of the attendees anyway. At the smaller event, you may actually have the opportunity to have a longer, more meaningful interaction with many more of the attendees. Additionally, audiences at smaller events often appreciate sponsors and partners a bit more, not only because of the more direct or intimate nature of their interactions with your brand but also because they recognize that the event may not have taken place without your participation.

There are dozens of smaller social media events, in almost every region or city at this point, that bring together the influencers in the local social media community, the business community that hasn't yet taken the plunge, and occasionally a nationally recognized speaker. If you're a small, regional business or organization, look to attend and possibly sponsor some of these events in your area. If you're a national-level organization or brand that hasn't yet established itself in social media, these regional and local events provide an excellent opportunity to build relationships with community influencers, get noticed by members of these communities as a brand or organization that "gets" social media, and have your message heard and your products experienced by a good number of an area's social media community.

Better yet, these events can provide you a launching pad for more direct interaction specifically with your brand after the event ends. People who've met your people or your team or been impressed with your program at an outside event are more likely to agree to interact with you at an event that you put on that's specifically focused on your brand. So make a point of finding smaller, more local social media conferences or events, and pay them as much attention as you would a big-name event. You don't always need the grand-slam home run of an SXSW or BlogHer. If you get four runs via bunts and singles at smaller events, you've got the same score on the board at the end of the inning—probably without spending as much money or expending as much time as a big program at a big event might take. Either approach works, but if you're budget- or resource-constrained as the Oakland A's of the 2000s were, smaller events are a way to even the playing field and win just as big.

Think Globally, Act Locally

Thinking globally while acting locally is not just a mantra for environmental or social good; it's sound social media advice. Outside events and conferences aren't the only cases in which smaller can be equal or better. You should also start thinking about microtargeting or going hyperlocal in your own programs as well.

In his stump speech, my friend Jason Falls of the Social Media Explorer blog and author of *No Bullshit Social Media* explains how the connections with brands made via social media can bring people back to a "small town" kind of mentality. He points out how business is done in small towns where everyone knows each other. For example, you don't bank at Chase or Citibank; you bank with Bill, whose son plays Little League with your son. You don't buy a car or truck from Chevrolet or Honda; you buy from Dave, who goes to your church. You don't buy a house from Century 21 or Coldwell Banker; you buy from Diana, whose daughter is in your child's class and who volunteers on PTO programs with you. And so on. Individuals earn business in a small town by being known, friendly, and trustworthy—and if an individual you trust leaves one employer to go work for another, you may well follow the individual. Brand loyalty does matter, but it is those local, individual connections that in many cases generate brand loyalty to begin with—and can be as important to the ongoing relationship with the brand as product quality. National commercials and ad campaigns may grab attention, but those local connections just as often have more to do with what purchases are made.

This phenomenon also takes place in social media. National campaigns like the Old Spice Guy do a great job of raising awareness of the brand behind them, but how many people who saw it actually had their tweet answered via video by the guy in the towel? That campaign was remarkably successful in the sense that it drew the desired attention to Old Spice—but it only rarely drove actual interaction with the product or even with any of the people behind the brand. (In the campaign's defense, sales *did* go up 107 percent in the month after the videos and commercials aired.[2] I'm not arguing that the campaign wasn't successful, only that there was very little that was "social" about it. The Old Spice Guy was a traditional advertising campaign carried out on digital channels, not a social media campaign.)

While consumer knowledge of a product or brand is important, that can be accomplished through traditional advertising, marketing, or PR. To take full advantage of social media, brands need to focus on building relationships, showing a level of engagement in social media that is missing in traditional channels. Local activations provide the opportunities to build those relationships, to encourage that small-town feel that Jason talks about. In the well-executed online programs I just mentioned, that local or community flavor was missing, or at least wasn't fully exploited.

Chevrolet's program at SXSW in 2010, for example, helped GM announce to the world that the brand was back—not only as a social media player to be reckoned with but also as a healthy option in the marketplace for people looking to buy a new car—after having to go into reactive mode during the business crisis of 2008 and 2009. But the biggest benefit we got from that campaign came long after all the SXSW attendees had left Austin. We met literally hundreds of people with whom we started relationships that we pursued during the rest of 2010. (I'll describe in just a moment a few of the follow-up events we were able to do with some of these new friends.) While by traditional measures we had every reason to be happy—61 million online impressions, more than 13,000 mentions of Chevrolet on Twitter in nine days, more than 250 traditional media stories generating more than 80 million more media impressions—the big win for us at SXSW was *not* the visibility or the impressions. The big win was meeting people we were able to go back to in their own home locales later on, building on those relationships to do more meaningful engagement in more conducive environments. Of the 15,000 people who attended SXSW Interactive in 2010, we were only able to get a few hundred actually *into* a Chevrolet vehicle to experience our product. But at our follow-up local events, the percentages of people who actually experienced our products and not just our branding were far greater—and that's where the real benefit happened for Chevrolet, getting us the chance to see not just a good marketing campaign but also how we were helping change people's impressions of American cars and specifically what Chevrolet is all about.

Among the local programs we carried out in 2010 alone that I consider to have been at least equally successful as what we did in Austin for SXSW are the following:

- **"Pizza Crawls" in the Miami area.** Our southeastern regional social media lead, Jennie Ecclestone, invited Miami-area food and lifestyle bloggers on a rolling tour of south Florida's most well-reputed pizzerias. Transportation was provided by Chevrolet cars supplied by local dealers, but the focus of the event was the pizza. Dozens of bloggers who might never have given Chevrolet a serious thought were able to experience the vehicles *while* doing something they loved doing—and Jennie was right along with them, not pushing Chevy but simply joining in on the fun. Not only did we have the chance to change some minds about our vehicles, but we gave our guests a face and friend inside Chevrolet as well.
- **Tweet to Drive.** Tasked with reintroducing Buick to a younger generation that had likely never considered the brand (and probably hadn't been inside one unless at their grandparents'), our north-central regional social media lead, Connie Burke, worked with her agency partners to develop a unique twist on the test drive: instead of trying to persuade people to come to us, we went to them. We set up a Twitter account, @DriveBuickChi, and told the Chicago Twitter community that whenever they had anything they needed to

do—grocery shopping, a trip to the airport, whatever they wanted—they should send us a tweet, and we'd come to them with a Buick vehicle along with someone familiar with the vehicle, and they had the car for as long as they needed to use it. In just three months, the program gave out more than 1,000 rides in various Buick vehicles—and many of those riders did blog posts or shared video of their experience.

• **The Traveling Baby Shower.** Partnering with Winn-Dixie, Safe Kids USA, the USO, and central Florida Chevrolet dealerships, we conducted a series of baby showers for military families—women whose husbands or partners were deployed overseas and who found themselves facing impending motherhood and family separation at the same time. Many military families are stationed in areas where they have no other family nearby to help them—so together our organizations worked to provide these moms a little bit of fun time and gifts that they'd normally have gotten from friends at showers near their home. Chevrolet provided the moms and their kids transportation, while Safe Kids provided car seats for the new babies, Winn-Dixie provided other baby products the moms would need, and the USO facilitated the entire program. Chevrolet team members and dealership representatives also took part in the showers, being part of the new extended family trying to make things just a little bit easier on military families.

With the exception of the Tweet to Drive, none of these programs had a cost that entered five figures. (That may sound like a significant number, but when you consider what major brands usually spend on advertising and marketing, you get a sense of how very low the cost truly was, relatively speaking.) Each of them achieved its goal of providing a more direct engagement with GM not just online but also with our products—and our people—in a more intimate, personal, and real-world setting. More important, each of these programs allowed us to be rel-

THE SOCIAL MEDIA STRATEGIST

evant to the target audience by fitting our products and people into *their* interests. We didn't force them into interacting with GM or Chevrolet or Buick; instead, we found something that they would be interested in or that they'd need and found a way to fit our vehicles and our people into their lives.

GM isn't the only big national brand that's found success through playing this kind of "small ball." Consider:

- **Hogs with hearts.** A national radio network in the middle of trying to penetrate three new markets ran targeted local Facebook ads promoting upcoming local events. In one market, it ran an ad about an upcoming motorcycle event, "Ride for a Cure," targeting people living within 50 miles of that city and interested in cancer causes, Harley-Davidsons, or motorcycles in general. The ad reached more than 17,500 people for a fraction of the cost of traditional advertising, and the network knew exactly how many times the ad was clicked. After the event, the local marketing team reported the participation of a large group of motorcyclists who showed up despite never having heard of either the local affiliate or the national network before. These bikers were not brought in by friends, radio ads, or billboards; they heard about the event from the Facebook ads and began relationships with this radio network due to its Facebook activity.[3]

- **A walk on the wild side.** SeaWorld in San Antonio, in an effort to raise its Texas profile as a family destination, decided to specifically target "mom bloggers" in major Texas cities. It reached out to small groups from Dallas, Houston, San Antonio, and Austin and suggested that if they would be in the San Antonio area on a given date, they could drop by for a "meet-up" inside the SeaWorld park, a chance for the women to get together in a fun setting and to "camp out" overnight near the penguin exhibit at the park, bonding with each other and beginning to form a community. These women weren't transported to San Antonio or given anything other than free admission to the park and a behind-the-scenes tour of the facility. Anyone who was interested and signed up was part of this new group. A little more than two years later, that community has grown into the "Texas Wild Side Bloggers"—a group of 16 bloggers highly influential in the Texas "moms" community. A Google search for "Wild Side SeaWorld" reveals more than 3,000 returns—more than 3,000 blog posts and Twitter updates from 16 women in just two years. Not only that, but this group has bonded into a tight-knit community whose members interact with each other nearly year-round, reinforcing their connection to the brand and promoting the community and the park within the Texas mom-blogging community. Three thousand opportunities for SeaWorld San Antonio to have its brand repeatedly promoted as a Texas vacation destination among Texas moms, for the cost of a few free admissions, letting some people "sleep over," and investing the time to have some of SeaWorld's people get to know these women in an off-line, real-life setting. Talk about a return on that investment!

That's one of the most critical lessons about social media success: it is as much about your off-line effort as it is about your online efforts. Online is a great place for you to *begin* relationships, but to *cement* them takes an off-line, real-world interaction—even if it's a short conversation during a conference, a drink at a reception or Social Media Club chapter meeting, or inviting them to share an experience with you and your people. You need to consider real-world, off-line tactics that will reinforce your online ones if you want your programs to really win.

By thinking first of the audience's interests and needs and then finding a small, direct, local way to integrate with those interests, brands can build much stronger and more effective relationships with online influencers. Not only is it easier to track the posts and commentary people put up after the interactions, but also it's a lot easier to send personalized follow-ups to 10 to

20 people than mass e-mails to hundreds or thousands of names and addresses on business cards. Companies can also more readily track more tangible business results, such as whether anyone offered to organize another event with his or her audience for the brand or whether anyone actually purchased the company's product in the days, weeks, or months after the event.

The relationships developed in these smaller, more local interactions much more closely resemble Jason Falls's small-town model. In the GM examples, our people weren't "the GM people"; they became "Jennie, who works for GM" and "Connie, who happens to be at GM." People in social media began wanting to work with us not just because we represented GM but also because they knew and trusted our people as acquaintances and then even friends. (Actually, during the bankruptcy and its aftermath, some people worked with us almost *in spite of* our representing GM rather than because of it; the personal relationships we'd built and the personal approach we took in developing new ones were a saving grace that helped us weather the worst of the enmity and negative feelings that the business situation could often engender.)

Additionally, these events in fact drove more tangible business results for GM in comparison with big programs like SXSW or a national vehicle launch. While the big activations paid off handsomely in awareness, online "buzz," and contributing to the recognition of GM and its brands as significant innovators within the realm of social media, they could not—for reasons of size and volume alone—provide the in-vehicle, individualized, tailored-to-the-audience's-direct-needs experience that the local events could.

The other side of this coin is the kind of people you should invite to the local events. There's still a mind-set in social that you're aiming most for the "big fish," or the people with tens or hundreds of thousands of followers or readers—that an activation or program is only a "success" if people with significant followings took part or were "influenced." The big guns certainly help with a large-scale program like a SXSW, to be sure. If your goal is awareness and buzz, the bigger players help you get it. But with smaller, more local events, you're aiming not just for buzz or impressions but also to provide real-world interaction with your products. If you're successful, some of your guests will buy your products at some point, whether immediately or in the long term. This is where you have to redefine your concept of "influence."

Let's use Oprah Winfrey's book club as an example to demonstrate this point. Think of the effect that Oprah has on her audience; when she held up a book on her show and said, "This is the book I'm recommending that you read," more often than not, the book ended up at or near the top of the *New York Times* bestseller list within a matter of weeks or even days.[4] Oprah has, for her audience, earned enough trust to have that kind of influence. When she says something is good, her audience believes her, and her opinion is disproportionate in that community; winning her over is the key to gaining her audience's favorable opinion. Oprah isn't just influential because she has a huge audience; she's influential because her viewers inherently trust her.

There's someone like that in every online community, no matter the size. These people have earned enough trust to have disproportionate influence over the opinions of the other members of the community—and whether the community is large or small, if you win over the "Oprah" of the community, you win the community. The money spent on your product is the same whether it comes from someone with 50,000 followers or 50, whether they're following a social media superstar or a mom in Indiana with a hundred readers. A customer is a customer, right? You wouldn't stand for it if you walked into a retail store and were told you weren't influential enough to be waited on or valued as a customer, would you? Why treat online communities—your potential customers—that way? Readers or followers of a smaller community of 200 are just as valuable to your business as those of a community of 2,000, 20,000, or 200,000.

And while it's not impossible for trusting relationships to be built with mass audiences, it's common sense that it's easier to build closer relationships with a smaller number of people. In fact, there's a construct within psychology—Dunbar's number—that suggests there is a finite limit, dictated by the human brain and how it's wired, to the number of people a human being can maintain a stable social relationship with. There's no precise number agreed upon for the exact value of Dunbar's number—most agree that it's somewhere between 100 and 230, with 150 being cited most frequently[5]—but if that theory holds, then it might logically follow that some smaller online communities are perhaps more tightly connected and trusting as a result of their size and the amount of more individual interaction that takes place within them.

The beauty of social media is that it allows this kind of individual interaction and individual attention, even for big brands. You don't have to invest any more time or money in interacting with a "small" community's Oprah than you'd spend on reaching out to a superstar—but you might be more effective, because many "smaller" bloggers aren't as accustomed to being taken seriously by a big brand or organization as the bigger influencers are. The outreach may be more appreciated and warmly received.

So when you're considering these smaller, more local interactions, make your target audience a broader mix of both some "name" influencers in your target area and some that traditionalists might consider "too small" to warrant an outreach. Doing so gets you the ideal mix—the online buzz and social media credibility that the bigger names and prominent influencers can get you and the tangible results on business objectives you're aiming for in the long run. And if you string together enough of these small events that are executed well and drive lots of chatter in these small communities, people will begin to notice at larger levels. Rack up enough wins, and you start to have case studies and successes to share at conferences or webinars—and the social media world places increasing respect on actual results, so you'll find yourself in more demand (both at conferences and by the social and traditional media) to tell your brand's story. Score enough runs, and you'll be winning at the end of the game—and no one's going to ask whether you got them one each inning through bunts, walks, and singles or via a couple of three-run home runs. All that matters are the runs you put up.

Here are a few guiding principles for putting together successful, winning hyperlocal programs that can result in these bunts and singles for you.

1. **Get involved in the local online or social networks and communities.** Start earning the trust of the people you're hoping to reach before you start asking them for favors. Make it a point to identify groups, both online and off-line, of the social media community in the locality you're hoping to be active in. Engage in conversations with them online, and show up at their real-world get-togethers. Most social media groups have semi-regular meetings or tweetups you can attend. Make it a point to get to know both the leaders and the "regular" members of the communities you're hoping to reach. And when you talk with them, make sure you're soaking in the things that matter and are of interest to them.

2. **Do what your *audience* is interested in, and find a way to tie yourself to it.** When you ask Jennie Ecclestone, who was our stellar social media representative in the southeastern United States and ran dozens of very successful small regional programs, what's at the heart of a winning hyperlocal social media event, she's very direct: "You have to find what *they* [your target audience] want to do," she says, "and then integrate your product into that."[6] Don't lead with your marketing message or make the entire point of the program the interaction with your product. Frankly, very few people are going to care enough to take time out of their day just for the "privilege" of experienc-

ing your product. Find a way to *help people do what they already want to do.*

3. **Make sure your people are as much a part of the event as your product.** Your people are your best assets; in an environment in which trust is a key currency, it is your people and their personalities that will sell an audience on your brand as much as your product. If you're trying to humanize your organization, you have to let people meet your humans! Don't just outsource the execution of an event to a vendor or agency and expect a report back. Have your employees, the ones who do the actual interaction online, as involved as they can be. Put your people front and center in your program, and make interacting with them a big part of the day or event. After the event, it will be more natural for them to follow up with people they actually met. Your people need to be committed and convinced that their personalities are as important to the success of the program as your products—and you need to have some faith in your people and give them space to be themselves in order to make the relationships work.

4. **Ask for ideas!** There's no rule that says a good idea for a program has to come from within your organization. Members of the community often are creative and have good marketing instincts of their own—or they have events going on already and may have ideas as to how you might integrate into them. This will often involve a request for sponsorship or money of some sort. In and of itself, this is not a bad thing, but make sure that you have the opportunity to actually be part of the event, rather than just cutting a check or being acknowledged from the stage during the opening remarks. If there are people within the local or regional social media community whom you'd like to reach or find a relevant activity for, by all means ask them what they'd be interested in or if there's a potential idea they might have for you to work together. If they come up with something of mutual benefit, do it.

5. **Coordinate and integrate with traditional media when possible.** I've mentioned that half of success in social media is executing smart initiatives and programs, while the other half is making sure that people know what you're doing. One way to make more people aware of your social media efforts—not to mention extending the branding benefit of your program or event—is to make sure that your social media and PR or media relations teams are working together and getting the traditional media involved when appropriate.

   The traveling baby shower in Florida was covered by Tampa Bay television. GM talked with local newspapers and radio about events or programs we've done in Chicago, Los Angeles, and other cities. On occasion, even national media like *Fortune* have covered GM's local activities, such as a program its western regional team did with college students in Southern California. In each case, GM not only extended the message and awareness of the program to audiences outside of social networks but also increased awareness of GM as a brand active in social media and doing fun, innovative things in the social space.

   Partnering with your PR team to generate traditional media coverage for your social media efforts helps make others in the social community aware of a brand's efforts and its program, which in turn paves the way for other programs with other members of the community. Like any other marketing effort, getting the traditional media involved helps extend your effectiveness and promote your brand. Do it when you can— but pitch sparingly enough to not generate feelings among the social community that you're using them for publicity.

6. **Rinse and repeat.** If one of your local or regional teams comes up with a winning idea that works as well as or even better than planned, you'll absolutely want to share the lessons learned and best practices with your other regional teams or to replicate the effort in other parts of the country. GM has done pizza and

cupcake crawls in other parts of the country after Jennie and her team pioneered the idea in Miami, for example. Ask your people or teams to present to the rest of the organization on what they did and why it worked. See if they can put together a template or playbook that allows other members of the organization to replicate the program in their own regions. There's no such thing as a good idea that shouldn't be reprised elsewhere if it's executed properly.

Being Billy Beane

Resources and time are always scarce, and it's often especially difficult to persuade leadership to devote significant resources to social media before you've racked up a few successes that prove its worth. But you don't have to have a seven-figure marketing budget and a team of 20 people working on social media for you in order to win big. You don't *have* to be the biggest fish in the big social media event ponds in order to develop a strong reputation in the space as a leading and innovative organization. If you apply the basic principles of social media—keeping the audience's interests front and center and making the depth of the relationships you build a key priority—to small events, you can channel Billy Beane's Oakland A's and compete quite effectively with the brands spending more money in social media than you. Social media success is not always about acquiring the big free agents with the gaudy numbers and being the New York Yankees of the space; it's just about smart execution and creative thinking. Money is less important in social media than creativity and fidelity to smart principles—the basics and fundamentals of the game. It worked in baseball, and it works in social media.

CHAPTER 12

WHEN ALL HELL BREAKS LOOSE

In business as in life, things can and will go wrong. A customer occasionally has a bad experience with your product—or worse yet, your customer service department. A defective product must be recalled. A corporate officer attracts public attention for embarrassing reasons, or we run a television commercial that upsets or offends someone. None of these things are planned for or intended, but they happen in spite of our best efforts. That's life; stuff happens. The real test we face is not in avoiding these things but in how we deal with them.

The same maxim certainly applies to social media. One of your employees says or does something controversial or off-message within a social network; one of your campaigns is met with scathing criticism; worst of all, a crisis arises in your overall business that must be dealt with in the social Web as well as the traditional media. Just as in life, the true test is not always in the crisis itself but in how you handle it. But the strategies and tactics for successfully defusing or riding out a crisis on the social Web can be different from those used for traditional media.

The Opportunity to Shine

In the movie *Apollo 13*, there's a classic scene in which NASA leadership realizes that the astronauts are in life-threatening danger and that their loss in space is a very realistic possibility. "This could be the worst disaster NASA has ever faced," the director says. But Flight Director Gene Kranz, played by Ed Harris, responds with incredulity and determination. "With all due respect, sir," he says, "I believe this is going to be our finest hour."

It's a lesson businesses should keep in mind when a crisis befalls them, especially in the era of social media. The conventional wisdom might suggest that a crisis is frightening enough in an environment with a 24-7 news cycle. Add the prospect of hundreds of thousands, or even millions, of unhappy people tweeting about your organization or thousands of angry messages being left on your Facebook page, and the idea becomes positively terrifying. Most of the people at big companies I've talked to go a little pale at the idea of facing the public via a social network during a crisis.

It's true that in the social space there are dangers from rapid spread of misinformation or coming under constant attack from the "haters" who dislike your brand no matter what you do. But the other side of the coin, as it were, is that social networks provide a fast and effective way to convey information during a crisis, to have a much larger audience see you actively trying to resolve the crisis by doing the right thing rather than just trying to protect your reputation. Just as with NASA during the *Apollo 13* crisis, if people see your organization trying to fix the problem or address an issue rather than just protect its reputation, the way you handle a crisis can actually be a significant *opportunity* for your organization. This was true in 1970, and it is *especially* true in the era of Twitter, Facebook, and blogs.

First Things First: The Best Defense Is a Good Offense

If the first time your organization starts to act in the social Web is when you have a crisis, *you're too late.*

Think about it. Social networks are built on conversation and the development of relationships. In a crisis, you're asking people to trust you and accept the information you provide. But if you haven't ever been active in these networks before, how can you ask people to take you at face value? You've never talked to them before, but now when you've got a problem, you're interested? Why *shouldn't* they believe that you're just a team of spin doctors and PR people coming in to do damage control?

Here's an unpleasant but demonstrative parallel: Say that someone in your neighborhood is accused of a horrible crime. If the alleged criminal is someone who always stays in his house, never talks to or makes eye contact with anyone, is antisocial, and doesn't make a point of joining neighborhood activities or of getting to know anyone in the subdivision or building, how easy is it to believe that he's guilty—or at least capable of the crime he's charged with? You don't know the person; he's made no effort to get to know you, so you have no reason not to believe what's been said about him and what he's been charged with. If the next day, when the story of his arrest has made the local news and he's out on bail, he knocks on your door for the first time, sticks out his hand to shake yours, introduces himself to you, and asks you not to believe what you've heard or what people are saying, how would you react? Do you think you'd give that person the benefit of the doubt? Invite him in for coffee and ask him to tell you his side of the story? I didn't think so.

But let's take the same scenario, only this time the police charge a neighbor you've waved to over the fence for years or chatted with from time to time in the hallway in your building. Maybe your kids have played together. He goes around with all the other parents on Halloween night trick-or-treating, and he's active in the home owners' association with you. Maybe you've even had a beer or two with him in his living room while watching the game, or he and his wife have been to your house for dinner a time or two. *Now* think about how you'd react to that knock on the door. If he comes over and says, "I know what you've heard, I know what they're saying, but I'm asking you to listen to me and believe me when I tell you it's not like that." This neighbor would get far more benefit of the doubt, wouldn't he?

Trust is a capital commodity in social networks—and if you haven't invested in it before you have a crisis, you'll have none to draw on. Your best effort in using social media in a crisis is to use it before you have a crisis.

There's another reason to proactively get involved in social networks before you have a problem: if you're involved and you have established a presence in social networks before you have a crisis, you're less vulnerable to impostors.

In the spring and summer of 2010, Americans watched in horror and disgust as the Deepwater Horizon offshore oil well, operated by BP, spewed millions of gallons of crude oil into the Gulf of Mexico. While efforts to cap the well and stop the spill faltered, BP's public relations team also faltered. I'll stay away from discussing their many gaffes committed outside of the social media space, but within social networks, the company had not been particularly active. BP America did have a Twitter account, but it wasn't used very frequently and thus had only about 2,500 followers in early May 2010, despite having been in existence for nearly two years.[1] The company's sporadic use of Twitter as a communications tool meant that not many people on Twitter knew BP was present—and that left it ripe for impersonation.

On May 19, 2010—one month *after* the explosion and fire on the Deepwater Horizon rig—someone set up the Twitter account @BPGlobalPR. Though the account was a spoof, it used BP's logo and appeared at first blush to be affiliated with the company. In June 2010, both BP and Twitter instructed the account to make more clear that it was a parody, which is in fact consistent with Twitter's policy on parody accounts. The account own-ers initially complied, although a check in October 2010 revealed that they had reverted to the version of their bio they were using before the June action. [2,3]

The tweets from @BPGlobalPR were hysterical in a gallows-humor sense. They satirized every PR fumble committed by the real BP and presented the story of the oil spill in a light that was extremely unflattering to the company. In the month following its establishment, the false account picked up more than 150,000 followers. While many realized the account was a parody, some most assuredly did not. The devastating satire continued long after the well was finally capped; as of mid-October 2010, @BPGlobalPR had more than 10 times the following of the real company, @BP_America—187,191 to 18,411.[4]

While BP did have an official presence on Twitter before the Deepwater Horizon accident, the fact that it underutilized the channel as a communications tool certainly helped some Twit-ter users believe that the phony account actually represented BP. The company's underuse of Twitter prior to the accident also contributed, in my opinion, to the fact that virtually none of the conversation on Twitter was in defense of BP. In fact, I didn't observe anyone even referring critics to talk to the real BP via Twitter—something that might well have happened had BP had a more notable presence in the months prior to the tragedy.

A robust and active presence on Twitter will never be enough to prevent satirical or parody accounts. Nor will having an official Facebook page prevent dozens of anti-your-company Facebook pages or groups from springing up. But you'll be less vulnerable than if you're not present and active within these networks.

One other thing all companies and organizations should also consider doing: try to snap up as many variations of their names as possible to prevent phony accounts. Just as most wise brands now buy up domains that could be used against them (yourcom-panysucks.com is the most common example), you'd be well advised to grab up Twitter handles like @TheReal_YourCo or

@YourCo_PR, etc. If you don't get them, someone else will—and while Twitter does protect trademarks, it also protects free speech and the right to parody or criticize (as it should).

But even if you have been active on Twitter for a year or more, regularly interact on your Facebook page, welcome spirited debate on your company blog, and establish good trust capital and a strong network of advocates willing to defend you, it's inevitable that you'll face at least one of the varieties of social media crisis. Even the best programs from the leading companies in social media take an occasional hit. As we've said, however, the true challenge is not in the crisis itself but in how you handle it. What you should do depends on the kind of crisis you're facing—so it's important to understand each type and the basics of how to respond in each case.

Six to Fix: Crisis in the Social Media Era

All social media crises are not created equal. Many factors—the origin of the situation, whether employees or an external audience are affected, the nature of the perceived offense, and even your response—go into defining each individual situation, how bad it can get, and the course of your most effective response. But over the relatively short life span of social media (and specifically corporate or organizational involvement in it), most crises that have occurred can be categorized as one of six main varieties.

- **Individual-generated.** An individual employee within your organization does something within the social Web that reflects poorly on your brand and raises ire within social networks.
- **Customer service #fail.** Your company falls short in customer service somewhere along the line, and someone on the social Web decides to let the world know just how unhappy she is about it.

- **Campaign.** An activist group with a political, economic, or cultural agenda targets your organization online, whether on your own sites or within social networks.
- **Social media #fail.** The social media campaign, tactic, or content developed by or for your organization hits a sour note and is received poorly within the social media world.
- **Organizational brain freeze.** As an entity, your company does something ranging from insensitive to flat-out dumb, and the social Web calls you out on it. The damage is to your brand, but with rare exceptions, little more than someone's feelings are hurt. (That's not to diminish the importance of people's feelings; rather it's just to distinguish this kind of crisis from the next kind.)
- **Three Mile Island.** Organizational meltdown. You're experiencing a business crisis in which employees, customers, the environment, and/or the economy are seriously hurt or endangered. This is not a social media crisis in and of itself but rather a significant business crisis that plays out in many arenas—of which the social networks are only one front. (We'll discuss this kind of crisis in detail in the next chapter.)

Successful navigation of any crisis online calls for slightly different tactics depending on what kind of crisis you're facing. The confident tone you might strike when being campaigned would be disastrous when you're responding to a major business crisis, while the apologetic tone necessary when an employee screws up would weaken your position when you're being campaigned. There are a few basic rules that apply to each variety of online crisis—and understanding those rules and the reasoning behind them is critical to weathering the storm.

Social Media Crisis Type 1: Individual-Generated

By virtue of the fact that you've hired them in the first place, you generally trust your employees to demonstrate common sense. You train them on both corporate policies and social media use in particular. (As we discussed a few chapters ago, if you're not doing this, you really should be.) You expect that no one in your organization would set out to consciously do something that would get him in trouble and damage your brand. Even so, it's a fact of life: despite your best efforts, at some point, one of your people is going to do something stupid.

The perpetrator won't necessarily be a low-level staffer. Sometimes, even the CEO or founder is the guilty party. During the Egyptian revolution in February 2011, Kenneth Cole himself took to Twitter to use the situation in Egypt to draw attention to his company's spring fashion line. The Internet community correctly reacted with revulsion and disapproval and quickly forced Cole, both the person and the company, to issue a retraction and apology.[5]

The social Web did not create this danger. Yes, the existence of Facebook and Twitter, and the ability of every one of your employees to have a blog if desired, has added a new wrinkle to the fear of employees' doing unwitting (or even willful) damage to your brand and its reputation. This risk existed long before Facebook or Twitter or even the Internet, but the speed at which such blunders could catch like wildfire has obviously been amplified.

But it's not just a wayward tweet that could cause you heartburn. Before social networks, when a bad experience happened in the real world, the damage could usually be contained to that one affected customer. Today, social networks enable information to be shared instantaneously, and containment is wishful thinking. An incident in one store in Phoenix can be well known in Atlanta within minutes if the offended party decides to share the story; a confrontation or insulting statement in Boston can be common knowledge in Los Angeles before you even know it has taken place.

Don't blame Facebook or Twitter. The whole thing shouldn't have happened in the first place—so let's get past the idea of resenting social networks or fearing their impact.

That said, most individually driven social media crises *do* start within the channels of social media. Unfortunately, there are lots of examples.

Price Chopper #Fail

In September 2010, Price Chopper, a supermarket chain in the U.S. Northeast, faced intense criticism from social media influencers, everyday bloggers, and Twitter-ers alike after one of its employees reacted horribly to a negative tweet about the company. The initial tweet referred to conditions in one of Price Chopper's stores and compared it unfavorably with a competitor.

The individual employee—who was in fact a member of the company's PR team—did the unthinkable: she not only responded negatively to the criticism but also, upon discerning the customer's employer from his Twitter bio, contacted *his employer* and suggested that the person's tweet might impact future business relations between Price Chopper and that company. (There was no business relationship at the time.) The Price Chopper PR person then actually requested *disciplinary action* against the employee. You read that right; she basically tried to get him fired.

That's a bad enough situation. But the targeted individual happened to be friends with a professor at Syracuse University who teaches both undergraduate and graduate courses in social media. Predictably and understandably, the professor took the situation to the public via a blog set up specifically to discuss the incident, and the firestorm began.[6] Price Chopper was attacked across the social Web for not only "not getting" social media but also having gone far beyond the pale of what anyone might consider "fair game" for a company dealing with criticism.

However, Price Chopper—as a company and even within its customer service unit—knew nothing about the incident and had never authorized its employee's actions. When its customer relations team learned of the situation after being flamed via many derogatory tweets, they were as appalled as the audience had been. They were facing some of the most intense criticism a company can face in the social Web, only as a company, they weren't responsible for the offense. One extremely misguided individual employee had incurred the wrath of what seemed to be the entire social Web.

Price Chopper's reactions hold lessons as to how a company should respond when dealing with a crisis initiated by a rogue employee—lessons you should take to heart in case it ever happens to your organization.

Acknowledge the Situation Quickly and Candidly

Don't hope or assume that people will recognize that your employees were acting on their own. It might seem self-evident to you that no business worth its salt would deliberately offend customers, but many people have an inherent distrust of businesses, and you're often guilty until proven innocent in the court of public opinion. You need to make clear that, while as an organization you might not have known about or authorized your employee's actions, you accept responsibility for them, while rejecting the offensive or inaccurate statements, beliefs, or positions espoused.

Price Chopper correctly moved to swiftly acknowledge the individual's actions, take overall responsibility for the offenses, and make clear that the individual acted outside of its organizational principles. While it didn't mitigate all of the anger felt over the employee's action, it did show that Price Chopper was aware that the individual's actions were wrong and that it had taken steps to make sure the employee *knew* that she'd been wrong. Even in an environment where people want to believe in the idea of the lumbering, clueless big company, most recognize that sometimes individual people do dumb things that aren't endorsed by the organization.

Be Seen Learning from the Experience

Price Chopper's next move was even smarter: its communications team followed up with the Syracuse professor who'd broken the story and asked to come to his class for a discussion of both the incident and Price Chopper's social initiatives in general. Not only did the team bring a communications person, but they brought the president and COO of the company along for the discussion too.[7] While professional media wasn't allowed in the classroom, live Twitter responses from the students were allowed. And after the two-hour classroom session, students interviewed by local television actually gave Price Chopper credit, with one saying, "I don't think this mistake means that they don't know how to use social media; I think it just means that they are rolling with the punches of a whole new way of communicating."[8]

Price Chopper didn't have to publicly discipline the employee in question in order to win back goodwill. It just had to show a willingness to learn from the mistake—and to learn from the community, not just the usual consultants and high-priced agencies. Moreover, sending the COO to the classroom gave not just the class but also the entire online community a signal of the seriousness the Price Chopper team assigned to the situation. Showing people that they not only understood that they'd made a mistake but also wanted to learn from it made all the difference.

You may not always be able to bring your COO to meet with a class or a group or party offended by something your company or one of its employees did. But it's a great idea to make a good-faith effort to show that you want the mistake to be a "teachable moment" and that you genuinely want to learn.

One last piece of advice: If you become aware that one of your employees is anonymously tweeting or blogging something that would be embarrassing if it were connected to the company, *don't* hope you can quietly take care of the situation without anyone's finding out that one of yours was involved. That doesn't mean that you fire the person publicly or fall dramatically on your sword—but you should just assume that it's only a matter of time before he's discovered. There are too many tools and too many smart people out there who can track down the source of a particular posting.

First, take whatever action is appropriate to what the employee did, based on HR guidelines. Then prepare a public reaction. It may not always be advisable to publicize your own failures before someone else does, but you should be prepared. If an apology is due to a particular individual, make the apology—privately at first, and publicly if she chooses to make it public. It might sound counterintuitive to most PR people, but the social Web appreciates not only contrition but also organizations that appear more concerned with doing the right thing than protecting their flanks.

Social Media Crisis Type 2: Customer Service #Fail

No matter how much your organization trains employees to provide impeccable and polite service to every customer, your business will at some point let a customer down. This becomes even worse if your personnel or policies appear insensitive to the customer's plight. If the customer has any sort of prominence or notoriety in social networks, the situation can become an absolute crisis.

For lots of reasons, people generally like to believe most large organizations to be impersonal, insensitive, bureaucratic, and unhelpful—so a story of bad customer service tends to be believed prima facie, and people within the social Web will often quickly spread the story. When you're really guilty, you've got very little room to maneuver in your online response; time is perhaps never a bigger factor than in this kind of crisis, because the longer you take to respond, the more people will believe that your organization truly is that indifferent to customer concerns—and the more chance you give your competitors to move to take advantage of your failure.

Dooce Versus Maytag

One of the most famous examples of this kind of crisis occurred in the late summer of 2009. Heather Armstrong, a popular blogger who blogs at Dooce.com and has acquired millions of readers and followers on Twitter (as well as having penned a *New York Times* top 20 [bestseller] book and signed a television development deal with HGTV), had purchased a new Maytag washer, which unfortunately was problematic for her from the outset. She tried to get resolution through Maytag's customer service department but encountered a combination of bureaucratic policies and customer service personnel who seemed anywhere from indifferent to her plight to thoroughly annoyed at her for having a problem. In frustration, Armstrong took to Twitter to vent, recommending to her more than one million followers that they never buy Maytag, along with a link to her blog post about the whole experience.

Not only was the story quickly passed around Twitter and the social Web, making matters incredibly uncomfortable for Maytag, but also one of its main competitors took advantage of the controversy by offering Armstrong a free washer as a replacement (which she eventually donated to a shelter near her home).[9]

Millions of people got negative impressions of not only the company's product but also its willingness to take care of its customer service—and Maytag's competition took the opportunity to ride in on a white horse, not only offering its product but also arguing that it placed greater value on its customers. All this despite more than a hundred years of brand dominance, a clear commitment to customer service, and a public image—well fueled and reinforced through commercials—of products so reliable that its customer service people were lonely!

Educate Your Customer Service Teams About the Social Web

In order for your organization to provide outstanding customer service in the twenty-first century, your team must be aware of the power and impact of tools like Twitter, Facebook, and blogs—and that failure or poor attitude could cause a major headache for both the brand and themselves. The realization that any caller might potentially have hundreds of thousands of followers eager to hear of any bad experience might be just enough to incent your reps to treat every caller like an A-list Internet celebrity.

Keep a List of Prominent Online Influencers and Make It Available to Customer Service Representatives

In theory, every customer should be treated as our most important one and should receive the same treatment whether "Internet famous" or not. But the unpleasant fact is that those with bigger megaphones do hold a bigger stick—and someone with 100,000 followers complaining about you is going to get more attention than someone with 100 followers. A flag ought to go up with your customer service team any time a "super-influencer" contacts you; knowing that they need to take special care to satisfy this customer can make the difference for your reps.

Time Is Critical

Response time is one of the most critical factors in managing an online customer service crisis. The longer it takes you to reply to an angry customer online (and the thousands who may be following along with the story), the more indifferent you appear to the customer's plight, and the more tone-deaf you seem to the influence of online communities. Even if your first interaction is little more than "We're sorry that you're having a bad experience; could you DM me your e-mail address, and we'll start looking into this," you need to react to the customer as quickly as possible. You don't have to give the customer everything he wants or "cave" to Internet pressure. But you should respond with concern to the customer's bad experience or at least present another perspective on the situation. When you're not present in a discussion, it is very easy for others to present you as clueless, heartless, uncaring, or worse—and even easier for the community to believe it because you're not addressing or challenging it.

What You Say Is Almost Less Important than How You Say It

Anyone who's ever worked at a business knows that the old maxim isn't true: the customer is *not* always right. Customers sometimes make exorbitant demands, expect treatment or solutions that exceed the nature of the problem, or refuse to accept responsibility for their own misuse of the product or any behavior that contributed to the negative situation. But rarely do those things show up in online anger at a company or brand. Sometimes a customer omits parts of a story that show good faith by the business or irrational or even threatening behavior on her own part. But even when the customer is either wrong or at least perhaps not considering other factors like the effect placating her would have on other customers, for example, the tone of your response can still be problematic.

Most reasonable people can recognize an unreasonable request when they see one. Many people who have an initial issue with one of your company's policies will understand when the policy is politely and sympathetically explained. If the customer's been legitimately mistreated, solve her problem, apologize, and offer her something to make up for her lousy experience. If you feel for the situation he's in but cannot for whatever reason do anything more to help him, say so (with apologies, of course). A professional and empathetic tone from you will go far in defusing the crisis for you—and can even win you sympathy.

In cases like these, visibility matters. Contacting the customer privately and trying to take care of things behind the scenes will not cut it. You can't count on the person to post an update stating that you've called her, and the rest of the audience needs to see your organization being attentive to and concerned about your customers.

Social Media Crisis Type 3: The Campaign

The social Web provides customers and consumers unprecedented access to companies and organizations. Most often, it's a constructive and empowering relationship in which both sides benefit. Occasionally, however, an interest group with a political or social agenda takes advantage of the openness of the social Web to advance its agenda at the expense of the company providing the platform. These interest groups aren't interested in dialogue. Their intent is simply to embarrass, shout down, or drown out the company they've targeted.

Anything could trigger this kind of attack: a television program your organization sponsors that an activist group disapproves of; where you buy your raw materials or sell your products; perceived political ideology of your organization; or a commercial you've run that a group finds offensive or problematic.

An activist group may target your Facebook page. It may flood your blog with negative comments, start a mirror site or Twitter feed, or "Twitter-storm" your account with negative comments and charges. It may upload highly critical content (the accuracy of which you'd certainly contest!) to any site that you've opened to user-generated content. If you choose to engage, group members will rarely acknowledge any of your points or counterarguments. Often they'll respond by making personal attacks on the individual whose job it is to reply. They don't want to engage; they only want their point of view to take over your Web property until you change company policy or direction so that it aligns with their ideology.

Any number of major brands have borne the brunt of online campaigns organized by consumers or activist groups. Some companies have received credit for how they've handled the attacks; others have been roundly criticized as much for their response—even by supporters—as for the initial reason for the campaign. In telling the story most familiar to me, I hope to demonstrate some of the right ways to handle an online campaign against your brand.

General Motors and Rainforest Action Network

In January 2008, GM kicked off a new website called "GM Next" in support of the celebration of GM's hundredth anniversary. Part of the website allowed users to upload their own GM-related content. For the first two weeks, the site and its community worked as we had hoped they would, with enthusiasts and employees uploading photos and videos of their vehicles and interacting with one another in the comments fields. On the 13th morning of the site's existence, however, we noticed a couple of random photos uploaded to the "green" section of the site proclaiming that SUVs—and GM in particular—were responsible for climate change, American dependence on oil, and other related ills. GM, they charged, was "greenwashing" by placing a "green" section on our site.

We opted to let the photos stay up; we weren't afraid of differing opinions, and we didn't want to be censoring anyone. Within the next 90 minutes, however, more than 15 similar photos were uploaded, along with dozens of comments critical of GM for building SUVs. Many of the comments were either verbatim copies of earlier ones or copies with a word or two changed here and there, so we had a strong sense that they were coming from the same place, that we were being campaigned, and that the folks flooding GM Next that day were unlikely to be interested in anything we had to say.

Nevertheless, we decided to engage anyway. We had our then-head of environmental and energy programs post a comment trying to politely address some of the concerns being raised. Unfortunately, that just upped the ante. We'd tipped our hand that we knew they were there and that they had our attention. Instead of responding to anything Beth had said, the protesters increased the frequency of their "hijack" posts, this time including in their comments various personal attacks and slanders on the character of the individual who'd tried to engage them. (I described them to the media at the time as "the kinds of things for which you'd punch somebody for calling your sister." These guys were aiming to be as offensive as they could be.)

At that point, we knew we had no choice but to put a stop to the campaigning. We'd tried letting their point of view be heard, and we'd tried talking with them—their response was simply to step up their tactics and shout even louder. But we didn't want to give them what they wanted—the downing of the site or the removal of the discussion; we did not want to hand them the moral and PR victory to claim.[10]

In the end, we didn't remove a single photo or published comment, and we didn't take the site off-line. We did, however, decline to publish personal insults hurled at an executive, and we closed off the section to new comments, depriving the campaign of its platform. I wrote a post acknowledging that we'd heard their voices—and while we had no intention of letting them take over our site, we did want to address their concerns. We promised that we would hold a series of Web chats over the course of the next few weeks to discuss the very criticisms brought up by our critics, and we specifically invited members of the Rainforest Action Network (the group eventually revealed to be behind the campaign) to take part. Over the next few months, we held a series of six such chats on the site, addressing the issues raised in the campaigners' comments.

While the chat series largely failed to win over RAN (I doubt we ever had a chance to do that, because I don't think they ever really were interested in two-way dialogue), General Motors won acclaim from social media observers and PR industry pundits for how we handled the attack. Many other social media personalities, environmentalists, and "traditional media" reporters did follow along and participate in one or more of the chats. We learned a few things about what people were looking for from us in the environmental realm, and I'd like to believe that at least a few of the participants learned a few things about some of GM's environmental efforts—and that we maybe weren't as horrible as they thought.

Rules of Dealing with a Campaign

I'll submit with some humility as well as pride that in GM's handling of the RAN campaign against GM Next, we demonstrated many solid principles worth adhering to if your organization is ever targeted in a similar fashion.

1. **Don't censor criticism.** Nothing conveys a failure to understand social media like censoring or removing criticism posted to your brand's online properties. Doing so conveys a sense of vulnerability to the charges being made against you or fear of

the organization campaigning you. If you've posted your terms and guidelines for acceptable behavior on the site, any post that adheres to these terms really must be allowed to stay up, regardless of how vitriolic or untrue it may be.

GM's community standards for online properties are simple: no vulgarity, epithets, advocating violence against anyone, or written attacks on an individual. It's fine to say "GM are a bunch of idiots" if you want to, but not "Jim Smith in customer service is an idiot"—not because the individual can't handle the criticism, but simply because there is an expectation of civil conduct.

When RAN's first posts and photos began showing up in the moderation queue, GM had an obligation to publish them—no matter how inflammatory or harshly critical. When the comments became personal attacks on our executive after our attempt at engagement, we stopped publishing—because they violated our stated terms and conditions, not because they were critical. We stopped accepting repeat or verbatim comments, yes—but we left the core of the criticism on the site for the public to see.

Accepting criticism is part of being online; if you're not prepared to do it, you shouldn't be in the social Web. In a campaign situation, if you start deleting, removing, or censoring the comments of your critics, you've lost the high ground and handed them a rhetorical weapon that can cost you the support of even those inclined to feel empathy for you. Being thin-skinned or appearing to be so is one of the cardinal sins in social media for a big brand.

2. **Assess the critics' perspective; are they wrong or just in opposition?** It's hard to do in the heat of the moment when insults are flying and your bosses are demanding that you do something to stop all these criticisms from showing up on your site—but you need to take a moment to think objectively about what the critics are saying about your brand. Are they factually incorrect? Have they even invented "facts" that just don't exist

to bolster their position? Or is their criticism—as much as it might anger you or make you want to argue with it—a matter of perspective or viewpoint?

If they've got their facts wrong, your job becomes easier if no less stressful. There is nothing wrong with a brand's pointing out inaccurate arguments and reacting with *facts*. You don't have to worry about appearing argumentative or combative if you're rebutting with factual information or pointing out to critics that they've not bothered to get their facts right. Of course, you still respond at least somewhat politely, but you don't have an obligation to stand by while inaccurate information is presented just because you're a big brand. You need to get the accurate information to rebut, confirm that it's correct, then get it out onto the site and into the conversation as quickly as possible.

Keep in mind that Google and other search engines are cataloging what's being posted and the subsequent responses. Leave an incorrect fact or inaccurate information unchallenged, and it goes unchallenged in search results as well. That alone should be enough to motivate you.

If, on the other hand, the campaign's perspective is not a case of bad or twisted facts but a matter of reading facts differently from how your organization sees them, you have a different challenge. You're still not likely to convert any of the people involved in the campaign against you, but that's not your audience anymore. Instead, your audience is the *rest* of the community or network.

This is a distinction often lost in the heat of the moment, but it's an important one. It's entirely possible that no one at RAN was going to be swayed by anything we said in response to any question, and if we were measuring success in terms of winning RAN members over or dulling their criticism, the effort was largely wasted. But we weren't aiming to win over RAN members; we were talking to the broader audience watching along. In addressing RAN's concerns and issues, we were making our case to the broader public that our perspective was the more fair, reasonable, and logical one. We didn't argue members' perspective with them or tell them they were wrong—we just went out and tried to answer any questions we got as honestly as we could, trusting that our view would be seen as reasonable and that our willingness to answer the questions head-on would win us some admiration or at least gain us some credibility.

When we recognized that the audience we were looking to convince wasn't the activists but those watching along, we managed to have our perspective not only heard but also listened to more widely. So be proactive, understand who your true audience is, and don't be afraid to present your best case. (If you're worried about talking about your product or your point of view, you've got bigger issues than the social Web!)

3. **Don't be afraid to take control—but be *polite*.** When it comes to comments on your organization's site, you don't want to censor or appear to only publish positive comments or fawning fans. At the same time, it's your page, site, or blog; you wouldn't stand for people protesting in your lobby or shouting down conversations in your conference rooms, would you? If your company website or blog is being used as a vehicle for an attack, don't delete the criticisms you've already published—but turn off additional comments. You have the right to stop an outside group from coming in and taking over the Web property you have built and are paying for.

Dealing with an attack on your Facebook page can be more difficult because you don't have the ability to turn off comments for specific posts. If you've enabled comments previously, the only way to shut them down when you're being campaigned is to shut them down on the entire page—which gives the group campaigning you exactly what it wants: control of the conversation on your page, and the impression that they've "won" by shutting you down or impacting how you interact online. The next best thing is to be diligent about enforcing

your terms of conduct. Delete anything profane; acknowledge
the posts at least occasionally (or risk being accused of not paying enough attention to even realize the campaign was taking
place) and hope your community of supporters will get involved
and defend you (or at least express annoyance at the attack).

That said, there is an art to the act of trying to regain
control of your properties. Responding in a petty, sarcastic, or
insulting manner has the effect of not only further infuriating
those campaigning against you but also earning them sympathy from observers and making your organization look arrogant and aloof. Nestlé learned this the hard way in March 2010,
when an employee responded to Greenpeace campaigners on
its Facebook page not only by deleting their comments but also
by returning with dismissive, impolite, and arrogant responses.
The tone of the responses turned off or angered even many
who were not wholly sympathetic to Greenpeace's argument
and made Nestlé look all the worse to the general audience.
The negative press generated by the company's response to
criticism just highlighted the activists' point and ensured their
inclusion in the coverage of the kerfuffle.[11]

It can be hard to make the most radical social activists into
sympathetic figures, but an impolite or dismissive response
from you can achieve that feat. So be sure to take care to always
be polite, take the high road in any debates people try to draw
you into, and do *not* get sucked into personal spitting matches
or fights with people going after you on a social site, no matter how personal or inappropriate they get or what they say
to you. Being the bigger person (or brand) can require a lot of
self-control, but it's the only chance your social media team has
to win hearts and minds when you're being campaigned. Take
control of your sites; just be nice about it when you do.

4. **Once you've regained control, address the concerns.** Nothing adds fuel to a fire like not acknowledging the accusations
or complaints that led to a campaign in the first place. While
you have every right to reclaim control of your site, ignoring

the criticism altogether not only is rude but lends validity or credence to the campaigners' concerns.

If the campaign is based around something you're either proud of or not going to stop (advertising on a particular television program or radio show, for example, or using a particular supplier or facilities from another country—say, China), offer a direct explanation of why you've made the choices you have, and restate your intention to continue the action. If the business decision is to stay the course (we're going to keep advertising on "The Controversial Show," for example), the campaigners may be disappointed and angry. You chose to risk that anger and potential loss of business when you made the decision—so offer the campaigners the courtesy of an answer and an explanation. Besides, in situations with political implications, you run the risk of attracting a countercampaign from the other side of the aisle for having "caved" to pressure.

In other cases, a deeper exploration of the issues involved might prove beneficial—not only to earn credit for taking on the criticism but also as a way to turn the focus onto your side of the story. In the GM Next situation, the Web chat series we embarked on in the aftermath of RAN's campaign showed a company unafraid of the scrutiny or the criticism and a company willing to give its critics a share of the floor. But it also gave us the chance to further explain some of our environmental initiatives under a brighter spotlight than we might have had for them before—and it even gave us the opportunity to learn more about what the environmental community wanted or expected of us. We got credit from the PR and social media pundit class for how we handled it, we had traditional media covering our efforts to do so and the environmental initiatives we cited during those conversations, and we began a few relationships in the green community that taught us a few things as well. Not a bad outcome for what started as an attack on our website, right?

Social Media Crisis Type 4: The Social Media #Fail

Every company makes mistakes—especially when entering into a new space like social media marketing. Unfortunately for those of us representing a big brand or organization, the social media world seems to be more vocal than most other communities about airing displeasure with mistakes—and lookey there, it just happens to have the tools to make its displeasure broadly known in no time!

Every now and then, you're going to do something in the social space that falls flat. You'll know when it happens because there will be a flood of people in various social networks who will let you know just how badly they think you've done.

Your campaign could be slammed as too "market-y" or found offensive in some way. Your team could be accused of a lack of understanding of social media. Whatever the reason, if you find yourself being attacked or stormed over a social campaign you've developed and that you *thought* would work, here's what can help lessen the blow.

Get a Lay of the Land

Is there anyone who likes the program or campaign? Your first response needs to be determining whether you've really whiffed or if it's something that some people like as much as others hate. If you have people liking the campaign, it's useful to point your detractors to them—not as if to say "you're wrong" but just to point out that not everyone is receiving the campaign as negatively and that the situation might be less a "#fail" than a matter of multiple perspectives about what you're doing.

Of course, whether it's fair or not, part of your concern has to be *who* is airing disapproval of your program. Unfortunately, you have a bigger problem if a major influencer is knocking your efforts. His criticism will reach more people more quickly and will seem more credible because of who it's coming from. So as you start seeing the criticism coming in, note well where it's coming from.

Admit That You Goofed

If the reaction seems to be universally against what you're doing (or if your defenders seem to be largely people you've already won to your camp), then you're going to have to face it: you've misfired. Maybe it was a bad idea to begin with, and groupthink took over when someone should have been calling BS in the planning meetings. Maybe your intentions were good; it might even have made a lot of sense on paper. But for whatever reason, when it hit the interwebs, it flopped. You goofed.

It's OK; that happens. All individuals practicing social media professionally on behalf of a brand—even the ones who've won acclaim and awards and who seem to speak at a conference each week—can cite at least one program or campaign (if not more) they wish they had back. *Mistakes are part of social media*, and people will often understand this. Just as in other facets of life, people will tolerate a mistake if you're sorry for it. If you're unrepentant or you insist that your program was brilliant if people would only see it your way, the negative reaction will only ratchet up another 10 notches.

Publicly acknowledging the goof, with humility but without overly fawning or pleading for forgiveness, is the right direction to go in these situations. Write up something for your organization's or brand's blog or your Facebook page (and then link to it frequently in tweets, in comments on your critics' blogs, and anywhere else you can go to get the word out) saying what you were trying to do, acknowledge that the audience didn't receive it the way you thought they would, take responsibility for misreading or poorly anticipating people's reactions (or not understanding the unwritten etiquette of the social Web, if that's what's happened), *apologize* for any offense or breach of trust that occurred, and even consider asking the audience for what they would do in your position or how they might suggest achieving the goals you've stated.

It might sound embarrassing or humiliating to go apologizing. It's certainly not pleasant to have to acknowledge that something you put significant thought and resources into didn't work. But you don't offer the apology to just quiet people down or mitigate the damage. Done properly, your apology can serve the purpose of also reminding people of your brand's humanity—that you make mistakes too, just like anyone else—and can even earn you some credit for being willing to publicly step up and acknowledge that you're still learning. You can point out that reactions like the one you're experiencing are part of why some big organizations fear the social Web—they don't want to get crucified while learning on the fly. The humility apparent in being willing to acknowledge a mistake in public earns more credibility in many online circles—and asking the community's opinion as to what you can do better takes that credibility up another notch. Inviting critics to offer a constructive solution and to be part of helping you do things better doesn't just make you look good, either. It also can mute or negate some of them. Think about it: if you've asked your critics what they would do, there are three possible responses from them:

- They'll offer constructive, solid advice for you, and you'll learn something from your community about what they're expecting from you in the future.
- They will be unable to offer a better solution or a stronger alternative or will respond that they don't offer advice for free and won't back up their criticism with anything solid. People can see that the person either doesn't have a better idea or is criticizing partly out of self-interest. ("Your social program sucks, but it would be better if you hired *me*" is a

not-uncommon attitude, but most people can recognize self-promotion disguised as criticism for what it is.)

- They'll not engage you at all. They'll just ratchet up the criticism and bash you for "not knowing what to do" or being "morons" or bash your apology while continuing to hate on you. These folks are well known online as trolls, and if your brand is acting the grown-up while a troll does his thing, the community almost always turns on the troll.

In the first scenario, you win because not only are you getting ideas, but you're investing your community in the idea's success as well. It's a lot harder to throw stones at a program or initiative you had a small part in planning or creating. In the latter two scenarios, your critic is revealed as somewhere between an attention seeker and a reflexive troll; in either case, her criticism quickly loses credibility within the circles paying attention. Either way, you're better off for it. So while the idea of opening yourself up to advice from the masses might seem uncertain (especially when you're feeling vulnerable during a failure situation), doing so actually has a positive effect on how your brand's reputation holds up in the aftermath and can steer your future efforts in a more productive direction.

Finally, I'd suggest spreading your statements actively across the social Web. Putting them up on your own sites alone won't effectively mute the controversy around your flawed initiative. Yes, the word will get out, and people will spread the link to what you've posted—but given that not everybody is going to click that link or bother going to your site, you really want to try to go to as many blogs as possible (those that have been critical of what you've done, anyway) to comment and share the same sentiments with those communities as well. Engage on Twitter with as many of your critics as you can. Respond to the comments that come in after you've posted. Be as active and visible in engaging those critics, wherever they are. The more openly and frequently you interact with people in the aftermath of the criticism, the better your response will be received, and the more likely you are to actually get credit for social savvy (turning a negative into at minimum a neutral, if not a positive).

Note that these suggestions are all for when you undertake a social media campaign or tactic that backfires or is seen as a mistake within the online social realm. There are times when it's not just your social media program but your entire company that is seen as having done something dumb—and those crises also pop up online.

Social Media Crisis Type 5: Organizational Brain Freeze

In early February 2011, Groupon ran a Super Bowl ad that appeared to many to make light of the plight of the Tibetan people.[12] Critics howled at the idea of using Tibet's misfortune to sell discount deals. "What were they thinking?" many wondered. "How did that get through; how did that happen?" The chorus of criticism echoed through all forms of media but social networks in particular.

For many of us in the PR business, reports like these make us say a small prayer of thanks that our company didn't pull that stunt or chuckle in sympathy with the company's PR or online team who have to clean up the mess. Then we go on about our day.

Then one day, it's our company that screws up, and it's our team having to clean up the mess!

All organizations screw up and have palm-to-the-forehead moments. But in the era of social media, these moments are magnified, shared, and spread before the organization may even realize it has a problem. The odds are, at some point in your career or in your organization's development, you're going to have a situation like this to deal with. How you handle it—and how quickly you move into action—will have a significant impact on the amount of damage your business absorbs as a result of the error.

A Couple of Famous Examples

The Gap, in an attempt to symbolize its evolution to a more modern, sexier brand, unveils a new and completely revamped version of its logo. Reaction online is virtually universal: everyone hates it and takes to the social Web to say so. A hostile parody Twitter account becomes a popular vehicle for attracting and spreading the vitriol. A website even springs up allowing users to create their own "crappy" logo based on the new Gap logo. Suddenly the company's leadership is attacked for messing with its classic branding and investing so much effort only to choose a banal, uninspiring, and uncool new design.[13]

Leaders at Chevrolet, in an internal memo meant for only the Chevrolet marketing department, discuss the importance of consistency in *official* branding efforts, especially overseas, and suggest that in the future, the company stop using "Chevy" and more consistently use the full company name, Chevrolet. The executives jokingly suggest that the Chevrolet marketing department set up a playful "swear jar" to which employees would contribute a dollar for using "Chevy"—as a fun and playful way to get the team used to the idea. The memo, however, leaks to the media—but the leaker does not convey the context of the memo when passing it along. Within a few hours, the Internet is abuzz with the rumor, seemingly backed up by the leaked memo, that General Motors is trying to prevent everyone—employees, customers, and enthusiasts—from using "Chevy." The online community angrily and passionately derides GM and Chevrolet for attempting to control how people talk and for not recognizing the power of its most familiar and well-established brand.[14]

These online crises were not caused by social media; each was instead rooted on the floors of corporate offices in decisions that made the brand seem tone-deaf to its customers and unable to interact with real people. The social Web merely exacerbated the self-inflicted wounds by spreading word more quickly than had previously been possible. But in each case, the speed and nature of the online response helped determine how the crisis was resolved.

If You're Guilty, Plead Guilty

If you've ever caught your child sneaking cookies from the cookie jar only to hear him insist passionately that he didn't do it (as cookie crumbs tumble from his hands), you know how maddening the "I didn't do it" response can be. If you remember getting caught doing something as a kid or a teenager that you weren't supposed to do, you probably remember that the smartest course of action when you were caught red-handed was to confess and take whatever punishment you had coming. Trying to get out of it just made things worse.

Similarly, the worst thing a company or organization can do when having screwed up is to try to get out of it. People can smell a CYA tactic or response a mile away, and it makes them as mad as it makes parents when their kids try to avoid taking responsibility for something. No one wants to hear a big organization talk about how it really didn't mess up and claim that if people only understood its intent, then the controversy would be over. When you screw up, admit that you screwed up. Denials or evasions just exacerbate the crisis. You're not always going to be 100 percent in the wrong—but when you are, have the backbone to publicly say as much. You'll be amazed at how much a simple "our bad" gesture can do to defuse people's anger or frustration.

Address the Controversy Head-On

If you don't want to look tone-deaf, you need to acknowledge that there's a controversy brewing. The longer you take to recognize that there are people unhappy with one of your actions, the less it seems that you're listening. Even when you think you're right (or at the very least that you're being misunderstood), to ignore the clamor within social networks is to appear that you're unaware or not paying attention. Don't give in to the old saw that you'll make a crisis worse or bring further attention to it if you acknowledge it. That might have been true during the pre–social Web days, but in today's environment, nothing goes away—and if you're not involved in the conversation, it just makes people angrier.

Try not to dance around the controversy by trying to pass off dissension and disapproval as "debate"—admit that there are some people who just don't like what you've done. Practiced PR-speak that avoids candor does not go over well.

Speed Doesn't Kill—It Saves

The faster you can get a response out and begin interacting with people over the situation that's gotten them unhappy, the more likely you are to both contain it and get it resolved favorably. A well-crafted response that takes three days to draw up, word-smith, and run through multiple levels of approvals frankly does you no good.

This means everyone in your organization—from the communications team to the lawyers to the C-suite—is going to have to accept that the response may not be perfect. So will the audience—sometimes, there really are legal reasons why an organization can't fully respond to a criticism or controversy. But in cases of social media controversies like this, fast is better than perfect, and being "on message" isn't as important as how quickly you respond. As the situation evolves, your approach should be two-pronged: swift acknowledgment of public criticism and anger, followed later by a perfected message and more crafted response. Without the first, you may as well not even offer the second.

Use the Right Tools

The first reaction from some companies when faced with an online brouhaha is to issue a press release addressing the situation. Issuing a statement via the PR wires about a situation taking place online makes about as much sense—and will have about as much effect—as the French building the Maginot Line to hold off the Germans prior to World War II. You can't use the tactics of the previous generation's war to win battles in this generation.

Utilize all the tools and options the social Web provides you. Issue your statement on your Facebook page (but be sure to respond to the comments coming in when you do!). Respond to individual critics via Twitter. Offer your perspective directly to the online audience, without filter from the media, either by text on your company's blog or through a video on YouTube. Depending on the situation, you might use Quora to ask an audience their opinion not only on the controversy but also on which actions they'd like you to take in response. The more people within these networks who see you responding and actively engaging your critics, the better off and more responsive you seem, and the more pervasively your message will spread.

If people inside your organization argue that it's more important that the "traditional" media see your response so that they can report it, remind them of two facts of social Web–era life: first, that most traditional media use social tools themselves and are just as likely to see your response on Twitter or Facebook as through a press release, and second, that to be covering the story of an online dustup to begin with, reporters have to have been paying attention online to this particular story.

The other reason that you want to respond using online tools is to make it easier for people to share your reaction through their own social networks. Remember, you're trying to reach as many people as quickly as you can. You'll have more success in that regard if you let the network—including some people who dislike you—help you disseminate that message.

Fix the Hole

This is perhaps the most obvious but most easily overlooked way to handle an online crisis. If you're being criticized for having done something stupid, and you in fact did do something stupid, fix it! Make it right! Redress the person or people who have been wronged. Do so publicly, without reservation. That doesn't mean falling on your sword out of fear of an Internet mob, but when you've genuinely screwed up, what better way to make it better than actually making it better? Apologize if it's necessary. Ask the audience for help in improving the next time, if it's appropriate.

Case Studies

I love Gap, but I think it could have responded far more adroitly to the criticism around its logo redesign. To start, it took too long to actually react—two days before it offered a public reaction to the storm of criticism in both the social and the traditional media. When it did respond on Facebook, its tone-deaf statement screamed, "We're not really wrong, and people don't really hate this."

"We know this logo created a lot of buzz, and we're thrilled to see passionate debates unfolding!"[15]

Seems pretty corporate, doesn't it? And very unwilling to say aloud or write the words that there were some people who didn't like the new logo. A lot of buzz? If by "buzz" they meant "parody Twitter accounts and disdainful websites springing up," then they got it—but no one was buying it. And did anyone really believe that people at the Gap were "thrilled" at the response? Nowhere in the phrase "passionate debates" did you get an acknowledgment that people just didn't like the new logo. Predictably, the online storm did not abate, and less than a week later, the company abandoned the new logo in the face of continued criticism.[16]

Gap's new logo certainly wasn't conceived online, and its critics were only given voice by the social Web, not created by it. This wasn't a social media crisis in origin. But by waiting too long to get engaged and then striking a tone-deaf pose that failed to fully acknowledge what was obvious and open to everyone else watching, Gap missed an opportunity to use social media to help resolve this crisis. (As I said, though, I like the Gap brand and am sure it will improve from a social standpoint.)

With Chevy versus Chevrolet, I think we did as well as we could given the circumstances. The story of the leaked memo started to catch fire somewhere around 9:00 or 9:30 in the morning; by 10:00 A.M., my team and I were trying to track down with our friends on the Chevrolet team the origin of the story, and by 10:15, we were exchanging worried BlackBerry messages with each other: "We have to do something."

My team and I hopped onto Twitter and Facebook within 45 minutes of seeing the first Google Alert on the memo, frantically trying to reassure Chevy fans that we weren't trying to tell them not to call us "Chevy." We did our best to answer as many people directly as we could—but the tide was coming too fast, and we weren't getting the word to enough people quickly enough. Moreover, because there wasn't an official explanation from Chevrolet, people weren't all buying our explanation. So my colleague Joe LaMuraglia grabbed a mini video camera and promptly marched over to the Chevrolet offices; he sat across from Alan Batey (the author of the memo) in Alan's office, turned the camera on, and asked Alan point-blank, "Tell me, what's going on—can we use 'Chevy?'" Alan responded, "Of course we can," before proceeding to explain the intended meaning of the memo. Quick, casual, easy, done in three minutes. And somewhere around lunchtime, we had that video posted on YouTube.[17] A few minutes later, the company put out an official statement on our media website that pretty much reiterated Alan's comments—but the YouTube video went first.

We tried to stick to as many of the principles outlined in this portion of the chapter as we could. We moved fast—I'm proud of the fact that we had a response up within three hours of realizing that we had a problem. We used the tools of the medium to reach the social audience—we went to YouTube first before worrying about a press statement and used a handheld camera to simply capture the right information (rather than worrying about doing heavy production or anything). We acknowledged even before turning the camera on Alan that we'd been busy all morning answering people who were unhappy about the perception that we were telling people not to use "Chevy." We took it head-on and had Alan explain the intent of the memo and how it came about—so that people realized we weren't reversing course from the memo but simply clarifying what had been meant all along.

It worked—or it seemed to. Within 24 hours, that video had about 10,000 views. Blogs and media outlets reported on the video and frequently linked to it from their stories. The link was passed around Twitter all afternoon. We cross-posted it on the Chevrolet Facebook page. And for the most part, within a day, the furor had died down. There were some who still insisted that we'd been forced to backtrack by public opinion, but by and large, the more accurate version of the story had spread pretty pervasively. I've even heard Google representatives use the "Chevy vs. Chevrolet" video as an example of how companies should be using YouTube and Internet video—and my team and I are quite proud of that as well.

Social Media Crisis 6: Three Mile Island

Each of the situations we've discussed in this chapter has been troublesome for brands or companies but hasn't been a matter of life and death. Angry consumers or customers you've let down are not pleasant situations, and none of us like to disappoint customers.

But every so often, something horrible, catastrophic, and irrevocable happens. It could be a violent incident at one of your facilities. It could be an accident that spills crude oil into the Gulf of Mexico from one of your destructed wells. It could be that your company's products are found or alleged to be defective enough that people are dying as a result of using them. Or, as was the case with General Motors, the company could be facing Chapter 11 bankruptcy, threatening hundreds of thousands of jobs—if not millions—across North America and requiring highly unpopular federal government intervention to keep the company going.

Dealing with a crisis in which either your business or an individual or individuals may not survive is an entirely different level of crisis management—from a business standpoint, from a traditional media standpoint, and certainly in the social media. Few social media professionals will ever be so heavily challenged—needing to find the right tone in their conversations, needing to react to people's online anger in real time, and realizing that every word could mean legal trouble if you say the wrong thing. Such a situation will call for you to draw on every communications skill you have and lesson you've learned—as well as going with gut instinct and making things up on the fly as people respond in real time on the social Web.

In the next chapter, we'll take a long look at one such crisis and explore lessons to take from it. It's a crisis and case study I know like the back of my hand because I led the team that weathered it.

CHAPTER 13

THREE MILE ISLAND: THE GM BANKRUPTCY CRISIS

The most remarkable day of my professional career took place on June 1, 2009, in conference room C-11 on the 30th floor of tower 300 of Detroit's Renaissance Center, overlooking the Detroit River and the skyline of Windsor, Ontario. A team of about a dozen communications people were clustered around the table, with boxes of crackers, granola bars, and cookies scattered about the room and bags of Starburst and peanut M&Ms lying around the table. The team had spent most of the past 48 hours there, breaking only for four hours' sleep before arriving at six o'clock that morning.

Down the hall, in D-11, a virtually identical conference room, a similarly sized team had been preparing the communications plan around the largest corporate Chapter 11 filing in U.S. business history. They'd worked in seclusion, their plan known only to General Motors' leadership and communications hierarchy, a few people within the Obama administration, and a small handful of legal and bankruptcy consultants.

Communicating to the world about what was happening to GM that day had taken weeks of preparation, scenario planning, and strategizing. SEC and federal reporting requirements had been taken into account. Lawyers, consultants, economists, and representatives of the president's automotive task force had vetted every word in the press release. Nothing had been left to chance; it was as meticulously scheduled and orchestrated as possible, with the plan listing events and activities right down to the minute.

The careful planning, cautious and legally approved wording, and meticulous attention to detail that had gone into the plan built in D-11 made what was happening back in C-11 all the more remarkable. Because in C-11, the dozen or so of us in the room were preparing to first convey and then discuss GM's actions within the social Web—the antithesis of the planned, organized, and controlled world of the financial experts and lawyers. It is uncontrolled, chaotic, and virtually impossible to plan for, at least in any kind of detail.

The financial counselors, bankruptcy counselors, and lawyers knew this—and there was considerable nervousness about how the day would play out. One of the bankruptcy consultants candidly and pointedly told the social media team that our activity, our very existence, was "the biggest risk" General Motors faced on filing day. But due to an extraordinary show of faith by General Motors' leadership—and a realization that direct communication with (not *to*, but *with*) consumers was the only way GM could go forward—we had an imprimatur from Fritz Henderson, then CEO. Steve Harris, then head of communications for GM, mandated that the social media team be given as much leeway and freedom to respond as possible, trusting in the judgment and instincts that the team developed in more than two years of engaging online.

In the 18 hours that followed before we signed off a little before two o'clock the next morning, the social media team took part in nearly 900 conversations online (nearly 2,500 by the end of that week!), among corporate and personal Twitter accounts, the corporate GM page on Facebook, and various blogs posting articles on the situation. We'd not only managed to survive the day without making a "mistake" online but also actually started to receive *credit* within social networks for how the company was handling the day in the social Web. An Associated Press reporter covering the company that day noted on Twitter that "in the old days, a company would be hiding in a cave on a day like today."[1] By the end of the week, online influencers across the social Web were lauding the team and the company's efforts to use the social Web to keep people informed and to respond to concerns or criticism. As Pete Blackshaw, executive vice president at Nielsen Online, cofounder of the Word of Mouth Marketing Association (WOMMA), and columnist for *Ad Age*, put it on Twitter:

> *"TIP OF THE DAY: Eager to ramp up social media skills? Review & digest how @gmblogs managed feedback yesterday."*[2]

How did this happen? In the middle of the biggest Chapter 11 filing in business history—one complete with a very unpopular government intervention on the heels of the even less popular TARP assistance to Wall Street—how did General Motors not only stay active and involved in social media but also actually win favor and public credit that week? What did we do?

The answers aren't just academic, and this chapter isn't meant to be "the behind the scenes at GM's bankruptcy" tell-all. In reviewing what we did at GM during the biggest crisis of our existence (and one of the biggest crises any organization might ever face), it is possible to take some core lessons away about how your company or organization ought to react should you ever be faced with a crisis of similar proportions—a Three Mile Island–level meltdown. (Here's hoping you never are faced with one. While managing GM's social media presence through the bankruptcy and recovery was certainly a once-in-a-lifetime experience that gave me 10 years or more of learning in just 18 months, I don't wish anything like this on my worst enemy.)

There are a number of things I think we got right from a social media perspective during the Chapter 11 crisis—but none was more critical to our success than the foundation laid before the crisis reached its head.

Give the Social Media Team Seats at the Table— and Keep Them Informed Throughout the Crisis

Contrary to what some might think, we did not know as an organization that bankruptcy was imminent. Maybe some in leadership had a sense (there are other books written by people closer to the top than I that might give you a better sense of that), but as an organization, we didn't know it was definitely coming until only a week before. But once it was clear that Chapter 11 was coming and we were going to have to deal with it, the communications plan included social media from the outset—which was a critical difference maker. A great deal of the credit for our social media success that week rests with two people who aren't even remotely involved in social media for GM—Randy Arickx and Renee Rashid-Merem, who led financial communications and had the foresight to make sure the social media team was looped into all the planning for the big announcement.

One of the members of my team, Annalisa Bluhm, was embedded with the financial communications team; she learned just what they learned, as they learned it, and brought that knowledge back to the rest of our group. This knowledge—as well as Annalisa's sense from having been on our team of what language would come off as "corporatespeak" and needed to be "translated" for social Web audiences and made more casual—was vital as we developed our social media program. Nothing caught us off guard; no developments took place in secret without the social media team's being aware of them. Renee and her team treated Annalisa like an equal and a peer and made sure that she understood everything that was going on, at levels beyond what the rest of us picked up. It's safe to say that for a month or so, Annalisa was as much an expert on what was happening to

GM as almost anyone in the company, or at least certainly within communications.

Additionally, as the overall communications plan for the filing was developed and prepared, social media was given a seat at the table as well. As the director of social media, I was in the room with the rest of the communications leadership, our bankruptcy consultants, and occasionally business leaders as we talked through the timing of what would happen and how we were going to communicate it to various audiences. Demonstrating the value of a strong executive champion once more, our SVP of communications, Steve Harris, pushed to ensure that social media be considered in our plan and included in the overall communications strategy. (Steve's support was vital, as some of the bankruptcy consultants were unsure about our participation. Given the very structured and prescribed nature of what companies filing for Chapter 11 protection are *allowed* to say by the SEC—and the timing of what GM was to say being directed by the U.S. Treasury Department—one of the lead consultants on the project told my team pointedly that social media was the biggest risk the company was taking on June 1. That same consultant, it should be noted, acknowledged shortly afterward that social media also represented the biggest reward that week.)

Finally, the week before the bankruptcy, my team was given a crash course in bankruptcy law and regulation by our bankruptcy consultants, Alix Partners. In a multi-hour session the Wednesday morning before the filing, bankruptcy experts drilled us on various elements of bankruptcy law—what Chapter 11 filings meant, the differences between Chapters 11 and 7, the nature of Section 363 of the U.S. bankruptcy code and the nuances of how an accelerated 363 process would work for GM, and what the answers were to most of the questions we could anticipate in the aftermath of the filing. I can't say that we became experts on bankruptcy law, but we probably learned more about it than the overwhelming majority of the people who were going to be asking us questions did. We were prepared to answer knowledgeably and honestly—and one of the Alix team members was assigned to be on call to our team that day (in addition to all of his other duties) so that if we got any question we didn't feel we comfortably knew the answer to, we could instant-message him to get an immediate response that we could then turn around to the person in the social Web who'd asked it.

We were as prepared to face questions about bankruptcy and what it meant for GM as anyone in the company—because we recognized that people would be asking online, because we owed people answers (the U.S. and Canadian taxpayers were, after all, becoming our temporary owners), and because failing to respond or answer during the crisis would greatly hamper any social media efforts the company embarked on in the future. (If we weren't going to be out there answering questions and providing information when people really wanted us, how could we ask them to pay attention to anything we wanted them to know later on?) We distilled complicated legal filings into conversational, 140-character bites. When the release crossed the wires, we were ready to go and were sending tweets and Facebook posts at virtually the same moment explaining the information in the release to social Web audiences. We were *ready*.

What can you take from all of this, should your organization ever face a catastrophe and need to deal with it online? *Communications and business leadership have to keep the social media team as informed as anyone in the company and keep social media front-of-mind as the communications plan around the situation is developed.* The world is going to be asking questions and conversing on Twitter and on blogs about what's happening to you, whether your organization is there or not. Being out and trying to provide as much accurate information as possible allows you to inform the conversation rather than leaving it to the speculation of others and frankly can win you points with an audience for your forthrightness. But this only works if your social media people are informed and have the latest information to share.

You're not always going to have a week's advance notice that a crisis is coming nor the luxury of that much time to get your social team up to speed. In many cases, you may have a matter of minutes. But recognize that many of the people affected by whatever's happening to your organization—not to mention many in the traditional media—will be watching online to try to get information as quickly as possible. Social media provides you the opportunity to share bursts of information as you get it, without going through the formality of a press release or a news conference.

Of course, there will always be some things you can't talk about—whether for regulatory reasons, to respect the privacy of those affected or involved, or because your lawyers warn that giving specifics could expose the company to legal consequences. This is understandable, and almost no one would argue that the existence of the social Web means that companies or organizations give up the right to keep some things private. But the more proactive you've been in providing information, and the more candid and open you've been in your interactions, the more likely an audience is to accept those moments when you really can't discuss things or reveal information.

Assemble a SWAT Team, and Make Social Media Its Responsibility During the Crisis

Admittedly, in most circumstances it isn't realistic to expect that an entire group of people in your organization are going to be able to devote all of their time to being present on the social Web. But then again, we're not talking about most circumstances; we're talking about a crisis in which your organization's existence is threatened or someone's life is on the line. If ever a situation called for extraordinary measures, this would be it, wouldn't you think?

During the first week of GM's bankruptcy, we had a SWAT team battened down in a room together. Twelve communications professionals from across the company were pulled from whatever their "day jobs" were and were specifically assigned blogs, Twitter search terms, or Facebook pages (GM's page, pages for Chevrolet, Buick, etc.). We wanted to make sure that as few questions or comments went unanswered as possible that week. Underlying this desire was our core belief: *in a crisis of such magnitude, you cannot overcommunicate.* Ordinarily, we wouldn't be trying to blanket Twitter, be on every blog possible, cover multiple Facebook pages, and write posts for our own blog. But during this crisis, we didn't want to rely on thinking that "most people will see it if we put it here" or take any chances that anyone could have a conversation anywhere on the social Web that week about what was happening to General Motors without hearing from us and interacting with us or someone who'd heard from us.

If something this big is happening to your organization, make sure that there's at least someone in the organization who's working social media full-time during the crisis, hitting as many channels as possible. You want to be in as many conversations as you can. This may seem scary, to be so exposed during your moment of ultimate weakness, but keep in mind that the people in your organization are not the only ones impacted by what's happening. Outside audiences, including those using social networks, will want and need as much information as they can get, and part of your responsibility when jobs and lives are on the line is to be as forthcoming as possible.

There's one other benefit to being so active online during the crisis: search engine results. Your organization and the crisis are going to get Googled as the crisis rages. Your activity should increase the likelihood that at least something authored by you—or influenced by a conversation you had—pops up in a Google search related to your crisis. All those conversations that take place online about what's happening to your organization will show up in Google and Bing results (and remember, Google is forever); you want your perspective as widely represented as possible.

Listen More than You Talk, Answer More than You Promote, and, Above All, *Provide Value*

Another reason I think our social media efforts were so well received during the bankruptcy was that I set the tone for the team early on, even before the actual filing, that we would be active listeners online—in fact, that we'd do more interacting with people than pushing our information out. People would be more interested in having their questions answered, I reasoned, than in hearing what we wanted to say or trying to distill a complicated legal filing. Not only that, but also as taxpayers, people on social networks were absolutely involved in what was happening to GM and deserved as many candid answers as we could offer. Using what we'd learned through the bankruptcy education the week before to guide us on what we were and were not allowed to say, the team determined that no matter how ugly or angry the conversations got, we were going to ride it out, take our lumps, and answer as much as we could.

When the week was over and we looked back on it, somewhere between 75 and 80 percent of the tweets and posts we'd done were in *response* to someone's inquiry or post, rather than being proactive GM information. Granted, we certainly spent a lot of time making sure that the information we needed to push out went out; we had taken the bankruptcy filing and press release, for example, and had broken it into 140-character bits suitable for Twitter; we'd made the content as social-friendly as we could.

But this was mostly within the first 20 minutes or so. Once the basic information was out there, we spent most of the next 20 hours answering people's questions.

- Would their warranties be covered for brands being discontinued? *(Yes. All valid warranties would be honored by any GM dealer.)*
- What would happen if their dealer was being closed down? *(When the list of dealer closings was finalized, we would make it public as quickly as possible and help people identify the closest remaining dealership to them.)*
- When did we expect that we might get the loans paid back? *(We didn't want to make promises we couldn't keep, but our deepest wish and fullest intent was to pay back the loans as soon as possible. No one wanted the government out of the auto business more than GM and the government.)*
- Would the plant in their hometown be closing? *(In cases where a plant closing was already announced, we would confirm. As for the remaining plants and their fates, we were not privy to the list of unannounced closing plants at that time—so we legitimately answered by saying, "We don't know yet, but if or when we hear anything confirmed, we will let you know.")*
- Would their uncle or brother-in-law who worked at a plant somewhere be able to keep his job? *(It wasn't fair for us to speculate on people's jobs online before they'd had a chance to talk to their local union leadership, so we respectfully weren't going to talk publicly about specific job losses until employee communications had talked with all plants and people had had the chance to hear their fates from the company or union rather than learning about it from the Internet.)*
- How could we be online that day and not be ashamed to show our faces? *(Because we felt it was more honorable than not showing our faces and not answering questions. It was an unpleasant and humbling experience, but we felt we had an obligation to be there and openly communicating that week.)*
- Did we really think the government intervention was necessary? *(While no one was more disappointed than we were, the government intervention was the last remaining option to prevent the company's collapse. Further, the ramifications of a GM dissolution*

or auto industry collapse would be far more costly and have longer reaching effects than the administration's actions—so unfortunately, yes, the intervention was necessary.)

- Why did we get government assistance when other companies hadn't—why couldn't we go through bankruptcy like everyone else? *(The domestic auto industry and its related industries—suppliers, dealerships, etc.—provided millions of jobs and contributed billions of dollars to the U.S. economy; by some estimates, a collapse would cost nearly three million jobs and more than $150 billion in tax revenues to the U.S. economy over three years. We believed that the government intervention was not about saving General Motors, that it was an action to protect the U.S. economy and GDP, which is what made this situation different from a typical bankruptcy.)*

- What would happen to their existing GM stock—was it worth anything anymore? *(Unfortunately, with the Chapter 11 filing, the existing stock in General Motors Corporation no longer had value, and we were very sorry to have to tell them that news.)*

All these questions and more came in rapid-fire from all corners and from people expecting rather immediate answers. And we tried to not only answer everything we saw but also see as much as possible. When we did respond, we did everything we could to remove the "spin" from our answers. There were "key messages," sure—but most of the items on the talking points document we all had were the unvarnished answers to the questions we expected most often. When we gave answers that somewhat defended the company or the government's intervention, we genuinely believed the answer to be true; it wasn't a PR message as much as the facts as we understood and/or believed them (especially as they pertained to the economic impact of a domestic auto-industry failure).

It ended up being so important that we weren't trying to protect our reputation, working on positioning, or "bridging back" to a core set of messages; we were simply trying to get people the answers they needed most at a time of uncertainty and when misinformation and opinion masquerading as fact were rampant. Our job that week was simply to be as reliable a source of the most accurate, unfiltered, and "un-spun" information as people needed us to be. There would be time for reputational repair after the immediate crisis had passed.

Was it crazy to not only be online that week but also let the audience dictate most of the terms and tones of the conversations? Perhaps. But we genuinely believed that in a crisis of that magnitude, answering as many questions as possible and being extremely visible about letting people know we were listening was vital. It wasn't as if we could hide from what was happening to us, and we knew people were going to be angry. The only way to make them angrier, we reasoned, was to make them think we were sitting smugly in some office tower oblivious to the furor our company was generating. So out we went.

Amazingly, people reacted quite well to what we did. While there were certainly folks upset with what was happening, we got sympathetic responses from most everyone we engaged—people seemed impressed that we were out there and taking every criticism or angry barb, not dodging anything. We even started seeing "hang in there, guys—we're rooting for you" tweets by the end of the afternoon!

What can you take from this for your organization? While you're working on pushing as much information out there as possible, don't forget about that whole listening and interacting element to social media. Maybe you don't need to swing your balance as close to 80/20 as we did, regarding how many of your online posts are "push" as opposed to responsive—but also you shouldn't be any lower than 50/50. Not only does it give you a better chance to provide the information most relevant to an audience (based on the fact that they're the ones asking for it), but you actually can mitigate some of the anger or frustration at your organization by just being out there and listening to what people have to say. (Key in this, of course, is being genuinely sympathetic to people's dissatisfaction with what's happening—BP, for example, would have struck just as discordant a note in the social Web as was struck in the traditional media when its then CEO seemed less than sympathetic to or understanding of the frustration that so many had with the company.) Get out, hear what people are concerned about, address it, and take whatever lumps you have to if you have them coming.

On that front, the individuals who are your online faces during a crisis of this magnitude should be reinforced and thanked often—because in many cases, they personally take the brunt of anger or frustration that's aimed for the company. During the weeks leading up to the bankruptcy, my team endured insults, derision, rudeness, and even the occasional threat. Unfortunately, the anonymity of the Internet makes brave people out of some cowards. And can you imagine having to have been representing BP online during the Gulf spill crisis or on Toyota's team during its recall crisis—what it must be like to have to personally bear the brunt of anger that isn't your fault at all? Make sure you're checking in on your people regularly, giving them breaks when they need it, trying to offer a perk or two here and there. Incessant negativity or threats can drain even the most positive people. And of course, have your organizational security team's number on speed dial in case anyone online gets out of hand and any of your people feel legitimately unsafe or threatened. If your organization isn't large enough to have its own security department, be connected with your local law enforcement agency just in case.

Let Others Help You

As General Motors' bankruptcy plan was being announced, I did something unorthodox and that would likely have gotten me in trouble had my bosses known. I sent many of the details of what we would be doing from a social media standpoint—omitting any of the legal or SEC language that hadn't been released yet, of course!—to a handful of social media influencers I knew well and trusted: the fact that we had a small squadron of people ready to spend the week answering to people online; the fact that we intended to do more listening than talking; the blog posts that we intended to put up . . . all of it. There's no point in divulging to whom I sent it because it's not material.

I wasn't trying to turn any of these bloggers and influencers into advocates for General Motors. Not only would that have been ethically suspect had I imposed upon professional relationships or friendships to ask for advocacy, but also it would have been a very challenging position to take at that point for anyone with a broad audience! No, the point of tipping off social media influencers to our whole plan was that I knew the fact that we were planning on being not only active in social media but also proactive during that week was going to be of interest to anyone who studies or observes social media. I knew that the story would be hard to resist—and that any good blogger includes lots of links in her posts. I was counting on the bloggers' news sense to point people back to us.

Sure enough, as the story broke on Monday morning, the posts began to appear pointing out that GM had an active social media program going on during the bankruptcy, pointing to the opportunity to learn from how it went (either well or badly!), and most important, pointing audiences back to GM's FastLane blog, our Facebook page, and our Twitter feed—just as I'd hoped.

None of those influencers acted on GM's behalf that week; none of them were taking our PR line and handing it to their audiences. Actually, in simply reporting on a good story, they were doing one better; they were pointing people directly back to us, where we had the chance to effectively make our perspective heard. The number of people following GM on Twitter literally doubled in one day on the first day of the bankruptcy—and while much of that should be attributed to what was happening, I'd wager that at least some of those new followers found us (and knew which accounts were really ours as opposed to fake or satirical ones) through those posts by the super-influencers.

I'm certainly not advocating that you send your social media crisis communications plan out to a group of big-time influencers. That was a huge roll of the dice that could easily have worked against what my team and I were trying to do. But the general principle behind the idea remains solid: how you handle a Three Mile Island crisis in social media is going to be very interesting to the social media pundit crowd. In fact, they'll be writing about it and tweeting about what you do (or don't do) whether you engage them or not. So make use of it—do a coordinated outreach to some super-influencers explaining what you're doing. Don't necessarily expect them to become advocates for your organization or company, but in mentioning that you're active, they're going to point people to you, which is exactly what you want—people coming to your feeds for information or to ask questions as opposed to getting answers without you. And, if you're doing a good job with your social efforts, these influencers might even praise your social media initiative—which will go a long way in helping you with the next piece of this puzzle.

Follow Up—Over and Over Again

Forgotten in almost every crisis, but especially one of this magnitude, is the fact that weathering the crisis is only the first step in the job for your company or organization. When the immediate crisis passes, you've got the daunting job of repairing your reputation. Social media can be an integral part of that reputation repair—*if* you use it wisely.

Whether it's fair or not, one of the realities of the modern media environment is that audiences are cynical. There will be a significant portion of the audience—both online and off—that receives your communications efforts during the crisis with more than a healthy dose of cynicism or disbelief. It won't matter how sincere or candid or genuine you try to be; a big portion of the audience is going to think that you're "just" doing damage control or, in situations brought on by the business and not outside actors, that the only reason you're sorry is that you got caught. No matter how effective your immediate crisis management plan is, this part of the audience in particular is still waiting for signs that nothing's changed or that no lessons have been learned. Even the portions of the audience that want to back you up or support you still need tangible signs that their faith is well placed, that you're going to reward their support by getting things right in the future.

So once the immediate crisis has passed, you need to demonstrate change to the audience and reinforce any trust or benefit of the doubt that you might have earned during the crisis. If a mistake on the organization's part led to the crisis, you not only have say that things have changed; you also have to show it. Give people a reason to believe in you once again—and make sure that everyone who questioned you or reached out to you during the crisis has the chance to see it.

At GM, one of the first things we wanted to do after the company emerged from Chapter 11 protection was to focus attention back on our products. For the better part of 18 months, people had focused on our financial state rather than our cars and trucks when talking about GM, and we knew that in order to demonstrate that we had a strong future in front of us, we had to get people looking once again at the product. So the communications team began developing a "product showcase" for the media, which would involve bringing 100 media members to Detroit to show them not only our 2009 portfolio but products in the pipeline for the next three or four years as well, hoping that the unprecedented access would raise excitement about our prospects. It was a great idea and the right thing to do, but there was another step we could take.

Several members of the communications team—some of them on the social media team, some not—had the idea that if we really wanted to show change and get people talking, we ought to bring in "regular people" instead of just the media, and instead of having them write stories in traditional publications about what was coming from GM, our guests should use the tools of social media, such as Facebook, their blogs, and Twitter, to talk about what they were seeing.

Fortunately for us, we had a good selection of potential guests to choose from for the program. We had been keeping records of people we'd had extended conversations with in social networks or online during the bankruptcy and emergence. Some were supportive, and others decidedly not fans of GM. But we picked 100 of them—as equally blended a mix of supporters, neutrals, and cynics as we could manage, some the editors of widely read blogs, others college students or moms with a couple hundred followers on Twitter—from that list and invited them to Detroit the day *before* the media got their shot at the behind-the-scenes showcase.

It worked wonders. Not only were almost all of our guests excited about what they saw, but also they talked about it at high volumes on the social Web. Best of all, they didn't just talk about the vehicles but also spoke about the levels of access they were given to both upcoming products and GM leadership, as well as how willing we were to take on the tough questions in person. We answered everything. And the main takeaway our guests offered back was that GM really did seem different—that we listened, that we were open to feedback, and that we weren't the "same old" company that had been described so mercilessly by the press during the countdown to our bankruptcy. The showcase event went an incredibly long way toward rebuilding our reputation and standing inside the online automotive community and won us fans among other online communities that kept the relationship with us going long after that event had ended. (Several of them ended up buying one of our vehicles within the next year!)

There are two lessons for any company in this effort. First, as mentioned, in the aftermath of a crisis, you have to show that you've learned from any mistakes you'd made and that the future will hold a very different outcome from the past. In order to demonstrate this to as wide an audience as possible, you have to implement the second lesson: reputational recovery and repair requires follow-up. Lots of it.

As you go through your crisis, as busy as you'll be, take furious notes as to whom you're talking with, what their general outlook about you seems to be, and what their specific concerns are, and then follow up with them repeatedly in the weeks and months following the peak of the crisis. Ask them questions—and listen to their answers. Give them follow-up information specifically tailored to what they've talked with you about. You're in a fight for your organizational life, and every customer or potential customer won back through these efforts is a win worth celebrating.

In the aftermath of a crisis, size or amount of influence doesn't matter. You're in a position of needing to win people back, one by one if necessary. The beauty of the social Web is that it affords you the ability to have the kind of individually focused conversations that can achieve this for you. We brought a college student with a small blog and a protected Twitter account to the product showcase—because even though she wasn't a "major influencer" and perhaps had only a couple hundred people within her circle, her opinion was going to matter a great deal to those couple hundred or so. Not only did she end up buying a Chevrolet Equinox the following December; she also talked up our products to her friends in the ensuing year. We wouldn't have found or "created" a college-aged advocate (and the youth market is *critical* to GM's future) if we'd been looking at people in terms of pure numbers. Follow up with *everyone* you've talked with during your crisis after the flood crests, whether or not the person has a huge following or mass influence.

The work of rebuilding General Motors' reputation is ongoing (and will likely be perpetual). Everyone inside the company is determined to bring the company back and never consider the recovery "done," so it's likely that the internal attitude will continue to be "we have more work to do." Some smart social media programs are hardly the main reason the company's primed for a successful comeback, but what we did in the social media sphere *has* been *a* factor; people routinely tell us so online. Here are a few examples from Twitter:

> @charger—*Congrats on everything your social media team does. I'm partial to Honda but your work ensures I'll consider GM.*
>
> —@KarlSakas[3]

> *In my experience as a consumer—GM's use of social media has certainly warmed my perspective toward the brand.*
>
> —@MollyKDaunt[4]

> @charger *I never had a great impression of GM, but your social media work is really great and changes my perception. #howtowincustomrs*
>
> —@davideckoff[5]

I won't promise you that you'll survive a Three Mile Island business crisis on the back of just a smart social media program. But you can help mitigate it, should you ever be faced with one, by using the principles at the heart of GM's social media initiatives during the Chapter 11 crisis:

- Keep your social media team or people informed and part of all communications planning during the crisis; more than almost anyone else in the organization, they will need fast access to accurate information and will need to know "what's going on."
- Make social the *only* focus for at least one person—preferably a team of people—for the length of the immediate crisis. It's going to be so important an outlet and tool for you, it will deserve and need dedicated staff.
- Listen more than you talk, answer more than you tell, and focus on providing value and being a resource for accurate

information and answers more than positioning your organization or promoting core messages. There will be time after the crisis peaks to repair your reputation, but during the crisis, people want to feel that you're on their side and that you place their interests above your own.

- Let others help you do the lifting. Proactively reaching out to super-influencers can help point people in your direction and help you reduce the danger of false accounts or imposters making your situation worse.
- Don't forget that weathering the immediate crisis is only the first step in repairing your reputation—and that you need to do lots of follow-up with as many people as you can with whom you engaged during the worst of the crisis. Sincere follow-up, not simply words, is the key to winning people back over.

AFTERWORD

If there's one thing you can bet the farm on with your social media program, it's that you'll be thrown plenty of curveballs. I offer myself as support of this maxim.

When I began developing this book and for most of its writing, I led social media at General Motors. I fully expected to be in that position at the time of its release and at the time when you were reading it. Three weeks before I finished the first draft of the book, however, an opportunity arose to join an agency I've always greatly respected—Voce Communications—and I jumped at the chance. And suddenly the guy who was writing a book based on the premise that those outside a big organization often don't understand the challenges inherent in executing social media at such an organization was no longer working inside a big organization and had become instead one of those outside voices. A pretty good curveball if I do say so myself—although it hardly affected what I'd written and has no bearing on the validity of what we've just spent 250 or so pages talking about.

But that's the one constant in social media: things change—fast, and often—and you have to adjust on the fly as smoothly and in as undeterred a fashion as possible. Few of your initiatives will go quite as planned, and you need to understand and anticipate this before you start. In four years at GM, not one of the programs I was responsible for went precisely as I'd drawn it up. Our success can in many ways be attributed to our willingness and ability to adjust course in midstream and go in the direction the current was taking us (or in some cases, to adjust course quickly to avoid oncoming rapids and whirlpools!). Your success will also rest in part on how adroitly and smoothly you are able to adjust for rapid changes in the online environment or unexpected directions or developments in your campaigns or programs. To further the baseball analogy, you don't ever want to dig in too deeply at the plate because you don't know whether the next breaking ball will break down and away, up and in—or at your head! Don't get rattled; just adjust your swing and make contact.

"Nothing will go as planned" is just one of the bottom-line thoughts I want to leave you with. Here are a few others.

This Is No Fad, and It's Not Just for "the Kids"

I don't know that anyone in business still *really* thinks that social and online channels are a passing fancy anymore, or really believes that all this social media stuff is going to go away. (Some might *wish* it would go away, but you might as well wish that Santa Claus will bring you a unicorn for Christmas.) But there is still an attitude more pervasive than you might think that social is something for "the young people"—used primarily by Gen Y and the Millennials but not by the demographic with the most money to spend, and as a result is often assigned to any under-30 in the office regardless of interest, experience, or aptitude. This just isn't so. More than half of Americans over the age of 12 are now on Facebook[1]—dismiss social media as the domain of teen-agers and twentysomethings, and you miss a critical opportunity to become more relevant to not only future customers but your current ones as well. This isn't going away, and it's not just for kids. It's a vital business tool that's been added to your potential arsenal if you embrace it.

Don't Be Afraid to Fail

It's easy to get rattled or intimidated by the social media land-scape. There's so much jargon, so many bright and shiny objects in the form of emerging new tools to distract you, and it seems like there are unwritten pages upon pages of etiquette and online cultural norms to try to intuit.

It can seem that the online world is very unforgiving of mis-takes, too. Because of the cantankerous nature of some vocal online critics, it's easy to become afraid to leap for fear of falling down or attracting criticism and generating "how not to do it" case studies.

But fear of failure shouldn't deter you from getting involved in social media or developing your program. No one gets it com-pletely right the first time out of the gate. Most companies well experienced in social still occasionally stumble. You learn from each mistake, and people really are willing to forgive just about any error or failure you may have. If you never try anything for fear of what could go wrong, you'll never accomplish any big wins either. It's somewhat sanguine to drop a quote on you here, but Teddy Roosevelt's words about critics come to mind:

It is not the critic who counts; not the man who points out how the strong man stumbles, or where the doer of deeds could have done them better. The credit belongs to the man who is actu-ally in the arena, whose face is marred by dust and sweat and blood, who strives valiantly; who errs and comes short again and again; because there is not effort without error and short-comings; but who does actually strive to do the deed; who knows the great enthusiasm, the great devotion, who spends himself in a worthy cause, who at the best knows in the end the triumph of high achievement and who at the worst, if he fails, at least he fails while daring greatly.

If you fail, you fail. Pick your program up, dust if off, and try again. Don't sweat it. You don't want to dismiss critics when they're right or at least being constructive, but you have to understand that the social media world is full of backseat drivers who love to point out all the turns you've missed. Don't worry about the backseat drivers; if you know where you're going, just stay on the route you've got mapped out.

Keep Your Eye on the Ball

The world of social media can be intoxicating because of its tendency to magnify or amplify any light that shines on you. It's easy to get caught up in the idea of having Facebook and Twitter interactions that get people talking about your brand or organization, of creating videos that generate millions of views, or of getting feted by Mashable as a brand that truly "gets" social.

But that's all ancillary. Social media is a *business* tool that can help you achieve *business* goals. Never forget what you're trying to accomplish via the use of social networks—or that investing time or money in your social program means not investing them somewhere else. You have to make sure that your efforts pay off for your business and justify directing those resources to social media. Don't get caught up in the social media echo chamber and its occasional penchant for self-congratulations or adulation; don't let your organizational ego get caught up in pursuing social media buzz at the expense of achieving business goals, and don't let your individual people get so caught up in becoming "rock stars" or in their "personal brand" that they lose sight of the fact that they represent *your* brand, not their own.

There's No "One Way" Sign in Social Media

We covered this in the Introduction, but it bears repeating: there's not a One Right Way or a cookie-cutter template to make a program win in the social media marketplace. No two industries are exactly alike, and what works for a company in one business may not work for a company in another. Even within the same industry, there can be more than one path to success. In the automotive industry, for example, General Motors and Ford took very different approaches to social media and how they built their programs—yet each company's program is considered successful, ranking among the best (according to many social media observers) among the Fortune 500. It's just proof that there's more than one road to Oz, as it were.

Don't get caught up worrying about what other companies are doing in social media and why you're not doing it. You especially don't want to get caught up in a "keeping up with the Joneses" mentality when observing what your competitors are doing in the space. If you become too focused on what "they" are doing, you end up simply trying to replicate their programs rather than finding your own way and innovating in your own right. Observe what works for others and incorporate what makes sense for your program, but always err on the side of blazing your own path.

If You Want to Go Viral, Sneeze on Someone; Otherwise, Just Build Good Content

Remember back in high school? You could always tell which kids were trying really hard to be popular—because they looked very much like they were trying really hard, which just got them dismissed by the in-crowd for trying *too* hard.

The same mentality applies in social media, especially with video. By definition, something goes "viral" when an audience chooses en masse to share a piece of content with its networks. If you design video content and call it "viral" from the outset, what you're saying is that you actually believe that you know—and can dictate to the audience—what it will find enjoyable and choose to share. That's an arrogant point of view, to say the least, and is the digital equivalent of trying too hard to be popular. When you're developing video, just focus on creating *good* content—make it informative, make it entertaining, make it touching, or make it controversial. But *don't* make it while calling it "viral." That's a designation that the audience grants—and that you don't have the right to.

Grow into Success

While you should have a sense of urgency about building out a strong social media program, you shouldn't plow into it so rapidly and headlong that you make easily avoided mistakes in the rush.

We've all seen chipmunks running around with their cheeks stuffed so full of food that it looks like their faces will burst. We laugh at them, generally. If you have kids, you're probably familiar with telling them to take smaller bites and slow down, or else they'll choke.

Well, in a social media setting, biting off more than you can chew is similarly unwise, a much worse sin than not being everywhere you'd like to be. So assess what you really want to do and what you can effectively manage, and focus on executing those things well before you try to add more elements. Perhaps you start with a blog, or a Facebook page, and build up both a loyal community and some experience managing that community, before you plunge into the even more uncontrolled world of Twitter. Build in other elements—video production, or geolocation initiatives, or conference/event sponsorships and programs—when you've got the money, the cultural imprimatur, and most important, the *people*, to carry out each element well. There's nothing worse than an official Facebook page on which the community isn't responded to or an official Twitter feed that goes dark for days or weeks at a time or a video channel on YouTube with the same three videos (often commercials) for weeks or months. So don't "chipmunk" your social media program. Start with what you can effectively manage and do well, and then grow into further successes.

Find Smart Partners Who Are Committed to *Your* Success

No matter how effectively you draw your program up and how well you've resourced to support a social media initiative, the odds are very strong that you're going to need and want partners to help you out. Whether it's scaling to accommodate the high number of conversations and relationships your social activity makes your brand part of, helping to manage the communities you've joined or created, planning strategic direction and brainstorming, providing advice and counsel as to how to handle particular situations, or helping you build platforms of your own to publish your point of view, there are going to be multiple opportunities for you to ask for needed help. There's no harm in that; collaboration and working in tandem with others can bolster your efforts. Your agency partners, or any consultants you bring in, can be vital contributors to your success—as integral to your team as anyone working directly for your company. But take care to select partners whose first questions are always about what *you* want to achieve, about how *you* will measure success, and whose objective is to meet your objectives and get *you* credit.

I've seen situations where agencies have wanted to issue press releases proclaiming their latest client before they've actually even done anything for that client. To me, that's a sign that the partner is more about its own goals and reputation than yours. I've seen consultants who've come in to an engagement with a company paying for their insight, only to give their standard stump presentation, collect their check, and go on—without ever providing any actual strategic benefit for the company that engaged them. (Yet they're quick to add to their résumé and talking points that they've "worked with" that company as they continue to inflate their CV.) For partnerships to work, everybody has to be on the same page and working toward the same goals and the same ends. Just as a good manager recognizes that she looks best when her people are excelling, a good partner will recognize that when you look good, he looks good. Take the time to look beyond an agency's or consultant's name recognition and assess whether its counsel or proposals seem designed to elevate your brand, enhance its place in social communities, and achieve your business goals.

Go to Summer School

When you were a kid, the idea of summer school probably annoyed you. I just *finished* school for the year, you may have thought. Why do I have to go back and keep learning? The tendency to think we've got a handle on everything we need to grasp can follow us into adulthood, and it's easy to feel that after a few successes you have this whole social media thing down cold. Trust me, you don't.

It's not that you don't know what you think you do—it's just that this space evolves so quickly that what was innovative last year is already tired and passé this year. If you want to be a leader, you have to commit yourself to the idea that you never will know "enough," that you need to keep reading and learning and experimenting and failing and evolving your program and even your mind-set about how social media should work. You should be prepared to challenge the thinking of the top influencers in social media and to challenge your own thinking. You have to constantly be in a state of feeling as if you're a little behind the curve. Read social media blogs and sites voraciously; go to as many conferences as your schedule and budget will allow; interact with as many people as possible in the social space. You haven't ever completed the grade. There's always summer school to go to.

Remember That Success Rests with Meeting the Audience's Expectations and Needs

Yes, you have to keep your eye on your own expectations and goals, and you don't ever want to get into a position where you're pandering to an audience's every whim or letting the network lead your program away from what you want or need to achieve. But your program and your content cannot be just about your key messages, your branding, and what you want people to know about you. A truly successful social media program begins and ends with *listening* before you talk, with putting yourself in the audience's shoes and asking, "What will be relevant to *them*, and would I care about this content if I didn't work here?" If you stay committed to listening as much as you talk and letting the audience control the direction of the conversation most of the time, you're doing it right. Keep the idea of being relevant to your audience ahead of the idea of being relevant to the suits in your organization, and you'll do fine.

Social Media Is About *People*

This is the most important lesson of all. This isn't about a bunch of new technologies wreaking havoc on the old communications power structure, and it's not about leading with your logo. Ultimately, it still is about relationships, humanizing, and people liking your brand or organization because they like your *people*.

Humanizing your brand does no good for you unless people like the humans they meet from your brand.

So the most important asset you can invest in and the most important element of your social media program will *always* be people. The smartest, most expensive, and most well-marketed social media campaign in the world won't succeed without the right people to make it work. But if you get likable, credible, smart, and responsive people involved in your social media efforts, you're going to win every time, even without the biggest budget in the world.

When all the elements we've discussed are in place, and you've got the right mind-set instilled in your people and your organization, your social media practice can be the most rewarding and *fun* part of your organization—while still contributing to the business goals that got it funded in the first place. This isn't a fluffy "Kumbaya"; this is a business tool that can deepen customer loyalty, win new customers, and change the way you service the people who keep you in business. If it's not the best thing since sliced bread, it's pretty darn close.

So go knock it out of the park.

NOTES

Introduction

1. Jonathan Klein, CNN, as quoted by Fox News on September 14, 2004, http://www.foxnews.com/story/0,2933,132494,00.html.

Chapter 1

1. Richard Binhammer, phone interview with the author, February 9, 2011.
2. Ibid.
3. Michael Wing, phone interview with the author, March 17, 2011.
4. Ibid.
5. Richard Binhammer, phone interview with the author, February 9, 2011.
6. David Puner, phone interview with the author, November 28, 2010.
7. Zena Weist, e-mail interview with the author, January 17, 2011.
8. Richard Binhammer, phone interview with the author, February 9, 2011.
9. Zena Weist, e-mail interview with the author, January 17, 2011.
10. Federal Trade Commission statement, "FTC Publishes Final Guides Governing Endorsements, Testimonials: Changes Affect Testimonial Advertisements, Bloggers, Celebrity Endorsements" (October 5, 2009), accessed online February 18, 2011, at http://www.ftc.gov/opa/2009/10/endortest.shtm.

Chapter 2

1. David Puner, phone interview with the author, November 28, 2010.
2. Zena Weist, e-mail interview with the author, January 17, 2011.
3. Richard Binhammer, phone interview with the author, February 9, 2011.

Chapter 3

1. Zena Weist, e-mail interview with the author, January 17, 2011.
2. *Business Insider,* "After Diaper Incident, Alaska Airlines Has a Major PR Debacle on Its Hands," November 8, 2010, http://articles.businessinsider.com/2010-11-08/news/30039713_1_customer-service-alaska-airlines-agent.
3. Dave Carroll Music, video posted to YouTube July 6, 2009, http://www.youtube.com/watch?v=5YGc4zOqozo.
4. ESPN New York, May 13, 2011, http://sports.espn.go.com/new-york/nhl/news/story?id=6532954.
5. Richard Binhammer, phone interview with the author, February 9, 2011.
6. Ibid.

Chapter 4

1. David Puner, phone interview with the author, November 28, 2010.
2. Lindsay Lebresco, e-mail interviews with the author, September/October 2010.
3. Richard Binhammer, phone interview with the author, February 9, 2011.
4. Lindsay Lebresco, e-mail interviews with the author, September/October 2010.
5. Zena Weist, e-mail interview with the author, January 17, 2011.

Chapter 6

1. Scott Stratten, keynote address at BlogWorld Expo 2010, Las Vegas, NV.
2. Olivier Blanchard, "Basics of Social Media ROI," accessed via SlideShare March 3, 2011, http://www.slideshare.net/thebrandbuilder/olivier-blanchard-basics-of-social-media-roi.
3. Geoff Livingston, "Why ROI Will Never Die," March 3, 2011, http://geofflivingston.com/2011/03/03/why-roi-will-never-die/.
4. *Fortune,* "The Trouble with Twitter," online April 14, 2011, print issue May 2, 2011, http://tech.fortune.cnn.com/2011/04/14/troubletwitter/.

5. CNN.com, "Ashton Kutcher Challenges CNN to Twitter Popularity Contest," April 15, 2009, http://articles.cnn.com/2009-04-15/tech/ashton.cnn.twitter.battle_1_cnn-twitter-account-followers?_s=PM:TECH.
6. Peter Shankman, address at "BrandCamp University," Southfield, MI, October 8, 2010.
7. *The Guardian*, "Justin Bieber Is More Influential Online Than the Dalai Lama or U.S. President," January 2, 2011, http://www.guardian.co.uk/media/2011/jan/02/klout-social-media-networking.
8. Mashable, "Charlie Sheen Sets Guinness World Record for Twitter," March 3, 2011, http://mashable.com/2011/03/03/charlie-sheen-sets-new-guinness-twitter-record/.
9. Twitter, http://twitter.com/charliesheen, March 7, 2011.
10. Zena Weist, e-mail interview with the author, January 17, 2011.
11. Facebook statistics, accessed on website of KTWV radio, Los Angeles, March 11, 2011, http://947thewave.radiocom/2011/02/08/the-average-facebook-users-habits/.

Chapter 7

1. Lindsay Lebresco, e-mail interviews with the author, September/October 2010.
2. Zena Weist, e-mail interview with the author, January 17, 2011.
3. Richard Binhammer, phone interview with the author, February 9, 2011.
4. Zena Weist, e-mail interview with the author, January 17, 2011.

Chapter 8

1. Scott Adams, *Dilbert*, September 27, 2009, http://dilbert.com/strips/comic/2009-09-27/.
2. Richard Binhammer, phone interview with the author, February 9, 2011.
3. Michael Wing, phone interview with the author, March 17, 2011.
4. Ibid.
5. David Murray, "Rules for Blogging at Sun: Don't Do Anything Stupid," *Ragan's PR Daily Europe* (January 25, 2011), http://www.prdaily.eu/PRDailyEU/Articles/Rules_for_blogging_at_Sun_Dont_do_anything_stupid__2853.aspx.
6. National Highway Traffic Safety Administration, http://www.nhtsa.gov/nhtsa/announce/testimony/tread.html.

Chapter 9

1. Zena Weist, e-mail interview with the author, January 17, 2011.
2. Story cited via *Huffington Post*, March 9, 2011, http://www
   .huffingtonpost.com/2011/03/09/chrysler-twitter-account
   -_n_833571.html.

Chapter 10

1. CBSNews.com, August 24, 2011, "Peter Shankman Tweets at
   Morton's Steakhouse to bring him a porterhouse, wish granted,"
   http://www.cbsnews.com/8301-501465_162-20096527-501465
   .html.
2. Danny Brown, "Morton's Steakhouse: Great Customer Service or
   Great PR?" August 19, 2011, http://dannybrown.me/2011/08/19
   /great-service-pr/.
3. Sara O'Flaherty, SaraOFlaherty.com, "Put Down the Knives,
   BlogHers, the Nikon Debacle Does Not Call for Blood," July 25,
   2009, http://saraoflaherty.com/2009/07/put-down-the-knives
   -bloghers-the-nikon-debacle-does-not-call-for-blood/.
4. *Notes from the Trenches* Blog, "In Which I Piss Off a Lot of
   People and Do Not Care," July 26, 2009, http://www.notes
   fromthetrenches.com/2009/07/26/in-which-i-piss-off-lots-of
   -people-and-do-not-care/.
5. Lindsay Lebresco, e-mail interview with the author, October
   2010.

Chapter 11

1. *USA Today*, "USA Today Salaries Databases, 2002," accessed
   October 2, 2011, http://content.usatoday.com/sportsdata
   /baseball/mlb/salaries/team/2002.
2. Mashable, "Old Spice Sales Double With YouTube Campaign,"
   July 27, 2010, http://mashable.com/2010/07/27/old-spice-sales/.
3. E-mail interview by the author with the marketing professional
   responsible for the Facebook ad campaign. While the radio
   network did agree to have the basic story and numbers retold
   here, its representatives requested anonymity in the retelling.
   I am honoring their request.
4. Hardy Green, "Why Oprah Opens Readers' Wallets,"
   Businessweek (October 10, 2005), http://www.businessweek.com
   /magazine/content/05_41/b3954059.htm.
5. Wikipedia, "Dunbar's Number," accessed October 2, 2011,
   http://en.wikipedia.org/wiki/Dunbar%27s_number.
6. Jennie Ecclestone, interview with the author, November 19, 2010.

Chapter 12

1. Anna Driver and Kristen Hays, "BP Turns to Twitter, Facebook on Spill Information," Reuters (May 6, 2010), http://www.reuters.com/article/idUSTRE6455OR20100506.
2. Brenna Ehrlich, "BP and Twitter to @BPGlobalPR: Tell Them You're Joking," Mashable (June 9, 2010), http://mashable.com/2010/06/09/bpglobalpr-changes-bio/.
3. @BPGlobalPR Twitter page, checked October 16, 2010, http://twitter.com/#!/BPGlobalPR.
4. Ibid.
5. *Los Angeles Times*, LATimes Blogs, "Kenneth Cole inflames Twitter with Egypt-themed tweet advertising his spring collection," February 4, 2011, http://latimesblogs.latimes.com/chatter/2011/02/kenneth-cole-twitter-egypt-cairo.html.
6. Anthony Rotolo, "Price Chopper Attacks Customer's Job Over Negative Tweet," Price Chopper Fail Blog, undated post from September 2010, http://pricechopperfail.tumblr.com/post/1156969465/price-chopper-attacks-customers-job-over-negative-tweet.
7. Anthony Rotolo, "Price Chopper Class Visit, Twitter Digest," Price Chopper Fail Blog, October 5, 2010, http://pricechopperfail.tumblr.com/post/1295405155/digest.
8. CNY Central News (CW 6, NBC 3) in Syracuse, NY (October 5, 2010), http://www.youtube.com/watch?v=G9CUBTK_2PY.
9. Mitch Wagner, "Maytag Crosses Popular Blogger, Gets Spun Dry," *Information Week*, Global CIO Blog (September 1, 2009), http://www.informationweek.com/blog/main/archives/2009/09/maytag_crosses.html;jsessionid=SLUZEPU2BC4FZQE1GHPSKH4ATMY32JVN.
10. RAN claimed publicly that it would "shut down" GM's site with its campaign. The site never went off-line, we never stopped contributing content to it, we did not take the main criticisms off the site, and we kept the site up for the entirety of 2008, our hundredth-anniversary year. Only if you consider that choosing to stop accepting new comments on an existing post, without taking the post or initial criticisms down, equates to "shutting down" our site would this claim be correct.
11. Caroline McCarthy in CNet, "Nestle mess shows sticky side of Facebook pages," March 19, 2010, http://news.cnet.com/8301-13577_3-20000805-36.html.
12. *The Huffington Post*, "Groupon's Controversial Tibet Super Bowl Ad," February 6, 2011, http://www.huffingtonpost.com/2011/02/06/groupon-tibet-super-bowl_n_819353.html.

13. Ryan Flinn, "Gap Scraps New Logo After Backlash, Revives Blue Box," *Bloomberg* (October 12, 2010), http://www.bloomberg.com/news/2010-10-12/gap-scraps-new-logo-after-online-backlash-will-return-to-blue-box-design.html.
14. Gary Grant, "Chevy vs. Chevrolet," *The Garage Blog* (June 10, 2010), http://thegarageblog.com/garage/chevy-vs-chevrolet/.
15. The Gap, status update (October 6, 2010), http://facebook.com/gap.
16. Juli Weiner, "New Gap Logo, Despised Symbol of Corporate Banality, Dead at One Week," *Vanity Fair* (October 12, 2010), http://www.vanityfair.com/online/daily/2010/10/new-gap-logo-despised-symbol-of-corporate-banality-dead-at-one-week.html.
17. Chevrolet video, "Chevy vs. Chevrolet," June 10, 2010, http://www.youtube.com/watch?v=LaQXQmkMFGc.

Chapter 13

1. Kimberly S. Johnson, Twitter, June 1, 2009, 5:46 p.m., http://twitter.com/#!/kimberlysjohns.
2. Pete Blackshaw, Twitter, June 2, 2009, 8:05 a.m., http://twitter.com/#!/pblackshaw.
3. Karl Sakas, Twitter, June 2, 2010, 11:49 a.m., http://twitter.com/#!/KarlSakas.
4. MollyKDaunt, Twitter, December 2, 2009 (Retweeted by someone else, so original time is lost.), http://twitter.com/#!/MollyKDaunt.
5. David Eckoff, Twitter, June 26, 2010, 12:09 a.m., http://twitter.com/#!/davideckoff.

Afterword

1. Jennifer Kruger, "More than Half of Americans Now on Facebook," PMA Newsline (April 1, 2011), http://pmanewsline.com/2011/04/01/more-than-half-of-americans-now-on-facebook.x.

INDEX